More praise for *Rambunctious Garden*

"[Marris] challenges us to revisit the definition of nature in our increasingly unnatural world."
—*Nature*

"Ms. Marris's book is an insightful analysis of the thinking that informs nature conservation."
—*The Economist*

"Seamlessly intertwining lyrical travelogue with ecological science... [Marris] champions a controversial approach to conservation."
—*Discover*

"Marris argues that the conservation and appreciation of nature can take place at far less exotic locations, such as backyards, city parks, farms, and even parking lots... This gracefully written and well-argued book deserves a wide readership."
—*Reason*

"A fascinating voice in an ongoing conversation about our environment... An interesting read for anyone who wants to expand their ecological world-view beyond the usual finger-pointing and hyperbole."
—*Library Journal*

"Insightful, probing and well-written, *Rambunctious Garden* is a look at the often-overlooked players of the modern ecology and conservation movement."
—*Grid Magazine*

"Into her lively reporting, [Marris] weaves a fascinating story of the history of environmentalism and the controversies that occupy it today. It's a stimulating examination of the questions of stewardship and the future of our delicate planet that will challenge any simple answers."
—*Publishers Weekly*

Rambunctious Garden

RAMBUNCTIOUS GARDEN

Saving Nature in a Post-Wild World

EMMA MARRIS

BLOOMSBURY

NEW YORK · LONDON · OXFORD · NEW DELHI · SYDNEY

Bloomsbury USA

An imprint of Bloomsbury Publishing Plc

1385 Broadway
New York
NY 10018
USA

50 Bedford Square
London
WC1B 3DP
UK

www.bloomsbury.com

BLOOMSBURY and the Diana logo are trademarks of Bloomsbury Publishing Plc

First published 2011
This paperback edition published 2013

ISBN: HB: 978-1-60819-032-4
PB: 978-1-60819-454-4
ePub: 978-1-60819-455-1

Library of Congress Cataloging-in-Publication Data

Marris, Emma.
Rambunctious garden : saving nature in a post-wild world / Emma
Marris. —
1st U.S. ed.
p. cm.
ISBN: 978-1-60819-032-4 (hardcover)
1. Nature conservation. 2. Wilderness areas—Environmental aspects.
3. Restoration ecology.
I. Title.
QH75.M363 2011
333.95'16 — dc23
2011021807

10

Typeset by Westchester Book Group
Printed and bound in the United States of America by Sheridan Books, Inc

To my mother, Kathrine Beck, for sending me to Audubon Day Camp.

Contents

1 | Weeding the Jungle

We have lost a lot of nature in the past three hundred years—in both senses of the word *lost*. We have lost nature in the sense that much nature has been destroyed: where there was a tree, there is a house; where there was a creek, there is a pipe and a parking lot; where there were passenger pigeons and Steller's sea cows, there are now skins and bones in dimly lit museum galleries. But we have also lost nature in another sense. We have misplaced it. We have hidden nature from ourselves.

Our mistake has been thinking that nature is something "out there," far away. We watch it on TV, we read about it in glossy magazines. We imagine a place, somewhere distant, wild and free, a place with no people and no roads and no fences and no power lines, untouched by humanity's great grubby hands, unchanging except for the season's turn. This dream of pristine wilderness haunts us. It blinds us.

Many ecologists spend their lives studying the most pristine places they can find, and many conservationists spend their lives desperately trying to stop wilderness from changing. We cling to fragments of "virgin" or "old growth" forests, to the "last great places," the ever-rarer "intact ecosystems," but they slip through our fingers. Like slivers of soap, they

1

shrink and disappear. And we mourn. We are always mourning, because we can't make more of such places. Every year there are fewer of them than the year before.

This book is about a new way of seeing nature. Yes, nature is carefully managed national parks and vast boreal forest and uninhabited arctic. Nature is also the birds in your backyard; the bees whizzing down Fifth Avenue in Manhattan; the pines in rows in forest plantations; the blackberries and butterfly bushes that grow alongside the urban river; the Chinese tree-of-heaven or "ghetto palm" growing behind the corner store; the quail strutting through the farmer's field; the old field overgrown with weeds and shrubs and snakes and burrowing mammals; the jungle thick with plants labeled "invasive" pests; the carefully designed landscape garden; the green roof; the highway median; the five-hundred-year-old orchard folded into the heart of the Amazon; the avocado tree that sprouts in your compost pile.

Nature is almost everywhere. But wherever it is, there is one thing that nature is not: pristine. In 2011 there is no pristine wilderness on planet Earth. We've been changing the landscapes we inhabit for millennia, and these days our reach is truly global. Inhale. That breath has 36 percent more molecules of carbon dioxide than it would have had in 1750.[1] There is no going back. Certain stories are especially symbolic of this: bobcat families moving into foreclosed suburban homes;[2] Yellowstone moose birthing calves by roads where human presence protects them from bears,[3] songbirds giving full throat to complex car alarm sequences. But more significant are global phenomena like climate change, species movements, and large-scale transformations of land.

We are already running the whole Earth, whether we admit it or not. To run it consciously and effectively, we must admit our role and even embrace it. We must temper our romantic notion of untrammeled wilderness and find room next to it for the more nuanced notion of a global, half-wild rambunctious garden, tended by us.

This garden isn't restricted to parks and protected areas. The rambunctious garden is everywhere. Conservation can happen in parks, on farms, in the strips of land attached to rest stops and fast-food joints, in your backyard, on your roof, even in city traffic circles. Rambunctious gardening is proactive and optimistic; it creates more and more nature as it goes, rather than just building walls around the nature we have left.

Many conservationists are opening up their definitions of nature and embracing a whole suite of possible goals beyond the familiar "pristine wilderness" goal. They find that when they do, they can use all sorts of new tools and approaches, the stories of which will be told in the chapters to come. As they experiment, they are finding that the values that got them into conservation in the first place are still relevant. We can cherish evolution in action even if all the species struggling for existence aren't "native." We can protect ecological processes like soil formation and water filtration that benefit us. We can marvel at the diversity of life and fight its disappearance, even if that diversity occurs in unfamiliar places. We can find beauty in nature, even if signs of humanity are present. We can see the sublime in our own backyards, if we try.

But changing our ideas about nature isn't easy. It's hard for you and me; it's probably hardest for those who have spent their lives studying and protecting wilderness. The scientists who are trained to be dispassionate are often the most passionate and opinionated when it comes to what counts as nature and what is worth saving.

Even those who are interested in expanding their conception of nature run into problems. The notion of a stable, pristine wilderness as the ideal for every landscape is woven into the culture of ecology and conservation—especially in the United States. Take the *baseline*. Virtually every scientific study of environmental change uses or assumes a baseline. Baselines are reference states, typically a time in the past or a set of conditions, a zero point before all negative changes. In the past, a place's default baseline was often before Europeans arrived. Today, as we learn more about how indigenous inhabitants of places from Australia to the Americas changed their surroundings, it is sometimes set to before any humans arrived. For many conservationists, restoration to a prehuman or pre-European baseline is seen as healing a wounded or sick nature. For others, it is an ethical duty. We broke it; therefore we must fix it. Baselines thus typically don't just act as a scientific *before* to compare with an *after*. They become the *good*, the goal, the one correct state.

When conservationists restore a site or manage a park this way, they first set a baseline. Then they characterize the site at that time. What species existed then, in what proportion? Where were the rivers? How deep and wide were they, and how fast did they flow? Where was the shoreline? What properties did the soil have? Once they have picked a baseline and characterized it, they have to get down to the heavy lifting of wrestling the area backward in time. Some species are removed, others reintroduced. Rivers are engineered, islands are built of sand, trees are killed and left to provide rotting habitat for beetles, and so on.

But ecosystems are slippery, and setting a baseline is not straightforward. Take Hawaii, some of the remotest islands in the world, home to hundreds of species that live nowhere else, many of which are rare and at risk for extinction. Earlier ecologists might have used 1778, the year Captain James Cook landed in Hawaii, as the baseline date for the island chain. But restoring the islands' ecosystems to the way they were in 1777 would be restoring them to a state very much shaped by the Polynesians who had been living there for at least one thousand years: a semidomesticated landscape filled with species the Polynesians brought with them, including taro, sugarcane, pigs, chickens, and rats, and missing others, including at least fifty species of birds, who were hunted out by the first arrivals.[4]

But if we set a date thousands of years back, safely before any humans arrived, we run into another problem. Ecosystems are always changing, whether humans are involved or not. Ancient forests with trees thousands of years old may feel timeless to us. We are a short-lived species with a notoriously bad grasp of timescales longer than a few of our own generations. But from the point of view of a geologist or paleoecologist, ecosystems are in a constant dance, as their components compete, react, evolve, migrate, and form new communities. Geological upheaval, evolution, climatic cycles, fire, storms, and population dynamics see to it that nature is always changing. On Hawaii, volcanic activity wipes the slate clean on any given slope every few hundred years, and occasional new arrivals to the islands, washed ashore or drifting in on the wind, adapt to their new home and find a place for themselves in its ecosystems.

Once we pick a date from amid this muddle, another problem emerges. Even when we use all the scientific tools available to look backward in time, from fossil pollen records to the climate information enshrined in tree rings, we don't always know what places looked like thousands or even hundreds of years ago.

The final and perhaps most vexing issue with prehuman baselines is that they are increasingly impossible to achieve—either through restoration or management of wild areas. Every ecosystem, from the deepest heart of the largest national park to the weeds growing behind the local big-box store, has been touched by humans. We have stirred the global pot, moved species around, turned up the thermometer, domesticated a handful of plants and animals, and driven extinct many more. We have definitely changed the entire planet, and it is getting increasingly difficult to undo all these changes at any one place.

I saw the scale of the challenge first hand when I visited Hawaii in 2009. The lush tropical plants out the hotel window looked gorgeous, but I knew that many of them had been introduced by people and were now considered a threat to the native species. I also knew that Hawaii has been called "the extinction capital of the world," and that many of its beautiful birds are either gone or near gone. Here was "the biggest ecological catastrophe in the United States," in the words of a *St. Louis Post-Dispatch* reporter,[5] and yet the islands are thick with conservationists who have not given up on the ideal of Hawaii as it once was.

My first stop was a group of experimental field plots testing the feasibility of restoring lowland forests on the Big Island's wet side. The plots are hidden in a forest on the Hawaii Army National Guard Keaukaha Military Reservation. Growing on flat land with plenty of rain, most forests of this type had been cleared for agriculture. What was left, or what grew back, is now dominated by plants from places other than Hawaii.

Rebecca Ostertag of the University of Hawaii at Hilo explained why these "invaders" are so prevalent on Hawaii. Hawaiian plants, having evolved in isolation for up to 30 million years,[6] generally grow slowly and use resources less efficiently than continental plants, which evolved with more competition. Similarly, Hawaiian birds and other animals are mostly helpless against introduced diseases. Avian malaria has knocked off many bird species; there were no mosquitoes on the islands until recently, so birds there never evolved any defenses to the mosquito-borne disease. Hawaiian raspberries and roses have even lost their thorns, and Hawaiian mints their minty defense chemicals, because there were no plant-eating animals around to fend off.[7] Such mellow Hawaiian species are pushovers for the scrappier mainland species that humans brought to the islands. Today half of the plants in Hawaii are nonnative.[8] In many lowland forests only the large trees are native; under them grows a carpet of introduced seedlings, just waiting for the day the giant natives fall. Some ecologists call such places "forests of the living dead."

At the army base, mynah birds from Asia stood in the road. The air was soft and humid. Ostertag and I met up with her colleague, Susan Cordell of the U.S. Forest Service, and a graduate student named Joe Mascaro from the University of Wisconsin, Milwaukee. Together we headed out to the study plots. After hopping a fence intended to keep out feral pigs, we pushed through a jungle of foliage from everywhere: trumpet tree with its huge star-shaped leaves, a native of Mexico, Central America, and Colombia; bingabing, a small tree with big parasol-like leaves, from the Philippines; tasty strawberry guava, from the Atlantic Coast of Brazil; purple-flowered Asian melastome; "Koster's curse," a little shrub originally from Mexico and parts of South America; and albizia, another immigrant from Southeast Asia. Many of these species were introduced not only deliberately but methodically—aerially seeded in the 1920s and 1930s after large forest fires to prevent erosion. The experts figured that Hawaiian plants would grow too slowly to do the job effectively. The resulting cosmopolitan forest is green and dense, with creepers hanging everywhere. Underfoot, dead leaves like starched, crumpled brown napkins made a terrific crunch.

Suddenly we stepped into a clearing. Here plants were spaced widely apart, with black lava rock covered in chartreuse moss visible in between. This was one of the study plots: small squares in which every single nonnative plant had been ripped out by hand. To get these spaces to a purely native state, researchers had to pull up and remove almost half the vegetation, a process that took about a week's worth of labor per thousand square feet for the initial clearing and epic bouts of weeding thereafter.[9] As a result, the plots look a bit sad and empty, like someone's living room in the middle of a move-out.

Here, I could get a better look at the typically less showy Hawaiian natives, including tree ferns; lama, a hardwood in the ebony family; the vaguely Mediterranean-looking 'ōhi'a tree with feathery bunches of bright red stamens; and the sweet-smelling maile vine, used for making fragrant leis.

The plots weren't created to be showplaces, however, but as experiments to see whether a native Hawaiian forest would bounce back if all the introduced species were removed. With all those aggressive tropical invaders exiled, would the native flora tap into the soil nutrients, rain, and newly available sunlight and grow vigorously to fill up the space? When I visited, it had been five years since the experiments began. Disappointingly, the mature native trees had grown very little. As Ostertag and Cordell put it, "The native trees may either be responding to the treatments very slowly and still undetectably, or they may be unable to respond at all."[10] The researchers were pleased, however, to see quite a few native seedlings appear on the sun-dappled forest floor.

These removal plots were weeded out for a specific experiment. But they also represent, in miniature, what many conservationists would love to do for huge swaths of the planet: rip out the introduced species, make way for the natives, and return the area to the way it used to be, making the baseline the goal.

But Ostertag and Cordell's lowland wet forest, like just about everywhere else on the planet, has baseline problems. The area was burning-hot lava no more than fifteen hundred years ago,[11] so there is a chance that humans had already arrived on the island by the time plants were reestablishing the area, leaving no clean prehuman window of time to look back to. However, the researchers can get around that by looking at nearby, similar forest that predates human arrival. More problematic is the characterization of that moment in time. No one catalogued this kind of forest early enough, so there may have been other native species here that disappeared without a trace, lost to record or memory. "There are only about five native tree species here," said Ostertag, as she looked around at the unassuming native plants. "It seems to me there probably would have been more than five."

And the final problem is the sheer amount of work involved. Their baseline just isn't achievable without spending a huge amount of money and time. "I think that people that are interested in protecting Hawaii's flora and fauna have resigned themselves to it being in postage-stamp-size reserves," said Cordell, sadly.

Of course, Osterag and Cordell's forest is in particularly bad shape. But are ecosystems that aren't so trashed perhaps redeemable? The answer is no, at least not in Hawaii. Nothing is going to go all the way back to the way it used to be, not even the Laupahoehoe Natural Area Reserve, so valued for its pristineness that it is used as a reference area—a contemporary baseline—for all similar forests. Scientists have erected a data-recording tower as tall as the canopy of the forest for characterizing the ecosystem. The idea is that instead of recreating the past, they will use this place as a proxy for the past. But even as they built their tower, scientists knew they were grasping at straws. The forest is just changing too fast.

I visited Laupahoehoe after leaving Ostertag and Cordell's poignant little plots. My guide was Christian Giardina, a lean, silver-haired government ecologist. To reach the data-recording tower, we had to drive up the side of a mountain. As we climbed, the most obvious human influences fell away one by one. Down low, pheasants from India scampered across the dirt road. We drove by dense forests of nonnative strawberry guava, until they thinned out. At some point we passed beyond the reach of the mosquitoes that bear avian malaria (they can't take the cold). We made a quick stop at the "valley of the giants" to look at enormous hundreds-of-years-old native 'ōhi'a and koa trees. Tall straight koa, prized and liberally used for canoe building, are now rare on the islands.[12] These giants towered above an increasingly tangled understory of introduced plants like ginger and strawberry guava.

At last, up on the heights, we found the reference forest. Compared to the bustling jungle below, everything growing here felt large, well established, widely spaced, and dripping with moisture. The result was an impression of tranquillity. Tree ferns unrolled their fronds five feet above Giardina's head, and we walked on spongy dark turf littered with the perfect crescent-moon leaves of the koa tree. For him, this is Hawaii at its best. But visits are bittersweet. Even here, in the most unchanged place on the Big Island, its native character may already be anachronistic. "We know it is not pristine," said Giardina. "The carbon dioxide is elevated; key fruit dispersers and pollinators are extinct. But it is the best that we have." He mused on the inevitable changes that would occur when the "invasion front" we passed on the road up made it to the top of the mountain and the climate warmed. Already there were signs. Between the koa leaves, the forest floor was pinpointed with tiny seedlings of introduced species poised to inherit the space. "This will be transformed," he said. "Aesthetically it will be very different. The species composition will be different. You won't be able to walk through. I get sad thinking about it: a forest type unique on the planet, and it will just get snuffed out."

Despite knowing in their hearts that they cannot turn back the clock, many conservation and most restoration projects explicitly try to recreate a former time, like Ostertag and Cordell's plots, but on a larger scale. This still seems like the most obvious goal to many conservationists. But these projects are often incredibly difficult and expensive, which means that unless the governments of the world suddenly decide to spend vastly more money on conservation, they will always be small, like little islands of the past. Or at least little islands *like* the past.

Such "islands like the past" spangle the planet here and there. Many U.S. national parks are managed to look as they did in colonial or frontier days. This has often meant that managers focus on stopping things from changing—which in these days of climate change means much more than keeping hands off. But other places have been actively restored, and it is here that things get most difficult and expensive.

In the summer of 2009 I visited one of the thousands of such restoration projects. The Australian Wildlife Conservancy is attempting to return a small area of the outback to the conditions of 1770, when Captain Cook (same Cook; he got around) first landed in Australia, some 40,000 years after people first arrived. "Australia can give up on a pre-aboriginal landscape, but there is a chance to go back to pre-European times," says Matt Hayward, an Australian Wildlife Conservancy ecologist. Easier said than done.

Scotia Sanctuary is a 250-square-mile tract of land about 90 miles upstream of the confluence of the Murray and Darling rivers, northeast of Melbourne, Australia.[13] Many species of eucalyptus grow here, emerging from red sand and splitting at ground level into many small trunks, each shedding bark and sporting branches with small, tough leaves adapted to the arid heat. Underground, these trunks all grow from a swollen root called a lignotuber, some of which are perhaps one thousand years old, which will survive even if fire destroys the aboveground tree. In between the trees are fairy rings of dagger-sharp spinifex grass.

The Sanctuary includes two fifteen-mile-square areas enclosed by what looks like a prison fence—serious, sturdy, tall, and electrified. The landscape inside these fences looks much like that outside, except the ground is pitted with numberless fist-sized holes, the traces of several threatened species of mostly nocturnal marsupials, including woylies, boodies, numbats, bilbies, and wallabies. These little creatures have been declining continentwide since Europeans—and their favorite animal companions—arrived. They have two strikes against them: they evolved without many predators to keep their survival skills up, and they aren't terribly bright. Some scientists argue that the poor soils of Australia created a world where big brains were just too energetically expensive.[14]

Several of these marsupials were brought here from their last wild haunts, offshore islands free of introduced predators. Cats and foxes, introduced as pets and for hunting, respectively, are devastating predators for the crew. Some species have only a few hundred individuals left. A population of bridled nailtail wallabies, kept inside another fence within the main fence, are the "backup" reserve for the whole species, which is poised on a knife's edge.

Over coffee at the communal table at Scotia's main building, I interviewed Tony Cathcart, a mild-eyed fellow in thick glasses, a V-neck sweater, and baseball cap who got rid of all the introduced cats, rabbits, goats, and foxes in Stage Two, the second of the two fenced blocks. His previous jobs had included bellhop, computer technician, and painter, but feral animal control may be his true calling. The job requires an incredible patience and commitment. Leave just two rabbits alive inside the fence, and in a few years the nibbling hordes will be back. You have to get every last animal.

Cathcart told me how he cleared Stage Two. He was able to shoot out the goats in a matter of days. Rabbits were harder. Every day he put out carrot bait, so that every rabbit's hole—and there were thousands of them—was within about five hundred feet of some carrots. The rabbits would tentatively nibble and learn to trust the new food source. On the third or fourth day, the carrots would be poisoned. Cathcart repeated this routine three times, running through 12,500 pounds of carrots, killing the majority of the rabbits. Then he switched to "spot cleaning" to get the remaining few.

Foxes have large ranges, so only about a dozen lived inside the fence. But they are also smart. For each fox, he learned its habits and was eventually able to find perfect places to trap or poison them. He also trapped the cats. But they too are smart. "The average in Australia is that it takes one hundred nights per cat," he said. "My first cat took one hundred eighty-seven nights." When he finally arrived, one dawn, at the trap to find a gray figure inside, he had mixed feelings.

The whole process took eighteen months, and the key to making it work, he says, was "perseverance, perseverance, perseverance." Eighteen months is actually pretty darn fast. It took Cathcart's predecessor five years to clear Stage One.

"It isn't really about the killing," he said, as we rinsed out our coffee cups. "It's about seeing the grass come back or the animals you haven't seen before—the little cute-and-furries." There are further effects as well. All that digging the cute-and-furries do turns the earth; their holes catch organic detritus and moisture. Scientists at Scotia are looking at how these changes affect soil nutrient turnover, bugs, and plant growth.

More than six years of effort for about thirty square miles: unless the whole country decides that its number-one priority is ridding Australia of feral animals, these little fenced islands are all that pristine-focused conservationists can hope for. Luckily for the marsupials, they'll never know their territories are inside de facto zoos. And the cats, foxes, and rabbits are a continuing threat, just outside the fence. To hold the blocks to a simulacrum of 1770, conservationists must shoot, poison, trap, fence, and watch, forever watch, lest the excluded species find their way back in.

The day after a rare rain, I went out into the reserve with Matt Hayward and his family. Streamers of bark blew in the wind. Dead leaves and twigs rot very slowly here, so they blow about and form little drifts in marsupial holes or against the base of spinifex clumps. The wet had brought out countless shiny brown cockroaches, and Hayward's girls—Madeleine, three and a half, and Zoe, nearly two—were intrigued. They ran around after them and asked their daddy to pick them up. They watched as a scorpion pulled one into his burrow—at which point their mother suggested they put shoes and socks on. We visited a malleefowl nest—a huge raised platform of earth and sticks and leaves, maybe six feet across, all made by one male malleefowl, a bird the size of a chicken. Zoe patted the nest thoughtfully with a stick. In some mud, we spotted kangaroo and emu tracks. In an odd way, these girls are just as oblivious as the marsupials. They are spending their childhood in an anachronism, an Australia where numbats and malleefowl are all around them, where bilbies come out at night with shining eyes.

Holding small areas like Scotia to states that resemble historical baselines may be possible, depending on where the area is and what date one would like to return it to. But to do it will take human intervention, both in the beginning and indefinitely into the future. A historically faithful ecosystem is necessarily a heavily managed ecosystem. It is not quite the "pristine wilderness" many nature lovers look to as the ideal. And there's the paradox that unravels the idea of "pristine wilderness." If we define *wild* as "unmanaged," then the ecosystems that look the most pristine are perhaps the least likely to be truly wild.

To be sure, this is not to say that reserves like those at Scotia are not worth having, or that Cathcart spent eighteen months chasing a dream. Even if we don't care about 1770, we may need such fenced islands if we want to avoid the extinctions of the cute-and-furries. Managed, fenced areas may well be the only places that many native Australian animals can live, given the unlikelihood of ridding the whole continent of foxes and cats. "Maybe in a hundred or a thousand years they evolve resistance," says Hayward. "That's more likely than eradication of predators."

But managing to avoid extinctions is subtly different from managing to recreate 1770. For one thing, managing to avoid extinctions is actually achievable.

In the last ten years or so, many scientists have moved beyond the notion that the goal for any piece of land is returning it to an unobtainable baseline. They are rejecting a view of the world that says a place must be completely "pristine" to count as nature; that view would imply that there are only two possible future states for most ecosystems: perpetual weeding and perpetual watching, or total failure. They are embracing instead a wider vision of nature managed for a wider array of goals. Instead of focusing on the past, they are looking to the future and asking themselves what they'd like it to look like.

Back on Hawaii's Big Island, as we thrashed through the nonnative-dominated forest that encircled the weeded plots, Ostertag and Cordell mostly saw failure. But Joe Mascaro, the grad student who accompanied us, saw something less value-laden. He saw the future, and as an ecologist, he found it interesting. He saw plants interacting together in new ways, with new creatures dispersing their seeds, new competitions for resources. He expects that there will be some casualties when species come in contact for the first time—"local extinctions and whole ecosystem types that will evaporate," he predicts—but he does not expect that the resulting ecosystems will be worthless just because they are changed. They will still store carbon in the bodies of their trees, keeping it out of the atmosphere where it would contribute to global warming. They will still harbor many species. They will still smell cool and green. At the very least, he says, they should be studied, because they are probably more representative of today's Earth than any so-called "pristine" forest. "These ecosystems, like it or not, are going to be driving most of the natural processes on Earth," he says.

Forests like the one we walked through can be managed to achieve a smorgasbord of alternative goals, based on the various things that people care about. One section might be managed as part of a carbon-sequestration project tied into the global carbon-trading market. This wouldn't require native trees, just lots of them. Other sections might be semiweeded into quasi-gardens where Hawaiians can gather plants of cultural importance to make leis, canoes, and so on. Another section might look a bit like Ostertag and Cordell's plots and be used to teach schoolchildren about the ecological history of their home state. And if there are any species in the forest at special risk for extinction, such as birds threatened by avian malaria, sections could be managed by scientists specifically to support them.

Around the world, no single goal will provide for a sensible, well-rounded conservation program. For example, if we focus only on avoiding extinctions, then we could end up with a zoolike world where all species are carefully tended by man but are separated from the ecosystems in which they once lived, died, and evolved. Similarly, a conservation program that focused only on what ecosystems can do for humans would have no time for ecosystems or species that don't contribute to human well-being in an obvious way.

Layering goals and managing landscapes with an eye to the future, rather than the past, is the cutting edge of conservation, but some ecologists, conservationists, and citizen environmentalists just aren't there yet. Among some conservationists, reverence for particular historic ecosystems can approach the religious.

One May evening at a Hilo restaurant, over a glass of wine, I talked to Giardina, my guide to the Laupahoehoe Natural Area Reserve, about his professional quest to eliminate introduced strawberry guava from the island. Giardina believes that historical ecosystems are superior to the new mixes of species emerging in the human-dominated present. And it both shocks him that other people do not share this view, and occasionally unsettles him that he, a scientist, believes it so implicitly.

"Are we so religious about this biodiversity ethic that we need to be called out on it?" he wonders. "I mean, one plant is photosynthesizing as well as another, right? The chloroplast in one plant is the same as the chloroplast in any plant. The rest is just window dressing—a series of tubes to get water or nutrients to that chloroplast. Who cares if it is a chloroplast in 'ōhi'a or guava? If you really dig down to why we should care, you end up with nothing. You are running on faith that we should care."

This faith that native ecosystems are better than changed ecosystems is so pervasive in fields like ecology that it has become an unquestioned assumption. One often finds it built into experiments, which sometimes automatically classify any human change to nature as "degradation." Until recently, it lurked behind conservation organizations' mission statements, which exalted the untouched places above all others. And it still saturates nature writing and nature documentaries, where the wild is always better than the tame. But it wasn't always so. The cult of pristine wilderness is a cultural construction, and a relatively new one. It was born, like so many new creeds, in America.

2 | The Yellowstone Model

I drove into the little hamlet of Mammoth Hot Springs one October to attend a scientific conference on the future of Yellowstone National Park. Mammoth is entirely inside the park and features a hotel, staff housing, a couple of private houses, and lots of parking. In the fall it also features rutting elk. As I pulled into a parking spot, I saw two big bulls, their heads lowered and antlers entangled, push each other in slow circles. All around them stood tourists, photographing and filming, some as close as a dozen feet away. In the truck next to me, a man watched the spectacle through his windshield as he polished off a Dairy Queen blizzard. Welcome to Yellowstone, the wildest place in the lower forty-eight.

Yellowstone National Park covers 3,472 square miles in Wyoming. Its unique features are geothermal—hot molten rock rises very close to the surface here, providing the heat and pressure behind geysers, hot springs, fumaroles, and bubbling mudpots. Otherwise Yellowstone is a high plateau, much of it covered in subalpine forest dominated by lodgepole pine. Bears, bison (also known as buffalo), elk, wolves, pronghorn (also known as antelope), and bighorn sheep live here in great numbers. The sky is big, the canyons are deep, the quiet is startling, and the valley bottoms, in the fall, are covered with buttery gold grasses and red-stemmed stunted willows.

Many call Yellowstone the "mother park." In the story of its creation one can read the story of the rise of a certain set of ideas about nature in America—ideas that excluded humans and that presaged the conservation movement's persistent focus on wilderness. While European conservationists focused on sustainable human use and avoiding extinctions, America perfected and exported the "Yellowstone Model," based on setting aside pristine wilderness areas and banning all human use therein, apart from tourism.

Much of Yellowstone spent millennia buried under a shifting landscape of ice, until about 13,500 years ago.[1] Initially, the surroundings would have been more like arctic tundra than the pine forest that makes up much of the park today. But well before the vegetation took on its modern look, the ancestors of modern Indians arrived. Archaeologists have found their spear points and other artifacts dating back to 10,000 to 11,000 years ago, some made of obsidian from the park's famed black Obsidian Cliff.[2]

Euro-American mountain men, trappers, and hunters first visited Yellowstone in the early 1800s, but official parties didn't systematically explore the area until the 1860s.[3] This long delay may have saved the park, for by 1860 a shift had taken place in American attitudes toward wilderness.

Wilderness has been seen throughout Western history as a source both of inexhaustible resources and of real peril, a domain of mushrooms and monsters, timber and timber wolves. Many European colonizers preferred towns and fields, where things were altogether safer, and they thought it progress when the land claimed for civilization expanded and savage nature shrunk.

It wasn't until societies attained a little safety, prosperity, and leisure that nature in its wildest aspect began to seem rather romantic. Eighteenth- and nineteenth-century British Romantics such as William Wordsworth and Percy Shelley took issue with older ideas that nature was inevitably desolate and terrible, that it was a soulless clockwork machine, or that it existed just as a heap of raw materials from which man could build civilization. On the contrary, they cried, nature was the stuff of life, the warp and weft of the great unity of which everything was a part. It could, in places, be sublime, ego shaking. Venturing out into the wild, to some place awe-inspiring, ideally with lots of vertical drops or gloomy forests, Romantics compared their own puniness to the overwhelming forces of nature, and experienced a mix of pleasure and horror.[4]

It took some time for the colonists and pioneers of America to come around to the idea of the sublime. While Romantic Europeans were swooning over the beauty of craggy mountains, the glory of solitude, and the handwriting of God in Nature, life was harder in the New World. Land was still being "conquered" for civilization, and bears, wolves, and cougars threatened human lives. In the words of wilderness historian Roderick Nash, "The pioneer, in short, lived too close to wilderness for its appreciation."[5]

By the nineteenth century, some few American men—mostly in the East, where the wilderness had been sufficiently beaten back—began to sing the praises of rugged nature. But these early American nature-lovers did not make a very firm distinction between wilderness and the pastoral in their general celebration of all things natural. In 1836 Ralph Waldo Emerson wrote *Nature*, about the transcendent possibilities of "essences unchanged by man; space, the air, the river, the leaf." He enjoyed "perfect exhilaration" whilst "crossing a bare common, in snow puddles at twilight, under a clouded sky."[6] As a "common" is a bit of land held in common for everyone in town to graze their livestock, it is hardly what we would call wilderness.

At just about the same time, in the late 1830s, a trapper from Maine, Osborne Russell, uses the vocabulary of the Romantics to describe the Lamar Valley, now inside Yellowstone National Park, as a place "where happiness and contentment seemed to reign in wild romantic splendor surrounded by majestic battlements which seemed to support the heavens and shut out all hostile intruders."[7]

Emerson's protégé and tenant was Henry David Thoreau, still considered by American conservationists as a sort of Abraham of their creed. Emerson owned Walden Pond, to which Thoreau famously retreated in 1845 to be absolutely alone and free. The pond, which has come, for many, to be an icon of nature, was not very deep in the woods or really very wild. It was a mere mile and a half or so from Concord Village in Massachusetts, and Irish railroad workers lived in shanties as close as half a mile to Thoreau's cabin, thanks to a railroad line from Boston to Fitchburg that ran right by the pond.[8] Thoreau apparently walked along the line to get to town "every day or two."[9] He wrote, "The men on the freight trains, who go over the whole length of the road, bow to me as to an old acquaintance, they pass me so often, and apparently they take me for an employee."[10]

But this proximity to civilization didn't spoil Thoreau's sense of being out on his own. The important thing was that his cabin was far enough removed from town for him to escape the common mode of life, which he saw as a recipe for the bleak "lives of quiet desperation" that most men lead.[11]

Thoreau did not describe Walden Pond as "wilderness," but he did discuss wilderness in a 1862 essay, "Walking," in which he made a distinction between cities and wilderness and associated wilderness with the qualities of being uncivilized, publicly owned, and generally speaking, due west or far north of Concord. Indeed, he may have preferred to contemplate some truly wild places in small doses. A trip to the Maine woods terrified him in the accepted manner of Romantic encounters with the sublime. On top of Mount Katahdin, he felt his surroundings to be "savage and dreary," "a place of heathenism and superstitious rites—to be inhabited by men nearer of kin to the rocks and wild animals than we."[12] Such intense experiences were good for the soul but not for everyday wear.

Thus Thoreau, who is often seen as a great defender of wilderness— among his most frequently quoted lines is "in wildness is the preservation of the world," which is often misquoted as "in *wilderness* is the preservation of the world"—actually preferred a middle ground between the truly wild and the truly civilized.

The reason we now often read Thoreau as a champion of wilderness may have much to do with the influence of one of his biggest fans, parks advocate John Muir. Muir was a Scottish-born explorer, reverent Christian, ecstatic naturalist, and energetic nature preservationist active from the 1860s until his death in 1914. In forest "temples" in the Sierra Nevadas in California, he saw "sparks of the Divine soul" in every rock and leaf.[13] Throughout his career he whipped up American enthusiasm about nature in magazine articles and other writings and advocated for national parks. He saw himself as a John the Baptist figure, trying to bring civilized humans to God through the glory of His mountains and forests.[14] He even looked the part. His friend, magazine editor Robert Underwood Johnson, recalled that "he looked like John the Baptist as portrayed in bronze by Donatello and others of the Renaissance sculptors—spare of frame, hardy, keen of eye and visage, and on the march eager of movement."[15]

Muir was a great admirer of Thoreau but altogether more picky when it came to nature. Only wilderness would really send Muir into ecstasies. According to historian Roderick Nash, "Much as he admired Thoreau's philosophy, Muir could not suppress a chuckle at a man who could 'see forests in orchards and patches of huckleberry brush' or whose outpost at Walden was a 'mere saunter' from Concord."[16]

But what did "wilderness" consist of for Muir? It must not be changed radically to suit man—"ploughed or pastured," "hacked and trampled."[17] Most economic uses of the land would therefore be ruled out. Muir also mentions the availability of solitude as one necessary component.

But although Muir, like Thoreau, has often been cast as an early champion of reverence for pristine wilderness, his writing reflects a more open mind toward people than many remember. For example, he does say that any man can live in harmony with nature, build houses, raise crops there, even do a little low-key mining, as long as they are not "mere destroyers . . . tree-killers, wool and mutton men, spreading death and confusion."[18] So while he sees "white gold-hunters" as "spoiling" the Black Hills of South Dakota, he classes the "free trappers of the early romantic Rocky Mountain times" with the "picturesque cavalcade of Sioux savages" as the rightful inhabitants of the place.[19]

Muir's ideas about wilderness as sacred space are his chief legacy, however, and he undoubtedly helped create an American conservation movement that often focused on protecting pristine wilderness rather than on achieving coexistence between humans and other species. He was certainly more interested in nature for nature's sake than many of the men who set up the first parks. Muir fought for California's Yosemite because he was inspired by its untouched beauty,[20] while Yellowstone was made a public park in 1872 with the encouragement of the Northern Pacific Railroad mostly to prevent the geysers and springs from becoming private, for-profit tourist attractions.

Yellowstone's plants and animals were hardly considered when it was made a park, and initially hunting went on in the area as usual. In the 1880s George Bird Grinnell, editor of *Forest and Stream*, visited the park and began to write about the toll hunting was taking on the wildlife, and in 1883 hunting of traditional game species was banned in the park.[21] The nascent wildlife-conservation movement that Grinnell spoke for was a product of what historian Nash calls the "wilderness cult," a national fad for all things wild that emerged in the 1890s, just as urbanizing, industrializing Americans settled down to enough safety, prosperity, and leisure to enjoy the wilderness.[22] Wilderness historian William Cronon suggests that this movement was an eighteenth-century version of primitivism— "the belief that the best antidote to the ills of an overly refined and civilized modern world was a return to a simpler, more primitive living."[23] To my mind, the wilderness cult can also be seen as the Americanization of an essentially European Romanticism, with less swooning and more shooting; less poetry and more adventure stories.

In 1893 the influential American historian Frederick Jackson Turner famously declared the frontier closed. In his speech to the American Historical Association, he posited that the frontier had created much that was good in the American character: independence, toughness, democracy itself.[24] Americans believed him and mourned the death of the Wild West by going camping, starting Boy Scout troops, and reading Jack London stories about hardscrabble life in Alaska. "The wilderness cult comprised a broad spectrum from those who sallied forth to those who read animal stories to their kids," says Arizona State University historian and ecologist Matthew Chew. "The former were less numerous than the latter."

Americans found wilderness salubrious. Writing in 1901, Muir said that wildness was a necessity for "tired, nerve-shaken, over-civilized people" suffering from "the vice of over-industry and the deadly apathy of luxury."[25] And a version of this idea—wilderness as tonic for the "neurasthenia" and garden-variety "overstrain" of fast-paced city life—is still with us. Wilderness was considered such a tonic that it was actually prescribed by some doctors. Among them was Silas Weir Mitchell, the nerve doctor who famously prescribed a disastrous "rest cure" for the writer Charlotte Perkins Gilman. She turned her ordeal into a short story, "The Yellow Wallpaper," about how easy it is to go around the bend when there's nothing to occupy your mind. Mitchell took a different and possibly more successful tack with his male nerve patients. To them he offered a "west cure" in which patients were instructed to head west, engage in a "sturdy contest with Nature," and write about it.[26] Among his patients so prescribed was Owen Wister, whose 1902 novel *The Virginian* about his experiences out west started the American fad for cowboys. Wister blanched at the idea of building an elevator at the Grand Canyon of the Yellowstone as a "vulgarization" of "a supreme piece of wild natural beauty."[27]

Wilderness cultist supremo Teddy Roosevelt famously advocated a "strenuous life" for American men, filled with hunting, fishing, physical hardship, and derring-do. *The Virginian* was dedicated to him. Roosevelt believed that the proper stage for the strenuous life was the wilderness, where game and fish are there for the taking. Roosevelt, of course, also found the wilderness beautiful, but for him, its key role was as a kind of many-faceted opponent against which to test oneself. The difficult fact was that triumphing against this opponent often meant diminishing it by, for example, making roads, ribbons of civilization cutting through the wilderness, or by hunting or trapping and removing specimens of its wild animal life. The near-extinction of the American bison was a case in point. "He is a truly noble beast, and his loss from our prairies and forests is as keenly regretted by the lover of nature and of wild life as by the hunter," Roosevelt wrote in 1897.[28]

The solution was parks. Parks would become a source of game, which would overflow onto lands where they could be hunted. Roosevelt described Yellowstone as "a natural breeding-ground and nursery for those stately and beautiful haunters of the wilds which have now vanished from so many of the great forests, the vast lonely plains, and the high mountain ranges where they once abounded."[29]

And parks became a place where Americans could get a look at the vanished frontier. They could see the West, even after it was won. Or as Grinnell put it in 1882, Yellowstone could be like a "rock" around which the "tide" of immigrants heading west to farm would break, "leaving it undefiled by the unsightly traces of civilization" for "generations yet unborn."[30]

Grinnell's idea about the value of Yellowstone's pristineness was echoed eighty years later. In the early 1960s, a committee of scientists led by A. Starker Leopold, son of the famous conservationist Aldo Leopold, met to consider some of the vexing management problems at the United States' national parks. The report they produced, known as the Leopold Report, may be among the most frequently quoted documents in American conservation history. Here is their view on what the goal of wildlife management in the parks should be: "As a primary goal, we would recommend that the biotic associations within each park be maintained, or where necessary recreated, as nearly as possible in the condition that prevailed when the area was first visited by the white man. A national park should represent a vignette of primitive America."[31]

The influence of this report has been enormous. Over time, according to Yellowstone historian Paul Schullery, it has developed an "almost scriptural aura."[32] It neatly encapsulates a long and widely held opinion in American conservation that natural areas *should* look like they did before Europeans showed up, that this is their correct state, the holy baseline. Ever since, managers at Yellowstone have obsessed over the state of the area in 1872, when it was made a park. They have pored through historical accounts to determine how many elk were there, and whether they wintered in the park. They have used old photos to determine the density of aspen. The National Park Service still aims at protecting parks' "natural condition," which it defined in 2006 as "the condition of resources that would occur in the absence of human dominance over the landscape."[33]

This high opinion of pristine wilderness and low opinion of human changes to the landscape have always coexisted in America with a more pragmatic school of thought, which seeks to combine human use and nature preservation. And the pragmatists have arguably been the victors in real terms. A map of U.S. national parks, which instantiate the pristine wilderness idea, shows a white continent flecked with green here and there. A map of lands managed for resource use by the Forest Service, the Bureau of Land Management, and other agencies looks like the West has been tie-dyed. The Park Service manages just 84 million acres out of 650 million acres of federally owned land.

Then again, through the Wilderness Act of 1964, the wilderness purists were able to layer their ideas on top of those public use lands. The act takes a pristineness approach, saying, "A wilderness, in contrast with those areas where man and his own works dominate the landscape, is hereby recognized as an area where the earth and its community of life are untrammeled by man, where man himself is a visitor who does not remain."[34] Any federal land can be designated wilderness, and once it is, the agencies running it must preserve its wilderness character. One of its key provisos bans permanent roads. One hundred and nine million acres have so far been designated wilderness in the United States. Sixty six million acres of that are not already parks.

Acreage aside, the pristine wilderness idea has been incredibly influential, and not just in America. It underpins the Yellowstone Model of nature preservation. The formation of Yellowstone—or perhaps, the ban on hunting in Yellowstone—was a breakthrough in conservation. Never before had a society voluntarily restrained itself from using natural resources in deference to "higher" uses of nature, such as pure enjoyment. Since Yellowstone's creation parks and nature reserves have been set up around the world. By one count, about 13 percent of the Earth's land (and a paltry 1 percent of its oceans) are protected areas, and it is undoubtedly the richer for it.

Americans and Europeans from the very beginning of the "wilderness cult" days made it their business to push for nature preservation in other countries, on the Yellowstone Model.[35] Countries with lots of land inhabited by few people—or by people with few rights—began their own national parks. From the 1870s to the 1890s, Australia, Canada, New Zealand, and several African countries opened parks.[36] With their own wilderness increasingly used up, westerners formed organizations like the International Union to Preserve Nature (now the International Union for Conservation of Nature or IUCN) and the World Wildlife Fund, in 1948 and 1961 respectively. These organizations continued to fight for new parks and other protected areas throughout the world. Soon the focus on protected areas got scientific support. In the late 1970s and early 1980s conservation biology was born as a scientific discipline. Two of its founders, Michael Soulé and Bruce Wilcox, wrote in the field's first textbook that "protected areas" are "the most valuable weapon in our conservation arsenal."[37]

But protected areas are not without their problems. Most early parks were chosen both for their perceived lack of value as working landscapes and for the value they could deliver to tourists seeking scenic beauty and the sublime. Early parks are all craggy, bedecked with grandiose vistas and tall waterfalls. Preserving something less sexy, like a swamp, just because it was a rare ecosystem, would have to wait until the 1940s.[38] Existing protected areas are disproportionately steep, rocky, barren, and covered in ice—useless for economic gain, and unrepresentative of the full spectrum of ecosystems on the planet.

Parks located on more fertile, flat, and workable land have another problem: people often were already living there when the protected area was created. And because the Yellowstone Model requires "untouched" nature, the people were often kicked out. Both Yosemite and Yellowstone were populated before they were parks. Yosemite Valley was the on-and-off home of the Miwok Indians, a group of whom were expelled to make way for gold miners in 1851 by the "Mariposa battalion" under the authority of the Mariposa County sheriff. But they didn't stay out.[39] Later Muir himself called for the expulsion of all Indians from Yosemite National Park.[40] A few lived in the park in the early decades of the twentieth century, on display, in an "Indian village." The last family left in 1969.[41] In Yellowstone, an initial agreement to let Indians stay was called off in 1877, and the area's residents were forcibly removed.[42]

According to journalist Mark Dowie, about half of the Earth's protected areas were "either occupied or regularly used by indigenous peoples." Millions of people have been moved in the last century to protect nature, but the irony is that they were doing the least harm—after all, that is why their land had sufficient nature to interest conservationists in the first place.[43] Today's conservation organizations are increasingly realizing that a protected area doesn't have to be depopulated to work. But Dowie believes that new "conservation refugees" continue to be created."[44] The "no people allowed" baggage of the Yellowstone Model is hard to shed.

Depending on the goal at hand, protected areas can indeed be the most valuable weapon in our arsenal. But even good weapons can misfire, causing collateral damage and casualties by friendly fire. And we mustn't believe that protected areas are the *only* weapon in our arsenal.

The mother park is also a good place to examine the tenacious idea of the "balance of nature." When conservationists guess what a park would look like in the absence of human domination, they assume that it would not have changed much on its own. Historical baselines are useful only for stable ecosystems. In the second half of this chapter, I'll explain how ecologists first embraced, then discarded this idea of a static or stable nature. Yellowstone, as it happens, is a great example of a place that has no stable state we can hang our hat on. It has always been in flux.

Although people didn't think in terms of ecosystems in 1882, park historian Paul Schullery believes that when George Bird Grinnell wrote about the park as a rock above the tide of immigration, he expected Yellowstone to persist, unchanging forever: "It seems pretty likely to me that, within the reasonable natural variations as he surely understood them (harsh winters, and so on), he was imagining that some ongoing and relatively stable Yellowstone landscape would result from just setting it aside and keeping it undeveloped."

That would have been the general view in the nineteenth century. "I think the implication is clear among those people that it was possible to set it aside and keep it as something that would just go on and on," says Schullery—though he adds, like a true historian, that it is foolish to make generalizations about what "everybody" in the nineteenth century thought based on the written documents they left behind.

The idea of nature as unchanging or fluctuating only modestly around a stable equilibrium, often called the "balance of nature" view, goes back a long way, at least to the ancient Greeks.[45] The American proto-conservationist George Perkins Marsh summed up his generation's view in 1864 by writing that "without man, lower animal and spontaneous vegetable life would have been constant in type, distribution, and proportion, and the physical geography of the earth would have remained undisturbed for indefinite periods, and been subject to revolution only from possible, unknown cosmical causes, or from geological action."[46]

At the end of the nineteenth century, early ecologists such as Eugenius Warming gave the "balance of nature" scientific credence. Warming and others looked into the question of "succession"—the changes in a particular landscape over time, leading to a final and stable endpoint. A fire might wipe out a forest, and a completely new set of plants might grow up from the ashes. But early ecologists noted that those plants would slowly be replaced by another suite of species, and those by still another, until eventually the original species that characterized the forest returned and took their rightful place.

Most influential among these early ecologists was Nebraska native Frederic Clements, active from the turn of the century through the 1930s. Clements saw newly available land as being colonized by a random, unstable suite of plants that would, over time, gravitate toward a predictable cast of characters, determined by climate. This grouping of species, the "climax," would go on forever, barring disturbance such as fire, windstorm, plow, flood, or ax.[47] Clements believed that climaxes would stay the same forever because they are perfectly balanced—in a state of stable equilibrium, in which any deviations from the mean tend to decrease over time, like a swing slowing down to hang still after a child has hopped off it.

With the help of animal ecologist Victor Shelford, Clements extended his succession arguments to all organisms in nature. So the animals, as well as the plants, were included in the climax community, which inexorably sprang up in any given climate.[48] Clements believed that every place on Earth had one single correct climax community, which he considered to be a kind of "organism." All the activities of plants and animals within this organism would eventually cancel each other out; if acorns were plentiful, squirrel populations would increase and eat them, then decrease as the food supply ran out. Oaks and squirrels would always ultimately return to an equilibrium state. Clements believed that no internal force could push the community to a new state.

Ecologist Henry Gleason at the University of Michigan, a contemporary of Clements, disagreed with this idea. Gleason believed plant communities were assembled mostly by chance, based on what got there first and what was able to hold on in the face of competition by other species. But Clements's idea of climax vegetation lodged itself firmly in the heads of many ecologists for years for come.

While some ecologists, including Marston Bates, tried to move away from Clementsian ideas in the 1950s, other ecologists hewed to the idea of stable equilibriums, especially the growing "systems ecology" group that studied energy and nutrient flows through ecosystems in the 1960s and 1970s. Such ecologists could model a lake, a forest, or even the whole Earth as a kind of large machine with inputs and outputs.[49] At the end of the year, they believed, most of these systems balanced out. The sun went up, photosynthesis occurred, nitrogen and other nutrients moved around, decomposers broke things down, big guys ate little guys, and the sun went down, with the ecosystem pretty much the same.[50]

This notion of stability persisted through the decades, even as ecologists learned more about how ecosystems responded to what they called *disturbance*. Many plants, it emerged, could not only tolerate disturbance but actually thrived on it. In some species, seeds can't germinate until they have been through a fire. In forests, light-hungry species depend on tree-falls that open up the canopy to make their move. But instead of upending the status quo, this expanding understanding that disturbance was not the enemy of nature was neatly folded into the overall stability theory. By the late 1970s, American ecologists were talking about the importance of patchiness in an ecosystem,[51] and describing a forest composed of patches of different ages as a "shifting mosaic."[52] But this shifting mosaic was, so to speak, the texture of the overall steady state.[53] The forest as a whole was still considered to be constant. The numbers and total mass of each species of plant or animal in any given ecosystem were believed to be stable over time, fluctuating only modestly. And unless disturbance was severe, ecosystems could "heal" themselves, returning to their original composition.[54]

Generations of field ecologists tried to make their observations fit this model, but the real world was stubbornly unpredictable. One of the quantitative ecological models that predict stable equilibriums in nature is the Lotka-Volterra equations, named after two ecologists. These equations predict that predator and prey populations will oscillate in an elegant symmetry: the moose will boom, providing more food for the wolves, who will then boom and eat most of the moose; with the moose all eaten, the wolves will starve, and once wolf numbers are down, the moose will boom again. Moose and wolf will dance this way together forever, or so the equations say. The problem, writes ecologist Daniel Botkin, is that so many contingencies are left out of this model. These mathematical moose and wolves are all identical. There is no infancy or old age, no disease, no parasites, no pack hierarchy, no vegetation scarcity, no cruel winters, no refuges from wolves, and no other prey besides moose.[55] Botkin, as an eager young ecologist, tried his best to squish data on moose and wolves that he and others gathered on Isle Royale in Lake Superior into Lotka-Volterra oscillations. It would not fit. For Botkin, the implication is that these predictable cycles are, in real life out in nature, swamped by sheer randomness (in ecological jargon, *stochasticity*).

Botkin wasn't the only one to fail to extract the expected curves from nature. Mathematical biologists have found that chaos, rather than equilibrium, is more common in the simple food webs they study. The authors of one such study wrote that in their Baltic Sea plankton community, maintained in a lab for over eight years, "predictability was limited to a time horizon of 15–30 days, only slightly longer than the local weather forecast."[56]

Botkin's experience on Isle Royale disagreed with the pervasive background assumption that ecosystems were fundamentally stable. In his 1990 book *Discordant Harmonies*, he characterized this assumption as "dominant in textbooks on ecology and the popular environmental literature," "the foundation of the twentieth-century scientific theory about populations and ecosystems," and "the basis of most national laws and international agreements that control the use of wild lands and wild creatures."[57]

While Botkin's book was well read among ecologists, he feels that the assumption of stability is still with us and is as tenacious as ever. "The balance of nature idea is so deeply ingrained that it is still dominant," he says. "If you ask an ecologist if nature never changes, he will almost always say no. But if you ask that same ecologist to design a policy, it is almost always a balance of nature policy."

As Botkin suggests, these days most professional ecologists do not believe in Clementsian succession. They admit that systems in true long-lasting equilibrium are the exception. Disturbances are so common in some systems that no stable endpoint is ever reached. Even in sleepy places where disturbances like fires, mudslides or volcanoes are rare, ecosystems barely have a chance to settle down into a serious self-perpetuating groove before the climate changes.

Feng Sheng Hu, a paleoecologist at the University of Illinois in Urbana, likes to quote the Greek philosopher Heraclitus, to his students: "the only constant in nature is change itself." As an example, he cites the magnificent old-growth forests of the Pacific Northwest. To the untrained eye, the seven-hundred-year-old Douglas-fir trees that dominate the scene look not only finished, somehow, but timeless, as if they had been sitting there, knee deep in the humus of their ancestors, for millions of years. But from a forest paleoecologist's perspective, they are *only* seven hundred years old. "This species in fact has the ability to live 1,000 or 1,200 years," Hu says. "But you don't see many of them that old. So what happened?"

The biggest driver of change in these forests, within the past couple of million years or so, has been what some researchers call *secular climate change*—climate changes that were not humanity's fault. Seven hundred years ago marked the end of the Medieval Warm Period, a dry and warm climatic episode that would likely have seen frequent fires. The cooler, wetter climate that came afterward allowed the "old growth" forests we see today to begin to develop. And that first generation of Douglas-firs is still growing up, with a good five hundred years left to go—barring any new disturbances. Here the climate changes faster than the life span of a single generation of trees.

"The point," says Hu, "is that there really isn't one unique state of natural conditions for any given landscape. What is more realistic is to set a range of natural conditions."

I asked Hu if he could identify a "quiet moment" where planet Earth's ecosystems stayed put long enough to be considered in some kind of stable equilibrium, something we could use as a baseline. His answer? No.

At the beginning of the Pleistocene epoch, 2.5 million years ago, the Earth entered an ice age, and we're still in it. The ice age has alternated very cold and icy periods—glaciations—with milder periods called *inter-glacials*. We're in an interglacial now. This pattern has repeated about fifty times, with cycles varying from about 40,000 years during the early Pleistocene to 100,000 years during the late Pleistocene.[58] Interglacials are much shorter than glaciations—only about 10,000 years long apiece—so if one wanted to establish a baseline by averaging the last two million years, that baseline for a lot of places in the northern hemisphere would be much colder than today, and in places like the upper Midwest, it would be ice. And we can't just average all the interglacials together either, because each one is different.

Pollen researchers, examining microscopic pollen that was trapped in layers of lake sediment to form a nice chronological record, have been able to trace the movements of plant species across several glaciations. Like seaweed that drifts in and out as the waves roll up and down the shore, many species have moved hundreds of miles over and over again. The planet will cool, the glaciers will expand, and juniper will head south. Tens of thousands of years later, the planet will warm, the glaciers will retreat, and juniper will head north again.

But every slow migration has its own idiosyncrasies. Some plants disperse faster than others; some may be also struggling with a pest or a new competitor; species adapt and evolve over time. Additionally, the glaciations haven't all been identical; some pushed much farther south than others. Occasionally, for reasons that may or may not be discernible from the present, a species migrates in the "wrong" direction, or makes an unpredictable foray to the east or west.[59] Gerald Rehfeldt, a retired U.S. Forest Service geneticist based in Moscow, Idaho, gives an example from climate-change models:

> Intuitively, one would think that the climate is warming, so the trend in vegetation would be Mexico flora moving north. That is not what the models show. In the Southwest, the desert expands, and the mountainous species in the U.S. move up and north and the mountainous species in Mexico move up and south. Deserts expand in both directions.

As a result, the distribution maps for plant species don't look the same from interglacial to interglacial.[60] Each climate change creates a new map, with new communities of species living together. Whole suites of species do not pick up en masse and decorously tiptoe south, making sure to keep together. It is rather a mad scramble—albeit in geological time.

Some of today's ecosystems have not fully bounced back from the last glaciation. One analysis suggested that thirty-six of fifty-five European tree species studied had still not spread out to the edges of their possible ranges.[61] Beech trees are notoriously poky. In North America they are still moving west across Michigan's Upper Peninsula.[62]

The whole planet doesn't get covered with ice during these Pleistocene glaciations. So do the hotter regions of the Earth show more stability? Nope. "Fifteen or twenty years ago most people would say that the tropics didn't change at all," says Hu. "That is not the case. There is plenty of evidence that they changed during the glacial periods. Forests were much more fragmented and the climate was certainly cooler. And if you think about the ocean, coral reefs have been affected because sea levels were so much lower than today." Meanwhile, the deserts of the American Southwest are apparently still drying out from the last ice age, when they were much more moist.[63]

The continent that might have changed the least in the near-past of geologic time is Australia, which drifted north toward the hotter equator over millennia as the global climate gradually cooled, thus maintaining a fairly stable climate in "an almost miraculous balancing act," according to Australian paleontologist and science writer Tim Flannery.[64] As a result, Australia has never been covered by glaciers, though its center did become a "vast dustbowl of swirling sand dunes where vegetation could not survive" during the last glaciation.[65]

On shorter timescales, ecosystems are prone to climate disturbances like planet-scale atmospheric and oceanic patterns such as the El Niño-Southern Oscillation, an ocean and climate phenomenon in which the central and eastern Pacific Ocean gets unusually warm and air currents across the equator change, spawning a complex series of consequences. Trade winds weaken, rainfall patterns change all across the world, and hurricanes settle down. Marine ecosystems in certain places fold up like accordions as phytoplankton die off in the heat.

Add to that the constant movement of sediment from erosion, rivers changing their courses, and biological irruptions like acorn masts or cicada broods, and you have a layering of asynchronous and often irregular patterns. What emerges is a picture of constant flux. Ecologists often try their best to factor out all these kinds of disturbances when studying natural systems. To them, they can be "noise" in their data. Another perspective, however, is that the noise is the data—that the changes, the disturbance, the outlying events, and the confounding factors are often the most important drivers of the system. Ecosystems are fundamentally stable entities afflicted by changes from without and within about as much as a ballet is a fundamentally static object afflicted with motion.

Thanks to the constant barrage of changes, ecosystems simply cannot stay unchanged for more than a few thousand years. According to one analysis, "There are few or no spots on earth where ecosystems have existed unchanged for more than 12,000 years."[66]

Yellowstone is among the systems that ecologists now believe are *nonequilibrial*.[67] Tree-ring studies done in the early 1980s by ecologist William Romme found no evidence that different successional stages always occupied the same proportion of the landscape, as predicted by the "shifting mosaic" model. Occasional huge wildfires—like the famous fires of 1988—can replace miles of mature stands with opened areas overnight, upending everything from wildlife habitat and food resources to streamflow levels.

And at such vulnerable moments, any changes in climate can have a disproportionately large influence. Mature trees can take the odd cold snap or drought, but seedlings in their first year or two are much more susceptible to extremes. If the climate is, say, too dry for lodgepole seedlings to survive, then a new landscape could replace today's familiar lodgepole-dominated forests. Douglas-firs could move in, or the forests could become a persistent meadow.

Once we understand that the ecology of Yellowstone is not stable over historical or prehistorical time, obsessing over 1872 is no longer as helpful to park managers. It doesn't help that 1872 was just at the end of a particularly cold snap, colloquially called the Little Ice Age, that came right after the Medieval Warm Period. Thus our baseline for Yellowstone is the ecosystem under particularly cold circumstances, which will be hard to hold to as the climate warms.

All of this brings me to Daisy Pass in the Gallatin National Forest, just north of the park. I'm standing at the snowline with Idaho State University ecologist Ken Aho. He's pointing out one of his study sites, an impossibly steep peak above our heads, partially obscured by white mist. Aho is studying the effects of mountain goats on the delicate, slow growing alpine vegetation that grows on such slopes. Every summer he and an assistant spend a few weeks camping in these mountains, subsisting on Power Bars, ramen, and melted snow, censusing plants and counting goat feces. His data will help park managers decide what to do about the mountain goats, which are not native to the Greater Yellowstone Ecosystem.

The powerfully built white goats with square faces seem just right for this landscape, but apparently they were moved here by Montana Fish and Wildlife officials in the 1940s for hunters. Their closest native range is two hundred miles away, and no fossils of mountain goats have been found that would indicate that they lived here in a former time. If Aho finds that they are hurting the alpine vegetation, or if other scientists find that the mountain goats are stealing food or turf from the bighorn sheep, the Park Service may get rid of them.

So far Aho hasn't found that they are doing much damage, though they may be speeding up plant growth by fertilizing the earth with their droppings. And ultimately the decision about what to do about the mountain goats may be moot. Climate models suggest that in a warmer future there won't be much alpine in Yellowstone to worry about. "You can't fight the climate," says Aho. "Eventually you have to throw up your hands if these things are inevitable."

Imagine Montana's Glacier National Park without any glaciers, Joshua Tree National Park with no Joshua trees, California's Sequoia National Park with no sequoias. Now come back in fifty years, and if the predictions are right, you won't have to imagine it. You'll be able to see it. What are park managers to do when faced with these overwhelming threats to the historical condition?

Let's say Aho and other scientists find that the mountain goats aren't changing Yellowstone's ecosystems very much. Park managers now have a philosophical decision to make about what to do about them. Should they be shot because they weren't there in 1872? Should they be allowed to stay because people like them and *think* they are native? After all, the authors of the Leopold Report admitted that "restoring the primitive scene is not done easily nor can it be done completely," yet "a reasonable illusion of primitive America could be recreated, using the utmost in skill, judgment, and ecologic sensitivity."[68] Would mountain goats have a home in that "reasonable illusion"? But with the climate changing, perhaps the reasonable illusion is no longer within reach. Perhaps on some of the lower peaks park managers should just abandon the alpine as lost and work on other ecosystems?

"There are changes all the time in ecosystems, directional and stochastic," says Aho. "You can't become attached to one particular snapshot. Part of the beauty of ecology is its change." Indeed, these days park managers are more likely to manage for "resilience" than for 1872 or any other historical baseline. Resilience is an ecosystem's ability to endure disturbances and changes without substantially changing in character. The idea is that a resilient ecosystem can sail into a warmer future with only minor adjustments, while a stressed ecosystem collapses at the first hot summer into something new, something undesirable. In essence, managers are admitting that change is happening and will continue to happen, but they are hoping to keep it gradual and subtle.

For Aho, change is beautiful, but man-made or *anthropogenic* change is not. He has actual nightmares about a restaurant opening on the summit of Grand Teton. He's not alone. Despite increasing evidence for Indian influence on the area that became Yellowstone, historian Paul Schullery writes, "even among those of us who know and accept this evidence there is a lingering feeling that things were somehow *right* back then, that some fundamental state of harmony existed between humans and the rest of nature and that North America was a kind of environmental Eden until Europeans arrived."[69]

But the search for the untouched is as vain as the search for the unchanging. Science tells us that ecosystems never hold still. History tells us that they are never pristine. We humans have changed every centimeter of the globe. Even, as I was to find out, ancient, virgin forest.

3 | The Forest Primeval

In 2008 I visited a shrine to the notion of the pristine wilderness: Białowieża Primeval Forest. The forest straddles the border between Poland and Belarus and is advertised as 580 square miles of untouched lowland temperate forest—that is, the kind of forest that many believe would have covered most of Western and Central Europe before people cut it down. The strictly protected inner core of Białowieża, some 18 square miles, has managed to slip through the entirety of European history without ever being clear-cut: if a climax temperate forest exists in Europe, this is it. Today it is a protected area and a site of pilgrimage for those who want to see what Europe looked like before people.

But as I was to find out, just because it was never cut down doesn't mean Białowieża is pristine. The subtle and complex influence of people on the forest illustrates the sort of human-caused changes that conservationists can overlook when holding natural places up as pristine. And if few places are as pristine as we once thought, then we can no longer use them to characterize prehuman baselines or revere them as the only nature worth saving.

The village of Białowieża is spread out on two long roads, and every other house features rooms for tourists or a massive rooftop stork nest. My guide to the forest is the former vice-director of the park, currently director of the University of Warsaw's Geobotanical Station: Bogdan Jaroszewicz, a slim man with close-cropped hair and a blue plaid shirt tucked into his jeans. We cross a field, at the far end of which is an abrupt dark line of trees, the very edge of history, past which we will plunge into the lost Europe of prehistory, the *Urwald* from which the continent's fairy tales and legends have sprung.

At the tree line, a large wooden gate separates the forest from the field. This is the strictly protected core, prohibited to unaccompanied visitors. All tourists must be escorted by licensed guides. Jaroszewicz stops at the gate and pulls out a can of mosquito repellent, which he solemnly hands to me. I apply a few squirts and hand it back. He sprays himself thoroughly from head to toe, including a good thick layer on top of his socks, in a ritual anointment indicating his separateness from the forest inside. Or perhaps he is merely being prudent.

Slipping through the gate, we enter a sun-dappled mingling of mostly broadleaf trees of all different ages and sizes: oak, spruce, hornbeam, and linden. Mossy limbs are bent in sinuous shapes, retaining in summer the contours they were pressed into by the weight of winter snow. Mosquitoes float picturesquely, catching the sun and filling the forest with dreamy motion—until they land on us and start sucking.

We are surrounded by green, but also brown, black, and red. Up to a quarter of the standing wood is dead, and it is the dead wood that really gives this forest its sense of great age, more so than the scampering of wild boar piglets or the musky, venerable presence of the largest remaining population of European bison. Here, unlike virtually anywhere else in Europe, dead trees are left to decompose where they die, organic matter is not constantly streaming out of the forest, and a whole host of species like beetles and woodpeckers that depend on dead wood can thrive. The dead wood feeds fungus: platelike shelf fungus in china white and explosions of orangey fungus in flower shapes. Death makes the forest feel natural in a way that a plantation of same-aged trees in neat rows does not.

The forest is brighter than I expected; I grew up in the Pacific Northwest, where old-growth forests can be very dark and dense. We stick to the path on this walk, though later I go with another scientific group off-trail, and it is surprisingly easy to move between the trees and over the underbrush (though nettles are common). The trees are impressively big: 600-year old oaks, big as castles; ashes and lindens 140 feet high in their third century; pussy willows 100 feet high.[1] The air smells like the little herb known as bear garlic and sounds like the sea as thousands of leaves rustle in the wind. We have moved only a few feet into the forest, but I feel irresistibly that we have traveled back in time.

But as Jaroszewicz explains, when Białowieża is called "pristine" in tourist brochures, it is a bit of an oversimplification. "This forest was used," he says. "It is not a virgin forest untouched by man."

This forest did not just happen to escape the ax. Białowieża was intentionally preserved in recent centuries—often as a game preserve for royals and other elites. Local people have also used its resources. Together all the small interactions between humans and the forest have influenced the ecosystem.

Białowieża sprang up after the retreat of the last northern European glacier 10,000 to 12,000 years ago, and its species composition changed as the climate warmed.[2] Its current composition is thought to date back 2,000 years.[3] The first human artifacts are almost as old. Iron-age settlements and cemeteries from the first to fifth centuries A.D., as well as Slavonic graves from the ninth through eleventh centuries are found in the forest.[4]

In the fourteenth century, as Poland and Lithuania were united under one ruler, it became a carefully managed hunting ground. In 1409 Władysław Jagiełło, king of Poland and Lithuania, held a big hunt among its trees, gathering game for an army preparing to fight the Teutonic Knights, a band of Christian mercenaries who claimed lands that Jagiełło claimed for Poland. The game was salted and sealed in barrels, and it must have nourished the army well, as they went on to decisively break the back of the knights at the Battle of Grunwald.[5] The Poles I met were still quite pleased with this victory. One told me that it provided some consolation whenever the Germans beat them at soccer.

The forest continued to change hands as history unspooled. Guards and wardens protected game and controlled forest access.[6] European bison, or wisent, existed here only because they were saved as game for elites. This species, which looks similar to the American bison, once ranged over Western, Central and Southeastern Europe. At eighteen hundred pounds, horned and shaggy, these largest of the European mammals had already been reduced to a few remnant populations by the eleventh century but were kept alive in the vast green pantry that was Białowieża.[7]

In the nineteenth century, under Russian rule, predators that competed with humans for game were killed to keep their numbers low. Bears were considered choice game until 1869, when they were relabeled as predators of bison and exterminated.[8] Wolves shared the same fate. Game numbers were inflated by large-scale feeding, which resulted in a forest fat with bison, wild boar, roe deer, red deer (a large species that closely resembles the North American elk), and introduced fallow deer, which all ate so many saplings that they may have changed the age and species structure of the forest. For example, spruce numbers increased in the forest beginning in the nineteenth century, and Jaroszewicz is trying to work out whether this is because of climate change or because of a high density of herbivores, which would have eaten the more tender broadleaf seedlings before they tackled the spruce seedlings. Spruce has been on the wane, though, since the 1950s. Again, the reasons are unclear. Is it because of an outbreak of spruce bark beetles, or are spruce numbers just settling down after their nineteenth-century boom? "We are seeing changes that we can't interpret," says Jaroszewicz.

During World War I, Germany set up an intensive logging operation, clearing 5 percent of the forest.[9] Troops went on a hunting spree to feed themselves, hitting the bison particularly hard.[10] An unknown and likely hungry poacher shot the last bison in the forest just after the First World War. Between wars the forest was logged by a British company and then by Polish foresters. A small portion was made into a strictly protected park in 1929. At the same time a few zoo bison were brought back to the forest but kept in a fenced yard.[11]

In the run-up to World War II, Hermann Göring, a passionate hunter, visited the forest to acquire bison for his personal menagerie and bag large numbers of deer and boar. When the war began in 1939, Białowieża fell into Russian hands almost immediately, then went back to the Germans in 1941. Göring took it over as his own playground. He ordered the game protected and the local people expelled from forest villages and murdered in large numbers. Their corpses were left just inside the woods.[12] Deeper in, Polish partisans hid in the forest fastness.

After the war Stalin agreed (as the locals have it, after several shots of vodka) to let the old-growth core of Białowieża remain on the Polish side of the newly erected Polish-Soviet border. Later on a six-and-a-half-foot barbed-wire border fence was put up by the Soviets.[13] Times have changed; instead of the USSR, Poland now borders Belarus, but the fence is still there, and still guarded, with neatly mown grass on each side. There is a crossing in Białowieża, but it is only for those on foot, on bicycles, or on horseback. I am told that few people cross on horseback, as the horse also needs a passport. On the Belarusian side, the forest is not very carefully studied or cared for. Rumor has it that the Belarusian leader since 1994, Alexander Lukashenko, uninterested in hunting, has had an extensive Rollerblading track installed among the trees.

These days the human influence continues. The European mink is locally extinct. New species, including many woody plants and the Asian raccoon dog, have moved in. Thirteen captive bison from the fenced enclosure were released in 1952, and another two dozen or so later.[14] Their descendants are still fed in the winter and culled in the summer to keep their numbers down. Park managers insist the bison need both the feeding and the culling to maintain a healthy population. Climate change, too, has come to Białowieża. Jaroszewicz and his colleagues are seeing obvious changes in the timing of events like flowering and leaf-out in the forest. The amount of rain is so far the same, but it falls in a different pattern throughout the year. This, plus the draining of bogs on the Belarusian side of the forest, is lowering the groundwater.

And the small size of the forest is a problem. Take spruce bark beetles. If the forest stretched for hundreds of miles, a boom of beetles could take out a large chunk, no problem. It could fill in later. But foresters worry that a major boom in Białowieża could kill all the spruce, and there would be nowhere for new spruce seedlings to come from. Or take lynx. "Lynx has a personal range of one hundred square kilometers," says Jaroszewicz. "So we can afford to have one lynx. We have three or four because ranges overlap, but not enough to sustain a population." The patchy dynamics of the forest—one bit filled with twenty-year-old trees, another with three-hundred-year-olds, still continues, he says, but in miniature. "The character of the disturbances is smaller in scale": a single tree falling, perhaps, rather than a fire. A forest fire that started here would probably be suppressed. "This forest is too small and precious to let it burn," he says.

In a way, the venerable moss-draped trees are camouflage for all the changes that have happened since humans first entered the forest nearly 2,000 years ago. Indeed, my sighting of a European bison is an excellent allegory for the odd marriage of wild and humanized that is Białowieża.

Bison researcher Rafal Kowalczyk has located a radio-collared beast for me by driving absurdly fast down narrow forest roads and occasionally hopping out and holding up what looks like an old-fashioned rooftop TV antenna attached to a box on a strap around his neck. Finally he hears a faint and fleeting noise, a *poink, poink, poink* sound just louder than the static. He has his bison. I follow him into the woods, trying as hard as I can to keep up without snapping sticks with my feet, and I sniff the air as we walk. Kowalczyk says bison have a distinctive smell, "not a smell as strong as wild boar or red deer. A bit like cattle, the smell of fresh milk." We enter a sun-dappled glade, alive with fat, drifting mosquitoes. Behind a bush, apparently unaware of our presence, stands a huge sienna-colored mass, a shaggy bison with a high hump, a ridgelike backbone, a skinny butt, black horns, and an undeniable reek of ancient days. He is an eight- or nine-year-old male, in the prime of life. Of course he has a radio collar, and his ancestors lived at the zoo, but none of that can quite diminish the timeless sensation of this scene: the silent bison browsing in the green, mossy, half-rotting forest. Suddenly Kowalczyk, a few steps ahead of me, turns around and, in a whisper, gives me a last-minute tip: "If bison charges, jump behind tree." The bison doesn't charge; I am not sure he ever sees us. A few minutes later he disappears noiselessly. "Sometimes they slip away like a ghost," says Kowalczyk.

The aura of the forest, the fascination of the ancient, remains for Jaroszewicz as well. He still loves to wander the protected core—appropriately anointed in mosquito repellent, of course. "Each time I see a new process or simply a new beautiful tree," he says. "The whole forest is mysterious and interesting."

Tomasz Samojlik, who grew up near the forest, has returned to study its environmental history at the Polish Academy of Sciences' Mammal Research Institute. He has investigated iron-age cemeteries, along with royal hunts, beekeeping in trees, and ore-smelting operations deep in the forest; he once found a fifteen-hundred-year-old sickle knife lying just under the tangled grass, untouched all these years. "After five or six years I have come to the conclusion that humans have always been connected to the forest," he says.

Samojlik is educating ecologists about the human influence on the forest, and historians and archaeologists are doing the same around the world. Our fingerprints are everywhere. In many parts of the world, people predate the last major climate change (Africa, Australia) or arrived as soon as the ice retreated (North America, Northern Europe). As in Białowieża, there was no humanless idyll. But often ecologists didn't consider earlier humans disruptive to ecosystems.

This blindness has generally been most apparent in countries colonized by Europeans. For generations, whatever state the landscape was in when the first white man stepped off the boat was considered "wild." Until recently, indigenous peoples were dismissed as too few and too undeveloped to seriously affect the landscape in which they lived. When the first calls went out to protect the vanishing American wilderness in the mid-nineteenth century, everyone assumed that the continent as Columbus found it was "untouched." "When Columbus first saw land, America was the sublimest object in the world," said historian Francis Parkman Jr., at Harvard's graduation ceremony in 1844. "Here was the domain of Nature."[15] Many observers of nature mentally classified indigenous people with the fauna of a place. Unlike "civilized man," they didn't spoil a landscape but belonged to it, as much as the deer or birds did; any presumably minor alterations they made to the place could therefore be classed with beaver dams or grazed meadows as natural.

In fact, America and Australia's first people might have made greater changes to the landscape than the European arrivals ever did. Sure, they never paved any of it, or dumped toxic chemicals into rivers, but they did kill off many of the species that once lived there.

Somewhere in the neighborhood of 13,000 to 14,000 years ago, the Americas lost a slew of large beasts, including wild horses, mammoths, mastodons, sixteen groups of ground sloths, the glyptodont (something like a four-thousand-pound angry tortoise with a spiked mace for a tail), short-faced bears that would make polar bears look puny, camels, saber-tooth tigers, lions, and cheetahs.[16] That's right. Not so long ago an American cheetah lounged around in the branches of the oak trees dotting the Great Plains. All of these large animals—"megafauna"—died out roughly around the same time in a burst of extinction.[17] Many scientists believe that humans killed them. Tellingly, humans arrived just before the extinction boom. Human fossils in North America mostly date from about 13,000 years ago, with a few sites going back to around 14,300 years ago.[18]

Only some species disappeared during this extinction pulse, and the ones that did tended to be the ones you would expect sensible hunters to go after. Most plants, small bugs, shrews, reptiles, and other miscellaneous creepy-crawlies made it through just fine. In general, the largest animals, with the most calories per kill, went extinct. And often the slowest big beasts went first.

Additional evidence comes from places where humans arrived later. Megafauna have a way of persisting on islands . . . until humans show up. For example, the most recent fossils of ground sloths on the mainland of North America date from around the time of the general large herbivore decline. But in Cuba and Hispaniola, dwarf ground sloths (animals often appear in smaller versions on islands, a phenomenon called "island dwarfism") persisted for 5,000 or 6,000 years beyond that, until just about when signs of human presence also show up on these islands.[19]

Similarly, North American mammoths went kaput during the general extinction pulse, except in two far-north islands. In 1999 hunters discovered a cave on remote St. Paul Island, off the coast of Alaska, already known to be the home of some very late mammoths. Named Qagnax̂," the Aleut word for bone, by a group of researchers from the University of Alaska and elsewhere, the cave yielded 1,740 bones, including 1,250 fox bones, 250 polar bear bones, and seven woolly mammoth bones. The mammoth bones included three teeth (mammoth teeth are huge and highly textured, looking something like a bunch of shoe soles glued together and turned to stone) and two head bones. They were dated to about 6,500 years ago and are now the youngest mammoth bones in North America. Scientists believe that St. Paul's mammoths died out only when rising sea levels made the island too tiny to support a mammoth population.[20] Wrangel Island, on the Russian side, had mammoths until even later, a mere 4,000 years ago.[21]

Another even later hanger-on was the Steller's sea cow, a titanic marine mammal weighing in at somewhere between 10,000 and 20,000 pounds; it went extinct on the North American Pacific coast around the same time as the rest of the land mammals. A population survived on the remote Commander Islands in the Bering Sea—until humans found them in 1741.[22] Within thirty years of their discovery, they were extinct.

The originator of what came to be called the *overkill hypothesis*, the late Paul Martin of the University of Arizona, tended to finger a group of people who lived all over North and South America about 13,000 years ago. "Clovis people" were named, in the archaeological tradition, for one of the first important sites where their tools were found, near Clovis, New Mexico. (The town itself was named for Clovis, the king who united and Christianized the Franks in the fifth century.) Clovis people are noted for their enormous spear points, which look designed for killing very big game. Indeed, these points have been found suggestively nestled between mammoth ribs.[23] Clovis culture only lasted a few hundred years, after which it was replaced by a number of local variants, usually featuring smaller spear points—perhaps redesigned for the humbler game left after the big Clovis spree.

However, newer dates for both people and megafauna extinctions in the Americas tend to push backward into time. Recently researchers have put forth a new and more precise date for the extinction of most North American megaherbivores, based on their study of the sediment of an Indiana lake that contains the spores of a fungus that specialized in eating herbivore dung.[24] These fungi lived it up on what must have been a continent rich with poop until they declined between 14,800 and 13,700 years ago, presumably because the herbivores that pooped out their lunch were declining at the same time.[25] As extinction expert Christopher Johnson put it in the journal *Science* in November 2009, "It is beginning to look as if the greater part of that decline was driven by hunters who were neither numerous nor highly specialized for big-game hunting. Clovis technology may have been a feature of the endgame, possibly reflecting an intensified hunting strategy that developed once megafauna had become rare, possibly wary, and harder to hunt."[26]

We don't yet understand precisely what role humans played in extinctions in prehistoric Europe, Africa, and Asia. These continents had large-mammal extinctions within the last few million years, to be sure. There are no more woolly mammoths, woolly rhinos, or cave bears in Europe, for example.[27] But they weren't all bunched up together in time, and they weren't as numerous. The reason, according to Martin, could be that humans lived in these areas for so long. Animals were thus able to evolve in response to humans' growing hunting prowess. Prey species could become faster, better at hiding, and more wary, as humans slowly learned better and better tricks for hunting them.[28]

This might help explain why the American beasts that did make it past the big extinction pulse tended to be those that had recently arrived on the continents themselves. Caribou, bison, elk, mountain goat, and moose all evolved in the Old World, presumably in tandem with their pesky bipedal pursuers, the humans.[29] They likely crossed over to the Americas several tens of thousands of years before humans did, and many have been here long enough to be considered separate species from their Eurasian kin, but chances are they were a bit better prepared for human hunters than the giant ground sloths.

But outside Europe, Africa, and Asia, extinctions and humans arrived hand in hand. If humans were partly or wholly responsible for these extinctions, then "untouched" nature has long passed away in the Americas, in Australia, and on the Pacific islands.

Australia today is a land of dangerous animals: huge crocodiles, many species of poisonous snake, and kangaroos that descend vertically in front of one's car at dusk. But it is not, particularly, a land of large mammals. The red kangaroo is the heavyweight champion, weighing in at up to two hundred pounds.[30] Many of the marsupials that characterize the native fauna of Australia are petite. This is partly because of the geological history and climate of the continent. The soils are old and low in nutrients; much of the inland is very dry. There is not a lot of vegetable productivity to support big animals. But the continent once featured a few more robust marsupials, such as the diprotodons—wombatlike creatures the size of taco trucks—as well as kangaroos more than twice the size of those that remain, horned turtles weighing more than four hundred pounds, and twenty-foot monitor lizards.[31] But about 50,000 years ago humans arrived, and shortly thereafter everything larger than themselves disappeared.[32]

The story in New Zealand is perhaps the most compelling, because humans first landed on the isle a mere eight hundred years ago.[33] Before people arrived, New Zealand was full of birds. Tim Flannery reports that the fossil record contains 164 species, many of them flightless.[34] Towering above everything else were the several species of moas, one of the biggest birds ever. Moas could be up to twelve feet tall and weigh 550 pounds.[35] They were feathered from beak-base to ankle and likely reddish brown, though some purple and white feathers have been found, hinting at splendid crests or tails.[36]

When people first arrived on New Zealand—they would become known as the Maori—they took one look at the moas and abandoned their chickens, which they had carefully transported with them in their canoes.[37] Moas were so big and so easy to bag that the Maori didn't bother to eat the whole bird. Heads, necks, and other less palatable bits were discarded; the Maori went for the drumsticks.[38] "Remarkably," writes Flannery, "absolutely no evidence of specialized hunting tools has been recovered from the excavated villages of the moa hunters. This may be because the moa hunters had to do little more than walk up to the enormous birds and spear or club them in order to obtain a meal."[39] Within four hundred years of human arrival, the moa were all dead.[40]

With the moa gone, the extinctions continued. Next to go were two species of seals and smaller birds. By the time Europeans came to New Zealand, the Maori were short on food and split into small communities.[41] War had been turned into an art; cannibalism was widespread.[42] They probably wished they hadn't been so hasty when ditching their chickens.

The story was the same all over Melanesia, Micronesia, and Polynesia. Among Hawaii's lost are *Thambetochen*, a duck, and *Apteribis*, a flightless ibis.[43] Perhaps surprising is the survival of the nēnē, a goose that is close kin to the Canada goose. Within the last 3,000 years, most of the many islands of the Pacific have lost a good chunk of their birds, and the extinctions can be traced in time, from west to east, in lockstep with the progress of ocean-going canoes.[44] An analysis by Richard Duncan of Lincoln University in New Zealand suggests that on Pacific islands, the birds most likely to go extinct were the slow, the large, and the flightless, a combination of factors that instantly suggests humans stepping off of boats with empty stomachs and clubbing on their minds.[45]

The consequences of all these extinctions rippled out through ecosystems and extended to every corner of the landscape. In many places, grasslands turned to forests when all those mega-herbivores that used to keep everything tidily grazed and browsed disappeared. In the upper Midwest of America, a savanna dotted with a few trees, mostly spruce, was replaced by a forest of black ash, hornbeam, ironwood, and spruce.[46] Fires markedly increased, fueled by the uneaten vegetation.[47] The new ash-ironwood-spruce forest was replaced with pines after a few thousand years. Later still, oaks began to dominate pines.[48] These changes may have been the result of both climate change and the continued unfolding effects of the extinction of the herbivores.

Scientists believe that the extinctions of 13,000 years ago even changed the climate. Regrowing forests reflect less sunlight than grasslands, so the earth may have absorbed more heat when forests expanded. And fewer large beasts meant 10 billion kilograms less methane emitted each year from their farts, according to Felisa Smith of the University of New Mexico in Albuquerque. And sure enough, ice core records show a sudden drop of methane levels from the atmosphere about 13,000 years ago.[49]

Humanity's changes to the landscape didn't stop when the extinction pulse was over. In North and South America, forget the idea of land besprinkled with a few low-impact tribes of people. As many as 112 million lived here, more people than lived in Europe at that time, according to recent estimates by archaeologists.[50] The reason these people escaped our notice until recently is that few Europeans saw any of them. European-borne disease, especially smallpox, killed as many as 95 percent of people in the Americas in the first century or so after contact (though the exact percentage is contentious).[51] By the time Europeans penetrated the conti-nent, most of its inhabitants were dead, its tribes and polities in disorga-nized fragments, its traditions already disappearing in the chaos of mass plagues. Only the very first European explorers, like Giovanni da Verraz-ano, who sailed along the East Coast of North America in the 1520s, saw a "densely populated" country packed with notably tall, healthy attractive people.[52]

The inhabitants of North and South America had grand cities, expan-sive agricultural fields, large-scale irrigation, and huge earthworks, includ-ing agricultural terracing, residential platforms above floodplain aquaculture works, and massive religious mounds—some in the shapes of animals. Near present-day St. Louis, one can still climb the central mound of the corn-crazy metropolis of Cahokia, a London-sized city that flourished from about A.D. 950 to 1250.[53] And nearly everywhere people had a way with fire. Many North American groups used fire to clear areas to promote new green growth, which would in turn attract grazing animals that could be hunted. The Haudenosaunee, for example, burned Manhattan every fall.[54] Many American prairies and grasslands thought to be "natural" were in fact artifacts of Indian land management.

In the east of North America, for hundreds of years before Europeans arrived, people supplemented their maize crops by using fire and tree plant-ing to create orchards. These orchards have now mostly melted back into the forest but can still be picked out by their high concentrations of chest-nuts, walnuts, pecans, hickory, and the like.[55]

People in the Amazon rain forest kept similar orchards, breeding trees such as the peach palm and dozens others into more appealing varieties.[56] While much of the Amazon basin has notoriously poor soil, some inhabit-ants planted their orchards and especially their row crops on a dark, fer-tile soil called "black lands" or *terra preta do Indio*. These Amazonian dark earths were made by pre-European residents of the Amazon rainforest. The darkest patches were the trash heaps of settlements and are cluttered with crescents of broken pottery. Larger and slightly lighter patches were once agricultural areas where charred wood was intentionally added to the soil to boost its fertility.[57] Researchers studying *terra preta* say that the expanse of such soil hints at an Amazonian population of at least 8 or 9 million at the time of contact. This is much higher than earlier estimates, which were based on the idea of Amazonia as a place of impenetrable jungles and poor soils supporting, at most, a few thinly scattered and unsophisticated peoples.

From the Amazon to the Yellowstone, the survivors of the repeated plagues of smallpox, measles, and influenza led lives much different from their ancestors. Displaced from their settlements and fields and traditional ways, they turned instead to such practices as slash-and-burn agriculture and foraging. As author Charles Mann says of the Yanomamo of Amazonia, "what is often pictured as an idyllic, 'natural' existence is in fact a life of poor exile."[58]

When Lewis and Clark crossed the Great Plains in the beginning of the nineteenth century, they saw massive herds of bison surging from horizon to horizon—and so those massive herds were treated as the correct baseline by later conservationists. But new research suggests that the herds were unusually huge because the main predator of bison—man—had just been knocked way back by disease.[59] The famously large passenger pigeon flocks in the early 1800s—so large as to blot out the sun for days running—may have been a similar freak population explosion attributable to the disappearance of their main competitor for maize and nuts.[60]

Australia, like the Americas, seemed to its first European colonizers a virgin wilderness. But people had been living there for 50,000 years.[61] And they, like the Americans, used fire to signal one another, to clear the way for travel, to encourage plants to grow for direct consumption, and to encourage plant growth to tempt herbivore prey.[62] Fires, judiciously set, maintained a population of medium-size marsupials that made good eating.[63]

Tim Flannery suggests that by killing off many herbivore species, Aborigines increased the amount of flammable plant material in Australia. This, combined with their fire-setting ways, may have changed the dominant species in many parts of the country. Fire-loving plant species replaced those easily killed by fire. Mangroves may have bloomed in the eroded sediment coming off of burnt slopes and traveling to river mouths. "I now see virtually all the continent's ecosystems as being in some sense man-made," says Flannery.[64]

If people have always been part of nature, where did we get this ideal

of pristine wilderness? First, the evidence for much of the prehistoric anthropogenic change is relatively new. Ecologists are just beginning to realize that many landscape features they have assumed were wild were in fact
man-made. Second, prominent early American nature-appreciators like Thoreau and Muir tended to seek wilderness to get away from people and
their works as well as to commune with the land, thus wedding the idea
of nature with the ideas of wilderness and humanlessness. Third, since
the early days of the field, ecologists have mostly studied ecosystems without people.

According to Arizona State University ecologist and historian Matthew
Chew, part of the reason we exclude humanity is an accident of history.
Ecology as a field inherited its scope of action from earlier natural historians. The natural historians defined themselves against historians who studied the doings of men. "There is a history of people and then this other
history," says Chew. "They said, 'We are studying the products of nature, not
anything imposed on nature.'" Ever since, ecologists have usually tried to
design experiments in which human influence is minimized, in part just to
keep the number of variables down. "Ecologists like to go out and find themselves in something they can call unsullied," he says. "But the so-called natural areas that we are studying, that we are trying to take as controlled
experiments, are vanishingly small numbers of places, and they were even
when ecology got started."

Clements of the climax, for example, grew up on the prairie, which before his eyes had been massively, perhaps permanently, changed by home-
steaders.[65] The land was in many places overfarmed and badly mismanaged.
For him, this was clearly a case of an outside force coming in and dis-
turbing nature. Thus man was not part of nature as he defined it, and
human-influenced landscapes were therefore not natural.[66] British ecologists working on an island notably short of wilderness didn't exclude people
in the same way. They felt less separation between humans and nature. Besides, as ecological historian Donald Worster points out, a strict "no humans" rule would "effectively deprive the [European] ecologist of a subject
of study" as no place in Europe could possibly have qualified for hundreds
of years.[67]

Finally, it is my own theory that the love of solitude and of unaltered nature evidenced by many nineteenth- and early twentieth-century conservationists became full-blown misanthropy for a few influential environmental activists of the 1970s to the 1990s.

Two central figures in this more purist conservation movement were Edward Abbey and Dave Foreman. Abbey was a writer, who in 1968 penned *Desert Solitaire*, a memoir about two summers alone in the wilderness, and in 1975 *The Monkey Wrench Gang*, a novel in which a merry band of saboteurs take on the forces of development in a battle for the soul of the desert Southwest.

Desert Solitaire, a meditation on a wild and harsh landscape and an angry indictment of the idea that "the world exists solely for the sake of man,"[68] was written from the point of view of an "Edward Abbey" that even Edward Abbey admitted was a literary character.[69] The real Edward Abbey, like his fictional counterpart, was a park ranger in the late 1950s at Arches National Monument in Utah. But the real Edward Abbey was also, some of the time, accompanied by his wife and infant son. The narrator of *Desert Solitaire* is, as the title implies, utterly alone in nature, so the nature around him can be utterly empty of people. According to critic John Farnsworth, Abbey also omitted to mention the nuclear testing that was going on a mere three hundred miles upwind of the ranger station while he worked there. The reason? He didn't want to give up "the trope of wilderness as paradise."

He nearly—nearly—goes so far as to kick himself out of the desert with all the other no-good humans: "I am almost prepared to believe that this sweet virginal primitive land will be grateful for my departure and the absence of the tourists, will breathe metaphorically a collective sigh of relief—like a whisper of wind—when we are all and finally gone and the place and its creations can return to their ancient procedures unobserved and undisturbed by the busy, anxious, brooding consciousness of man."[70]

Foreman is an environmental activist and cofounder of the radical group Earth First! (exclamation mark included as part of the name, as with the quiz show *Jeopardy!*). Foreman actually lived the kind of adventures described in *The Monkey Wrench Gang*. The group's motto was "No Compromise in Defense of Mother Earth." They were zany, male-dominated, beer-fueled, and hell-bent on protecting really huge areas of wilderness.

Where wilderness was all clapped out, they wanted to yank out roads and put it back.[71]

Earth First!'s heyday lasted about a decade, but its influence can be seen today in activists who occupy trees, protesters who dress up as polar bears to draw attention to climate change, and the thousands of people who every year decide that nature has rights that are being violated; rights worth fighting for. These more radical environmentalists often share Abbey and Foreman's uncompromising definition of nature. For them, nature must be wild, and wilderness must be virtually empty of people. Nothing else counts.

Interestingly, Foreman tells me that he doesn't agree with my reading of his ethos. He feels that the idea that wilderness must be absolutely pristine was part of a propaganda campaign by the U.S. Forest Service. By insisting on a strict level of purity in wilderness, the agency could limit the amount of land that could be officially designated wilderness under the 1964 Wilderness Act and thus be taken out of circulation for other uses. "The forest service and other agencies . . . often argued against protecting an area because of some ancient stumps or a two track road," he says. In Foreman's opinion, "minor intrusions do not disqualify an area from wilderness. We have said for fifty years or more that there are no pristine areas, and the word *pristine* does not appear in the Wilderness Act."

Indeed, most people who spend significant time in the wilderness, including conservationists, don't have the same strict standards of purity that many people who merely dabble in wilderness do. Real nature-heads know too much about how things have changed to fool themselves. Foreman quotes Aldo Leopold on the subject: "One of the penalties of an ecological education is that one lives alone in a world of wounds."

Foreman adds that his and others' focus on wilderness was in part strategic. They felt they could get more conservation bang for their buck by trying to get lands designated as wilderness, and thus be given the highest level of protection, than by fighting battles over the details of how to use "mixed-use" public lands. "Back in the fifties, sixties, and seventies, we conservationists worked really hard on overall management of the public lands—all designed to bring a little better multiple-use management to the Forest Service and . . . we would see the agencies thwart that legislation.

So more and more we turned to wilderness areas as a way to stop the Forest Service from industrializing the world."

But Foreman does have a bit of a purist streak. Because he feels that wilderness is "a place where you are making a deal with yourself, that you are going to interact with the land on its own terms," he dislikes the modern phenomenon of hikers toting cell phones there. "We do river trips here in the Southwest. I tell everyone that if I find a radio, a cell phone, an MP3 player, I am going to throw it in the river. I don't even like GPS devices."

These days the historical disinclination of American ecologists to study human-altered systems has been mixed up with an ideological dislike of such systems. Most ecologists are also committed conservationists who, in the correct manner, dislike "invasive species" and climate change and anything else that reeks of mankind.

A 2009 study suggesting that a tropical forest that has regrown after logging might be worthy of protection aroused "outrage" among more conservative ecologists.[72] Laura Martin, a graduate student at Cornell University, analyzed the top ten ecology journals from 2005 to 2010 and found that a mere 17 percent of terrestrial study sites were in human-dominated landscapes. Just 4 percent were in cities or suburbs, and 64 percent were in protected areas, despite the fact that 75 percent of the ice-free Earth is actively being used by people.[73]

And the 25 percent that isn't being used is by no means pristine. Zero percent is. In 1989 environmental writer Bill McKibben published a book about climate change called *The End of Nature*. As the title implies, the thesis was that nature is over—and if you use McKibben's definition of nature, it certainly is. For McKibben, "the thing that has, at least in modern times, defined nature for us" is "its separation from human society."[74] For McKibben, even the sound of a distant chain saw in the woods behind his house "drives away the feeling that you are in another, separate, timeless, wild sphere."[75] Climate change, like the chain saw's noise, "taints" a walk in the woods, except unlike saw noise, it is everywhere on the planet all at once. Everything has been tainted. Nature as a separate thing has ended.

For environmentalists like McKibben, the pristineness rule has been made very strict. A single rusty hubcap tucked under the ferns, a wildfire observation station visible on the horizon, a species moved, an atmosphere heated, a forest felled two hundred years ago—it doesn't take much to chase away "nature" if nature must be perfectly "untouched" or "pristine."

Having erected an impossible vision of purity as their ideal, such thinkers are doomed to perpetual disappointment. There can never be any more of this kind of nature, because once touched by humans, it is ruined for eternity. As McKibben says, "All we can do is make it less bad than it will otherwise be."[76]

One night in Białowieża, at a pub just outside the forest, I relaxed with researchers from the Mammal Research Institute. Kids chased each other and threw sticks into the river, and the researchers and their families drank żubr beer (żubr means "bison" in Polish) and ate deer steaks with fries and bigos, a hunter's stew. The conversation turned to aurochs, the wild progenitor of cows, now extinct. The last one was shot in a lost forest near Warsaw in 1627.

Fossils show that aurochs once inhabited Białowieża, but what role did they play in the ecosystem? Kowalczyk thinks that maybe they never interacted with the bison, that they kept to different parts of the landscape. Matt Hayward, my friend from Scotia in Australia, who was then a visiting scholar at Białowieża (his family shared a house with Kowalczyk's, where they kept dueling vegetable gardens), suggested that the aurochs had perhaps been the forest's bulk grazer, maintaining grass clearings in the forest where the bison could then also eat. "Maybe riverside scything and winter provisioning replaced this," he speculated. Maybe cattle could be let wild into the forest to take over this role.

Joris Cromsigt, a skinny bespectacled herbivore specialist from the Netherlands, suggested Heck cattle, domestic cattle specially bred to resemble aurochs. Several hundred of these cattle live without human interference at a reserve in the Netherlands called the Oostvaardersplassen. It was a Friday-afternoon conversation. No one seriously expected that anyone would let them release a bunch of novelty cows to run around in a forest that is still considered valuable to tourists and to science for its untouched character. But if it was up to Hayward and Cromsigt, the experiment might be tried. Why not? They don't believe the forest is pure, pristine, or unchanging. Or as Cromsigt put it that afternoon, "We don't really believe in a zero reference."

Before I left Białowieża, I went to a party in the forest held by the Mammal Institute for their summer school for European graduate students. I ate bread with lard and raw onions, drank warm beer, and watched my bison guide Kowalczyk leap over the bonfire. I joined a circle of dancers whirling around the fire and kicking up dust. We went faster and faster, laughing uncontrollably, until someone broke the circle and led us, in a great grimy line, on a romp into the cool night. All around us was the forest, much older, larger, and more solemn than we—but not unconnected to us and not unchanging. We were part of its unfolding story, as it was part of ours.

The pristine wilderness notion is a historically created idea about what ought to count as nature, and there is no reason we can't change it. Just as the definition of *citizen* has changed to include more kinds of people as political ideas changed, so could *nature* expand to include more kinds of areas. Many ecologists today argue that we *have* to expand it, as our increasing understanding of history and atmospheric chemistry has left us with no areas at all that have not been altered by humans. And once we do change it, a heretofore unthinkable, exciting, and energizing thought occurs: we can make *more* nature. We can make things on Earth better, not just less bad.

4 | Radical Rewilding

In the Netherlands, on land that was underwater as recently as 1967, stands a large grassy plain that evokes a past so distant, we know it only from natural history museum dioramas, watercolor re-creations, and cave paintings. This is the Oostvaardersplassen, a twenty-three-square-mile nature reserve half an hour's drive from Amsterdam, an entire landscape designed by an ecologist to run as it did 10,000 years ago, despite what might seem like a major handicap: the extinction of most of the large mammals that would have roamed there.

Frans Vera, a tall, energetic ecologist with a handshake like a hydraulic press, is the government scientist with the vision behind the Oostvaardersplassen. One misty morning in the summer of 2009, Vera took me out on what can only be described as a Dutch safari.

What if we take the idea of the pristine prehuman baseline to its logical conclusion, proposing that we restore not to 1491 (when Columbus landed in the Americas) or to 1778 (when Cook landed in Hawaii) or to 1872 (when Yellowstone became a park) but to 13,000 or more years ago, before humans drove any species extinct? The result is a new idea called *Pleistocene rewilding*. Of course, the state of an area before people arrived is not equivalent to the state the area would be in today if no one arrived; as we've learned, nature keeps changing with or without us. But by reaching back to a deeper past, the scientists behind the concept have begun to erode the notion that historical dates linked to colonial contact are the obvious go-to baselines. And thanks to the many extinctions that have taken place in the last 13,000 years, they've had to scrap authenticity and use "proxies" for those lost species. In doing so, they've really begun the project of designing brand-new ecosystems.

Vera and I drove into the reserve on a misty morning. Wind turbines, electrical pylons, and dim gray towers from nearby cities poked up from the horizon. Trains whizzed by, filled with Dutch commuters reading *De Telegraaf*. But inside the bounds of the reserve, all was green grass and wide vistas. Vera soon located a herd of horses, more than one hundred of them in all. They were small and stocky and creamy gray; some of their legs were striped. Stallions fussed at their harems and occasionally reared and nipped at one another in challenge. These equids look a lot like the wild horses called tarpans that once lived in Europe. They aren't though; they are Konik horses, a breed from Poland and thought to have similarities to tarpans. This breed, which was hardy enough to pasture outside in the winter, was disappearing as Polish peasants tried to trade up to more fashionable breeds in the 1800s and was almost lost. Years ago Vera traveled around Poland with a veterinarian, buying all he could find.

Red foxes with white-tipped tails slipped in and out of the long wet grass, and fox scat, violet with the iridescent shells of incautious beetles, dotted the earth. Farther along hundreds-strong herds of red deer moved across the wide-open plain like schools of fish, staying always some distance from our van. They moved in such tight formation that I was astonished that their antlers, all fuzzy and damp with mist, didn't become entangled as they ran.

In a smaller herd were Heck cattle, which I had first heard about in Białowieża. They were developed by two German brothers from a number of different cattle breeds with the express intent of mimicking the extinct auroch. Heck cattle are somewhat controversial, as the Nazis supported the breeding program for a time. They had their own motivations; they saw the auroch as a symbol of a glorious Aryan past.

The Heck cattle at the Oostvaardersplassen, naturally, are unaware of the history of their kind or the role they are called upon to play in the ecosystem. They don't look like Holsteins, but they also don't look completely alien. Large-bodied and wide-horned, they come in several colors, from black to brown to beige. "For me, the point was that they not look like dairy cattle," said Vera. He wants the public to see them as wild animals. Same for the Konik ponies. "If we had Iceland ponies here, there would be little girls lined up along the fence," he said.

Vera and I spent some time standing around the fresh corpse of a red deer. Its antlers were a bit bloody from where it had been rubbing its felt off, but it didn't otherwise have a scratch on it. We didn't know how it died, but we could guess how its death would unspool, what species would draw life from its carcass. Already its reddish flank was striped with the white dung of ravens; its anus had been gnawed into a large hole by foxes. Its eyes were gone. Eyes are always the first things to go.

As in Białowieża, the presence of death separates this place from a mere pleasure park. Death is important here. Carcasses have attracted a pair of rare white-tailed eagles to the Oostvaardersplassen. They perch by their nest, an enormous treehouse of bone-white branches. In 2005 the carcasses also lured a very rare black vulture from a French reintroduction program. The massive bird just appeared and probably would have settled down for good. Alas, it was killed by a train when dining on the tracks one day. Its corpse was donated to a natural history museum.[1]

Vera's project has its share of critics—mostly ecologists who don't agree that Europe looked like a savanna 10,000 years ago. But he must be doing something right, because he's attracted several species of rare bird: the white-tailed eagles and vulture, along with, in the marshy part of the reserve, hundreds of breeding pairs of graylag geese and great white egrets, neither of which had been known to breed in the Netherlands since at least the nineteenth century.

The idea of Pleistocene rewilding derives from *rewilding*, a term coined by Dave Foreman, cofounder of Earth First!, sometime in the mid-1990s.

Rewilding posits that the main factors necessary to keep ecosystems resilient and diverse are the regulation provided by large, top-of-the-food-chain predators; the room for these predators to do their work; and connections between predator ranges so they can meet, mate, and maintain a healthily diverse gene pool.

When predators are not around to kill the various prey species, the reasoning goes, the only check on their population is competition for food. Eventually this uncomplicated competition leads to one prey species squeezing others out until one is left with larger populations of fewer species. Whatever species ends up dominating would eat the heck out of its favorite plants, and this leads to a simplification of the plant diversity in the area as well. Simultaneously, the missing top predators make more room for medium-size predators like raccoons or snakes, who then expand and put significant pressure on little creatures such as songbirds. The result of all of this? Fewer species.

These ideas were laid out in a 1998 *Wild Earth* paper by conservation biologists Michael Soulé and Reed Noss.[2] To preserve diversity, they wanted to see restored "the entire pre-Columbian set of carnivores" to large swaths of North America, including wolves, bears, and cougars, which are currently restricted to small protected areas.[3] Many conservationists have taken up this call.

Once you start dreaming about a continent alive with large animals, you get greedy. You start thinking about all the really large mammals that used to live in America thousands of years ago, and you start wondering what ecosystems would be like if you could have *them* back too.

In 2005 Paul Martin, the chief proponent of the hypothesis that humans killed off the Pleistocene megafauna, weighed in on a National Park Service plan to exterminate feral burros from the Grand Canyon. The burros are the wild descendants of pack animals used by miners and prospectors at the turn of the twentieth century, and the Park Service long sought to remove them from the park lest their grazing hurt native plants. Besides, "the presence of the heavy-hoofed burros contradicted the notion that a national park should be a pristine wilderness," according to one account.[4] Martin countered that the species might be new to the area, but its general kind—equids—had hoofed it around the canyon for millennia before the big extinctions in the Pleistocene.[5] The plants in the area presumably had coevolved with very similar animals. So why not let them stay? The same went for wild horses. Sure, the Spanish brought them from Europe, but they aren't that different from *Equus caballus*, the extinct American horse. They could play that lost animal's part.[6]

Martin had similar ideas for the Pacific Ocean's islands, where many nearly extinct birds and other animals cling to life at just one or two tiny outlying islets. Why not reintroduce them to the islands they formerly inhabited? And while we are at it, why not move a few to islands outside their former range, where similar creatures have been lost forever—especially if they are threatened with extinction at home? In 2003 Martin, along with his former student, David Steadman of the University of Florida in Gainesville, proposed that a flightless forest bird called the Guam rail, eaten nearly to extinction by the accidentally introduced Australian brown tree snake, be moved to the island of Aguiguan, less than one hundred miles away. The Guam rail would presumably be safer on Aguiguan, which features neither snakes nor people. And besides, Aguiguan once had flightless rails of its own, now extinct, so the Guam rail could play the part of the lost Aguiguan rails in the Aguiguan ecosystem.[7]

These sound like reasonable ideas to many, but there are just a couple of slippery steps between allowing wild burros to live free, asking one flightless rail to play the part of another, and importing proxies for some other long-lost beasts. What about bringing cheetahs to Arizona or elephants to Missouri to play the parts of related megafauna?

In 2004 thirteen scientists and conservationists, including Paul Martin, Michael Soulé, and David Foreman met at broadcasting mogul Ted Turner's ranch in New Mexico to discuss the idea of bringing proxies of extinct megafauna back to North America. The group agreed that they would love to restore, if they could, the age when nature lived wild and large, when hairy mastodons and elephantine sloths heaved their bulk around the continent, and when deadly predators were big, fast, and ubiquitous. They outlined a plan for "Pleistocene Rewilding," which was published in *Nature* in 2005.[8]

One of those present at the meeting was field ecologist Josh Donlan. He ended up becoming the lead author of the paper that summarized their plan, and he has spent much of his time since as the unofficial spokesman for the idea. Donlan has spent his career removing nonnative animals from islands, where they can cause extinctions, often by eating up native species. "In some cases we were too late in getting cats and rats off of islands," he explains. "The extinctions had already happened." Once, when working with a cat-eradication team on islands in Mexico's Gulf of California, Donlan failed to de-cat an island before the extinction of a certain subspecies of wood rat—a much smaller and shier rat than the long, mean city-dwelling Norway rat. "So we started playing around with this idea of, well, should we take a wood rat from an island next door which almost certainly plays the same ecological role, and introduce it?"

Donlan and the group at the Turner ranch essentially took the rewilding concept as laid out by Soulé and Noss, moved the baseline back to before people came to North America, and widened its remit from just predators to all large mammals, including herbivores. The idea is to restore long-lost processes such as intensive grazing or population control by large predators, to restore "evolutionary and ecological potential" to populations of large animals just barely hanging on in their current ranges, and to inspire people to support nature conservation.[9]

"No one was around to document what were probably major ecosystem shifts when North America lost its sixty-odd species over one hundred pounds," says Donlan. "But we do know from the few long-term ecological studies that are out there now that when we remove large mammals, we see these unexpected, cascading ecosystem changes. And when we put 'em back—a perfect example is the reintroduction of wolves to Yellowstone— not six month goes by without a new groundbreaking paper coming out linking some unexpected ecosystem shift to the reintroduction of wolves." So reintroducing proxies for lost animals would be a grand-scale scientific experiment that would also restore some of what North America has lost since humans arrived. We can only guess how the ecosystems would change.

The plan the group put together starts out slowly, with less scary moves like reintroducing the endangered 110-pound Bolson tortoise to the United States from Mexico. Then they propose introducing Asian asses, wild horses, and Bactrian camels (from the Gobi Desert) to special private reserves in North America. All three are endangered in their current ranges and could stand in for the wild horses and camels that once roamed the continent. The group hopes that the camels would eat woody shrubs, like mesquite, that today cover much of the Southwest in a drab and disliked monoculture.

Then, if all went well, they recommend establishing populations of cheetahs, elephants, and lions on the reserves. Many of the proxies in their plan would come from Africa, which lost far fewer of its large animals in the Pleistocene, perhaps because they evolved with humans and didn't have to face them all at once after humans became hunting experts. Each had an analogue in Pleistocene North America—though these were different, larger species—and each is threatened with extinction at home. Move the cheetahs in there with some pronghorn antelope, and the pronghorns would have reason again to use their blazing-fast speed, which likely evolved under selection pressure from the extinct American cheetah. Elephants could eat and spread the seeds of the Osage orange, a cantaloupe-size green orb made of many small stone fruits welded together. The tree nearly went extinct after North America lost its elephantlike animals in the Pleistocene extinctions.[10] They could also dine on the honey locust's foot-long pods, another orphan that lost the animals it probably coevolved with.[11] The distributions of plants and the character of some landscapes might change, with grassland perhaps replacing forests in some places. And of course the condors would love it. With all those large animals and large predators would come large carcasses for large scavengers. The birds would no longer rely on the gut piles of human hunters.

The rewilded animals would be carefully separated from human habitation and intensively managed. In this respect, the concept tends to reinforce the line between humans and nature, rather than blurring it. "It's not like we're advocating backing up a van and taking out a bunch of cheetahs," says Donlan. Eventually, though, the reserves would be enlarged and linked together so that in places like the Great Plains, where human populations are declining, the majority of the landscape would be wild. Towns and farms would have to consider whether they wanted to fence themselves to protect against incursion from large animals. In many ways, this megareserve, though managed by humans and populated with nonnative species, would be far wilder than any part of North America is today. It would be more diverse, and more dangerous. Donlan and company suggest importing several kinds of animals, but it is the carnivores that give a lot of their critics pause. Donlan finds this critique—that North American people shouldn't have to live with the threat of death—arguably racist, given that we expect African people to do just that so that the world can contain lions. "African communities have to deal with large dangerous carnivores, and the United States doesn't?"

The Pleistocene rewilding idea was incredibly controversial. "I got five hundred personal emails from Joe Q. Public," says Donlan. "People either loved it or they hated it. We got everything from 'I want to quit my job and work for you' to death threats." The whole idea struck many as preposterous, not least because they saw it as an egregious case of human intervention in "wild" landscapes. "A big criticism of this is 'you are playing god,'" says Donlan. "Well, I don't buy that. We are already playing god." The leap, he says, is "admitting to ourselves that we live in an intensely managed world."

Indeed, the idea of African animals in America seems far-fetched to many despite the fact that it is already happening. The group points out in their paper that "77,000 large mammals (most of them Asian and African ungulates, but also cheetahs, camels and kangaroos) roam free on Texas ranches, although their significance for conservation remains largely unevaluated." I could sign up tomorrow to go hunting for zebra by the Guadalupe River, but the tendency of ecologists to ignore any area that doesn't look pristine means that no one is studying the fascinating question of how these "Texotics" interact with their new environments.

Since the commentary appeared, Donlan says, many people have come around to the idea. "I think that it is certainly gaining traction in the public view, and over the past five years," he says, "conservationists are starting to rally around this idea, almost certainly partly because it is proactive." That is, it is something that conservationists can do beyond holding the line against development and negative change.

Dustin Rubenstein, an ecologist at Columbia University in New York, has another critique. He argues that placing proxy animals in a modern landscape could spell trouble.[12] These ecosystems have changed, and existing species have evolved in the thousands of years since megafauna extinctions. Attempting to fill gaps that closed long ago with proxy animals could generate unpredictable results. The difference between rewilding with native species and Pleistocene proxy rewilding "is the difference between the known and the unknown," he says. Proxy animals, he suggests, could become invasive pests, or escape their parks and cause trouble with local landowners, who would then turn against the conservationists and conservation more generally.

Donlan doesn't buy the idea that he and his colleagues would be creating potentially runaway invasive species. He says that history suggests that large mammals are less likely than plants, fish, or insects to become invasive pests. And besides, he says, "we killed 'em once; we can kill 'em again."

Donlan's Pleistocene rewilding and Soulé and Noss's pre-Columbian version are both premised on the desirability of returning North America to an ambitious baseline—they just use different baselines. Donlan personally admits that all baselines are "largely a value judgment." But both plans also invoke a sense that large animals, and especially carnivores, are inherently wild. "Without these components, nature seems somehow incomplete, truncated, overly tame," write Soulé and Noss. "Human opportunities to attain humility are reduced."

Rewilding could further a number of the alternative goals we need to articulate in place of "pristine wilderness": protection of beloved large mammals by expanding their range, biodiversity maintenance (if the ecological theory that top predators support more diverse and complex ecosystems holds up), tourism, and aesthetic values. Many conservationists will argue for preserving the only-recently and imperfectly supplanted idea that the wilderness is a frightening place.

Part one of the plan cooked up by Donlan and his colleagues is under way. Those enormous Bolson tortoises are now living at the Turner ranch. "First time they have been in New Mexico in eight thousand years," says Donlan.

Meanwhile, outside the United States, threatened species of large tortoises have been translocated to islands around the world that have lost their own native tortoises. Donlan finds them to be an ideal candidate for testing out the rewilding idea. They are portable, appealing, unthreatening, and unlikely to become problematic invasives. If they cause trouble, they can be picked up, one by one, and taken away.[13]

And at the Oostvaardersplassen, all the introduced animals are fenced in. For the Dutch public, though, the biggest concern about Vera's experiment wasn't the threat of invasive wild horses, but squeamishness about that crucial ingredient in wild ecosystems: death.

As we drove around, we spotted an abandoned calf just a few feet off the road—its eyes glazed, its knees wobbly. Vera watched the calf for a few moments. Then he reached for his radio and called one of the reserve's staff members to come and shoot it, as per an agreement worked out with the Dutch government, which has strict laws against animal cruelty written with an agricultural context in mind. The Dutch public hasn't had to contend with nature in its raw, undomesticated form in many generations. Letting an animal starve to death, to many here, is too cruel to be allowed, even in the name of nature.

At the Oostvaardersplassen, death is not completely restored, for the Oostvaardersplassen is not completely rewilded. There are no predators here altering the number or behavior of the grazers. However, weary from battles over his theory of European ecological history and the management of the Oostvaardersplassen, Vera is in no hurry to hop onto the political minefield of wolf reintroduction, in a country in which livestock owners are such a powerful political force. Instead, he says, he will just wait for wolves to come to him as they spread out from populations in Central and Eastern Europe. "Wolves are expanding in Germany," he says. "The closest sighting was as close as two hundred kilometers from here. They are also in northern France, in the Vosges. They will come, whether we like it or not."

Predators, as Donlan and company have discovered, are the hardest sell. In central Saudi Arabia, the Mahazat as-Sayd protected area features reintroduced houbara bustards, reem gazelle, and Arabian oryx, an ungulate with two unicornesque horns that went extinct in the wild in the 1970s. These reintroduced species mingle with the African red-necked ostrich, a proxy for the extinct Arabian subspecies that once strutted here.[14]

Native vegetation and birds complete the picture of the Arabian Peninsula as it might have looked 2,000 years ago. Well, mostly. Notably absent are the wolf and cheetah—predators that would likely have hunted here.[15]

If anyone ever gets wolves into the Oostvaardersplassen, it will be Vera. The place is his baby. Vera was among those who originally advocated for it to be made into a permanent nature reserve. The area was once part of the freshwater Markermeer, a lake that was itself created by cutting it off from an arm of the North Sea in 1932. Engineers drained it in 1968, and it was supposed to be a temporary nature refuge just until the land was ready to be used as an industrial area. But Vera became interested when tens of thousands of graylag geese showed up and began changing the marshy landscape. Their grazing patterns created a mix of open water and reeds that attracted many other bird species, such as bitterns and bearded tits.[16] Vera was a birder from youth and became intrigued with the place, which seemed to run itself so well. At the time, according to Vera, the European model of reserve management was very hands-on. The area that became the Oostvaardersplassen was considered too big to manage without great cost, since it was assumed that humans would have to create open water to attract birds and that dry areas would have to be mowed to provide congregating places for the geese. Vera got together a proposal to run the reserve cheaply by letting the geese's grazing keep the water open and by letting wild cattle and horses' grazing do the "mowing" for them. At the time, he says, many ecologists felt this wouldn't work—that the geese could not form the character of the marsh, and that horses and cattle could not, by themselves, stave off the inevitable development of a dense closed-canopy forest, which they believed was the natural vegetation for most of Europe. But it did work, and the landscape that developed inspired Vera with new ideas about prehuman Europe.

Since then, Vera has tried to recreate at the Oostvaardersplassen the processes—principally grazing—that he believes ran Europe as the glaciers of the last ice age retreated, before people began changing the landscape. How is that different from traditional conservation, with its focus on pristine baselines? First, Vera is trying out a baseline thousands of years further back than most projects. And second, he's going into it knowing that exact fidelity to the baseline is impossible, since many of the Pleistocene species are extinct. In an odd way, then, his project looks to the past but creates an unprecedented ecosystem.

Vera's alternative goals are to create habitat for rare species and to perform a long-term experimental test of his ideas about the ecological workings of prehuman Europe. He is passionate about his theory. He has spent decades on it, scouring libraries for rare tomes describing the early landscape of Europe, and arguing, ceaselessly, with those who disagree with him.

Most ecologists see prehuman Europe as a huge closed-canopy forest: Białowieża writ large. Vera's vision is of a patchy landscape, in which any given area cycles between forest, plain, and shrubs. Much of it would be open grassland maintained by large herds of herbivores. Here and there light-demanding shrub species like hawthorn and sloe could pass through the dangerous tender-seedling stage and form hard thorns and woody stems to deter herbivory. Thus, a portion of the landscape would be covered with thickets of thorny shrubs. These patches would then become protective nurseries for tree seedlings that would otherwise be devoured by the many herbivores. Groves of trees would grow out of the thorns and eventually create a dense canopy with shade underneath. This shade would tend to kill the thorny shrubs and create the kind of open understory I saw in Białowieża. Once this happened, the herbivores would have no trouble getting into the grove and moving around on the ground, and would start eating all the little tree seedlings in the shade of their parents. The groves could therefore not replace themselves and would eventually, after hundreds of years perhaps, disappear as the old trees died and fell over. The spot would then return to grassland for an indefinite time, until thorny shrubs again went uneaten long enough to harden their spines and form thickets. And the cycle would continue.

Even Białowieża, Vera says, was once such a mosaic of open and closed spaces, what he calls a "parklike landscape." The only reason it remains a closed-canopy forest today, he says, is because the cattle were removed that were continuing the role of the aurochs and because herbivores are kept to such small numbers by nervous foresters, who worry that they would prevent the regeneration of the forest. The density of bison is so laughably low compared to what Vera believes the historical state of things was, he calls it a "homeopathic solution."

The notion of the closed-canopy forest was born, Vera says, when early ecologists considered old fields fenced off from humans and their domestic animals. Such fields inevitably turned into dense forests. But, he argues, the ecologists failed to realize that Europe before humans was not free of herbivores capable of keeping a forest from springing up. Auroch, wild horse, deer, elk, bison, and other species would have been grazing it down.

Vera relishes his maverick status in the field, and he also clearly believes his theory absolutely. He spent two days working on me with such energy that I found it difficult to resist his reasoning. Take oaks. Oak seedlings don't grow up to be adult oaks in the shade of other trees, and yet they are found in all of the continent's old forests, and in abundance in the fossil pollen record. Vera believes that old oaks mostly grew up in open areas, in those thorny nurseries, and then saw the forest fill in around them. Wild fruit trees and hazel also won't regenerate in the shade but are well represented in the fossil record.

His critics challenge much of Vera's evidence. They say oaks can regenerate in the shade, given the right kind of soil and the occasional gap in the canopy provided by a falling tree. They suggest that hazel can make a great deal of pollen, even when it is just clinging on in small gaps of sunlight. They point out that the composition of trees was not quite the same in the past, so competition between oak, hazel, and other species may have had different dynamics than it does today.[17] The critics add that there is very little grass pollen in the historical record.[18] Vera counters by suggesting that a well-grazed grassland never gets a chance to grow tall enough to make much pollen. Meanwhile, a researcher at Sheffield University, Paul Buckland, has used the fossils of beetles that specialize in different habitats to paint a picture of an ancient Britain that was fairly densely wooded, and had grazers at somewhat low densities. Buckland also sees evidence, in the form of beetle species that thrive on burned areas, that fire was an important part of the prehuman ecology of Britain. Fire is something that Vera, on the other hand, doesn't think was a major factor in Europe.[19]

The number of herbivores that once lived in Europe, including browsers, grazers, and generalists, is unknown. Earlier ecologists tended to imagine that they were forest animals living in low densities; Vera thinks that they lived rather more like African herbivores, in large dense herds out in the open. In the end, both sides are prepared to admit that some land was open and some closed—they just differ on what that ratio might have been and whether herbivores were the driving force that established it.

So far Vera's Oostvaardersplassen has shown that a high density of herbivores can certainly have a large effect on a landscape. The open plains that the cattle, horses, deer, and grazing graylag geese maintain look more like an African savanna than dark dense forests. In places in the reserve, trees are emerging from sloe scrub, illustrating the next phase of his cycle. "They need one year without being browsed to harden their thorns," Vera says. I wonder if wolves could change herbivore behavior or numbers enough to give the thorny shrubs a bigger foothold here.

The Oostvaardersplassen may be the best example of how one can make more nature through rewilding. It is so far from pristine, it's funny. Civilization is visible all around the perimeter. Some of the "wild" animals were trucked in (though many others followed of their own accord). The keystone species are domesticated animals posing as their wild ancestors. And as the icing on the cake, the whole place is fourteen feet below sea level. Let a few human-built and -maintained dikes crack, and the entire reserve will be underwater. And yet there may not be a wilder-feeling place in Western Europe. At the Oostvaardersplassen, when the sun comes out, thistle butterflies explode from the bushes in an orange mist. Bees drone; horses whinny; spoonbills methodically sweep the water with their sensitive upper beaks. The sun picks out the gleam of crushed beetles and white bones. Life and death are plainly on display here, and there is plenty of each.

I do not know whether Vera's theory about presettlement Europe is correct. To my mind, however, the experimental reserve he's running to test it is worth having even if Vera is wrong. Something interesting is happening there.

"My frame of reference is not a man-made landscape, but a natural-processes-driven landscape," says Vera. "A natural ecosystem is better than a cultivated one. Forget past versus present—it is really natural versus cultivated." And yet the whole place is cultivated, man-made, created. But that's not how Vera sees it, quite. "The only thing man did was create the conditions, and nature filled it in."

There is a seeming paradox here. The Oostvaardersplassen was man-made to be wild, created from nothing to look like it had never changed. Is the result a wilderness? A garden about wilderness?

5 | Assisted Migration

The American pika is a small flower-nibbling mammal with rounded ears that lives in the alpine boulder fields of the North American West. Pikas are disappearing from some of their lowest habitats—and no wonder. Experiments in the 1970s showed that the little furballs curl up and die after a few hours in 78-degree-Fahrenheit heat. As the global climate warms, pikas will have to move higher up to stay in their comfort zone. Unfortunately, on some mountains, they are already living at the peak. There is nowhere for them to go.

Imagine a pika sweating it out at the top of a peak in California, looking longingly north. The animal could never migrate on its own; the trip down to the lowlands to get to the next mountain would kill it. But what if a concerned human with a refrigerated crate were to come along? Conservationists are increasingly considering moving animals in advance of climate change to places where they might thrive in a warmer future. But they are hesitant and nervous; assisted migration is a long way from the conservation many grew up with.

Human-caused or anthropogenic climate change has been going on for longer than we used to think. As we saw, Pleistocene extinctions left traces on the atmosphere. And an analysis by climatologists at the Max Planck Institute for Meteorology in Hamburg, Germany, suggests that by the late Middle Ages, humans were increasing the concentrations of carbon dioxide in the atmosphere via large-scale burning to clear land for agriculture and via the indirect effects of deforestation. Carbon dioxide emission rates even show clear dips in preindustrial times in response to human events. The Black Death in 1347 saw about seventy thousand square miles of land turn from fields back into forest; the Mongol invasions of the thirteenth century saw even more. In the wake of these mass die-offs, trees growing up in the fields abandoned when their owners died captured enough carbon to decrease emissions, almost as if the planet caught its breath for a moment before marching forward toward the Industrial Revolution.[1]

Now, of course, anthropogenic climate change has begun warming the whole planet in earnest. I won't go over the arguments that this is so here; there are many excellent books and other treatments of the subject. Suffice it to say that scientists believe that anthropogenic emissions of gases including carbon dioxide and methane and of industrial gases like hydrofluorocarbons have changed the composition of the Earth's atmosphere such that it now retains more heat. The result is not just a hotter world but a world in which some places get more rain, others less, and climate patterns become, on the whole, less predictable. Anthropogenic climate change has already altered the natural world, from the timing of flowers opening in the spring to the whereabouts of animals. Ecologists are just beginning to get their heads around what climate change will mean for the ecosystems they study. It is the biggest single thumbprint humans have put on this planet.

Many species are expected to move due to climate change. Many already have. Most plants and animals prefer certain temperatures and certain precipitation patterns. Most also have thresholds of tolerance beyond which they do not survive or cannot successfully reproduce. Species that can't handle the new heat are expected get out of the kitchen as best they can by moving toward the poles and uphill over generations.

For example, American beech currently grows in the eastern half of North America, from northern Florida all the way to southern Canada.

With smooth gray bark and buttressed bases, beeches are a hallmark of today's eastern deciduous forests. When the climate warms, the beeches at the southern end of the range may not be able to grow and reproduce as well. Beeches like a lot of water and don't like temperatures over 100 degrees Fahrenheit. If northern Florida dries and heats up, the beeches there might die. On the other hand, more of Canada might warm to temperatures suitable for the species, and beech seeds dropped by blue jays farther north than the current northernmost beech might sprout and do well. So in one hundred years the range of the species as a whole may shift. American beech will march north into what is now the southern part of the conifer-dominated boreal forest. The boreal forest will march north into what is now the southern part of the tundra. The tundra will march north into what is now the southern part of the ice-covered Arctic. And the ice-covered Arctic . . . will melt.

Of course, it'll be a little more complicated than that. In 2006 a Canadian scientist and a Chinese scientist teamed up to look at beeches all over the world, matching maps of various specific climatic conditions with maps of beech.[2] They found that the most important variable—that is, the one that best predicted the actual ranges of beech—is temperature during the growing season. But the situation varies around the world. In China beeches could handle temperatures farther north of their current limit, but it is too dry up there for them to do well. And British beeches are nowhere near their potential northward limit, perhaps because they just haven't had time to get that far since the last glaciation.

Ecosystems are unlikely to march in lockstep. As during previous climate changes, some species will be friskier than others. And often, in today's world, there are barriers in the way: seas, cities—sometimes a single road will be an effective barrier to a little species. And since species have different environmental tolerances and different migration abilities, ecosystems as we know them are likely to be torn apart.

Butterflies, winged as they are, can move more easily across a landscape than can a plant. But many butterflies will lay their eggs only on a specific species of plant and so will have to wait for the plants to make the first move. On the other hand, many plants depend on insect or bird pollinators to reproduce. What happens if the pollinators fly north or up the mountain to cooler climes before the plant can get there? And some species—a lot of them, maybe—are just going to be too slow to outrun climate change. They may die out before they can disperse somewhere where they can thrive.

Many range shifts for individual species have already been documented. University of Exeter biologist Robert Jon Wilson found that in the Sierra de Guadarramas in central Spain butterfly ranges have shifted, on average, 200 meters uphill in the last thirty-five years. Species already living on the mountaintops are now shifting off the peaks into thin air— that is, they are going extinct. Apollo butterflies in the Sierra de Guadarramas, for example, are now restricted to north-facing slopes above 4,300 feet, which isn't a lot of real estate.[3]

Tree lines—the line on a mountain, visible from a distance, where the forest ends and an alpine meadow or similar ecosystem begins—have been moving up. In many places, notably the Swiss Alps, a recent end to grazing on these high meadows helps this shift along, since now there are no goats or other grazers to eat pioneering saplings.[4] But tree line shifts aren't neat and tidy. One analysis of 166 sites showed that only 52 percent of tree lines advancing. Forty-seven percent were standing still, and 1 percent were retreating.[5] Winter warming turned out to be a better predictor of movement than summer warming—a good reminder that "global warming" can be broken down into many subcomponents, each of which might have different effects.

And those are just the upward shifts. Pole-ward moves are also being documented. In 1999 a team led by Camille Parmesan, an ecologist then at the U.S. National Center for Ecological Analysis and Synthesis, found that of thirty-five European butterfly species they studied, 63 percent have shifted 20 to 150 miles north since 1900. (Butterflies are favorite model species for ecologists because they are often brightly colored and easy to see, relatively easy to catch, and not particularly large or fierce.)[6] Parmesan has been working on species' response to climate change ever since. She's contributed to the reports of the Intergovernmental Panel on Climate Change, or IPCC, those periodic tomes summarizing the scientific consensus on climate change. In 2003 she estimated that the average species's range—not just butterflies, but everything—moves 3.8 miles toward the pole every decade. She also estimated that spring events are occurring 2.3 days earlier per decade, which is not going to help keep current ecosystems in sync.[7]

The pole-ward movements are alarming, but the early extinctions due to this phenomenon will probably be mountain species. The reason is geometrical, says Parmesan: "If you imagine something going northward, there is plenty of land. But species that are restricted to alpine habitats are restricted to less and less land because of the shape of the mountain." If you imagine a mountain as a perfect cone, you can easily visualize this effect. The higher you go up the cone, the less there is of it.

But, says Parmesan, while "you can't make the mountain grow bigger, you could think about moving species to another mountaintop that is either higher or further north." That sounds pretty harmless, right? Not to most ecologists. After a lifetime studying the infinitely complex workings of existing ecosystems, the idea of taking a species from one into the other willy-nilly sounds like a terrible idea. The organisms could die, because you don't know exactly what they need to live—some specific soil microbes or microclimatic condition. Or, in a much worse scenario, they could do so well that they become a dreaded "invasive species" that takes over and pushes out native species. And it is one thing when humanity accidentally creates an invasive species. Humanity is dumb. But to do so these days, with all we know, on purpose? For many ecologists and conservation biologists, that is just insanity. But then . . . to do nothing and watch plants and animals go extinct because of climate change that we caused?

What is interesting about climate change is that it pits two common assumptions against each other: the pristineness myth and the myth of a correct baseline for each area. If humans are outside nature and humans caused climate change, then it follows that humans should make good— should make sure that species that would have survived without climate change survive, no matter what—even if it means moving stressed-out organisms to new places where they can thrive under the new climate. But if ecosystems have a correct baseline to which we must return—the second assumption—then we absolutely cannot move species from one area to another. To do so would violate the baseline and be tantamount to willfully creating invasive species.

This conundrum has paralyzed many scientists. Proponents of moving plants and animals threatened by rising temperatures to more hospitable locations are more concerned about the increasing rate of species extinction, while opponents are more worried about the integrity of coevolved ecosystems. But in general, scientists are pretty freaked out by the whole idea.

Another reason for their reticence is that moving species smacks of *adaptation*, which was, until recently, a dirty word in environmentalist circles, because they felt it distracted from the primary goal of reducing emissions. "Really it's been somewhat taboo to talk about it," says Jessica Hellmann, an ecologist at Notre Dame University in Indiana. "The IPCC has talked about adaptation, but really the balance has been to emphasize mitigation. I think this is a manifestation of that in biology." With the pristineness myth and the adaptation taboo freezing up conservationists and ecologists, it took a curious, eccentric citizen naturalist to force scientists to start a conversation about moving plants and animals.

Connie Barlow is an itinerant preacher. She has short, graying hair and wears wire-framed glasses, jumpers, and cardigans and has the general air of a cheerful schoolteacher. She lives in a van with her husband, the Reverend Michael Dowd. They travel the country giving inspirational presentations about science, mostly at Unitarian churches. The couple style themselves as "evolutionary evangelists." Their programs educate children and adults about "the fourteen-billion-year epic of cosmos, life, and humanity told as a sacred story, glorifying to all." If this sounds confusing, keep in mind the distinctive features of Unitarianism. With roots in a repudiation of the trinity in favor of a single god, today's Unitarians are politically liberal, pro-science, and antidogmatic. It is even possible—and not uncommon—to be an atheist Unitarian.

Barlow's motivation for these programs is to teach people to see the world with "deep time eyes." She's interested in looking at things within the context of the long sweep of time, rather than becoming fixated on how things have been for the last couple hundred years. And she's also a committed environmentalist.

In the 1990s Barlow learned about *Torreya taxifolia*, or Florida torreya, one of the world's rarest evergreen trees, and she visited it a couple of times in what is considered its native range. "I had grown really fond of it," she says. "I am really attached to the idea that individuals can make a difference by following their heart." Picking one imperiled species and fighting for it seemed like something she could take on. On her second visit, she says, she made a personal commitment to the tree.

T. taxifolia has egg-shaped seeds with a milky bluish glaze and flat, needlelike leaves that smell strongly of turpentine when crushed. The smell gives rise to one of its common names, stinking cedar. The native range of *T. taxifolia*, as defined by where naturalists have been able to find it growing wild, is just forty miles long—a bit of the eastern bank of the Apalachicola River on the Florida-Georgia border. One likely reason that it exists only there is that it is a "trapped glacial relic," in the words of Mark Schwartz, an ecologist at the University of California at Davis.

The idea is that 30,000 years ago *T. taxifolia* was widespread in North America. Then the climate changed, as it has so often during this ice age, and a glacier began to creep southward. This, the latest of our glaciations, would have pushed *T. taxifolia* southward and perhaps into little low-lying pockets, like the river valley in which it is currently found. Paleoecologists call these tiny warmer spots *glacial refugia*. About 12,500 years ago the glacier began to retreat, and many of the plants and animals it had pushed south began to move back north in its wake. But some of them had bad luck. Perhaps the new conditions immediately outside their refuges were not hospitable. Perhaps their populations were so small that they could not reproduce in sufficient numbers to expand.

If *T. taxifolia* got stuck in such a pocket, the warming climate may have become too hot for it to really thrive. That is, as the climate warmed back up, conditions in its former refuge, once nearly the last place it could be happy, were turning against it. In the 1950s the population crashed, for reasons still unknown. If the trees were stressed by heat, they could have been more vulnerable to a fungal or insect attack. In any case, the trees never bounced back. According to *The Shrubs and Woody Vines of Florida*, "old-timers report that the torreya was once so abundant that it was regularly cut for use as Christmas trees."[8] These days there are no adult specimens in the native range, just tiny saplings that die back and resprout, die back and resprout. None make seeds. Scientists don't know whether climate change has yet had any role in the tree's decline. But it isn't going to help, that's for sure.

When Connie Barlow talked this story over with her friend Paul Martin—the scientist who theorized that humans killed the Pleistocene megafauna—she looked at it with what she calls "deep time eyes." For her, the true or baseline range of *T. taxifolia* was not the puny refuge where it waited out the glaciation, but the much larger swath of land it might have occupied for tens of millions of years, before the onset of the ice age. With that as a starting point, the next step was obvious: replant torreya in its old stomping grounds, where it could grow to be the vigorous forty-five-foot-tall tree it evolved to be.

Around 2004 Barlow and Martin started corresponding with botanists, including University of California, Davis, ecologist Mark Schwartz, about moving the trees. Printouts of the e-mail correspondence are now archived in Barlow's storage locker in Ann Arbor, Michigan. "Those emails are just classic in terms of botanists thinking through this," says Barlow. "It just seemed so historic." And indeed, students of the history of ecology may someday handle the printouts with gloved fingertips in library archives. Time will tell.

The next step was a couple of editorials in the January 2005 issue *Wild Earth*. At about this time the idea of moving species got the name *assisted migration*. *Migration* here is used, not in the sense of birds moving south in the winter, but in a paleoecology sense, in which species move around slowly, in geological timescales, often in response to climate shifts. Barlow and Martin wrote a piece in favor of moving torreya. Schwartz wrote one against. His comments are worth quoting at length, as they so well capture how many ecologists feel about this issue.

> In most cases we use historical records to establish a baseline forest community toward which we manage our current forests . . . Without a baseline we have no target. Without a target, every kind of management, including those that result in lost native species, is arguably a success. I fear such success. Intentional introduction of species outside their current distributions in an effort to con-

serve them detracts from and trivializes this baseline and threatens to discount standards for conservation. From a visceral level, it seems likely that a range of people would say: Florida torreya has no place in southern Appalachian cove forests. As a consequence, assisted migration should, and will, result in rancor among conservationists. This rancor does not serve conservation.[9]

So though one species may be going extinct, the measures that could save it might endanger other ecosystems, might threaten the existence of the baselines that guide conservation efforts, and might piss off other conservationists. Weep if you like, but let the Florida torreya go.

That might have been the end of it, but Barlow put up a Web site about the controversy, in which she named herself and her sympathizers "the Torreya Guardians." It was then that the citizen-naturalist types got in touch. And they wanted to do much more than debate. They wanted to plant.

Meanwhile, ecologists were starting to talk about assisted migration— not in published papers but at the bar, after work. Hellmann remembers chatting with a paleoecologist named Jason McLachlan, who was hired in Hellmann's department at Notre Dame. When he flew out to Indiana to shop for a house and prepare for the move, the two caught a women's basketball game. As they cheered the Fighting Irish, they talked about the torreya case, and about how often this idea of moving plants and animals around was coming up, especially in the question-and-answer sessions after they gave talks about their research at conferences.

"There is always someone who raises his hand and says, 'Well, if you can predict which ones won't be able to disperse, why don't you intervene on their behalf?'" says Hellmann. "The impulse is to scoff and say, 'Well, this is nature. You don't *intervene on its behalf.*'"

But the questions kept coming, and Hellmann, McLachlan, and Mark Schwartz decided they ought to at least take the issue into the mainstream of scientific discourse—academic publication. And that's about all their first paper on the topic did. It was a conversation-starter, and didn't come out as pro or con. "One of things we said in that paper is that scientists have to debate this," says Hellmann. "If you say it is just not important, you are going to be shocked in twenty years when people are doing all this without guidance." The paper came out in March 2007.[10]

The immediate response was a long pause. In scientific publishing, most papers take forever to come out. Apart from a few big journals like *Science* and *Nature*, which can rush particularly hot discoveries into print, getting something published often takes longer than having a baby. And that's if it is accepted at the first journal to which it is submitted.

Eventually, a few papers did follow, including one biggie, a paper in *Science* with seven authors, including Camille Parmesan and famous Australian ecologist Hugh Possingham. These heavy hitters argued that assisted migration was sometimes a good idea, and they provided a back-of-the-envelope guide for deciding when to move species. Their first-pass analysis suggested that species should be moved if they are at high risk to extinction from climate change, if they can be feasibly transported, and if "the benefits of translocation outweigh the biological and socioeconomic costs and constraints."[11] Of course, that last decision is a real doozy.

They also called the practice "assisted colonization" rather than "assisted migration," and the scientific argument between various parties about what to call schlepping species around is arguably hotter at the moment than the argument over whether it is a good idea. A few more papers have followed, all theoretical and cautious. The International Union for Conservation of Nature has convened a working group to look into the question, with the goal of publishing an official opinion by 2012.

And that just about brings us up to date on the official scientific response to the idea—a tentative engagement with what they consider a very scary proposal. The citizen naturalists, however, have not been so slow. In the summer of 2008 the Torreya Guardians took action. They planted thirty-one *T. taxifolia* seedlings from nurseries in carefully chosen locations in North Carolina. The land is owned by two private citizens excited about saving the species. Each seedling was given the name of a historical personage associated with the Florida torreya or conservation more generally, including John Muir, Ed Abbey, and Aldo Leopold.

And here's an interesting twist. This action, which seems like the natural consummation of the conversations that Barlow was having with like-minded citizens for years, was finally catalyzed by the media. According to Barlow, *Audubon* magazine was interested in covering the torreya story. But the editors didn't want to move forward without some good pictures. Barlow organized the planting party to accommodate them. And she's pleased with how everything jelled as a result. As she put it in her essay on the action: "Were it not for the conservation biologists and land stewards who took alarm at the prospect of ordinary citizens acting on their own to move an endangered plant far north of its so-called 'native' range, there would have been little ground for the major media to pay attention to the desperate plight of one obscure species. And it was media attention that motivated us 'guardians' to consider that maybe now *is* the time, and maybe we *are* the people."

T. taxifolia is not very likely to become a hugely problematic invasive species. Even Mark Schwartz agrees with that. Unlike many species that have become pests, torreya seeds are not dispersed by wind; it reproduces slowly, and the trees are sufficiently large that, as Barlow puts it, "if you make a mistake, you can take out every single one." Nevertheless, a precedent has been set. And it was the amateurs rather than the professionals who set it.

Unintentional assisted migration is also well under way. An analysis of about 350 native European plants sold at nurseries in Europe has revealed that 73 percent of them are now sold farther north than their native ranges, with a mean shift of about 600 miles.[12] Pretty pink-flowered rock soapwort doesn't occur north of Germany, according to official ranges published by botanists. But you can buy it in Sweden and grow it in your garden. The researchers suggest that these commercial movements might help these species adapt as the climate changes. "While the debate on assisted migration continues," they write, "it is clear that, across the planet, we have already given many species an unintentional head start on climate change."

All in all, it looks like—as in the case of rewilding with proxies—the horse is out of the barn. What's not clear is whether scientists like Parmesan or citizens like Barlow will be running the show. Will squeamish scientists hang back while plants and animals (though probably fewer animals, as they are harder to mail and sometimes illegal to transport) are moved wholesale? Or will scientists convince governments to regulate this sort of thing? And which, in the end, would be better for the Earth?

Barlow thinks it makes sense for passionate citizens to do this work, and that's why she went ahead with her torreya planting party. "I didn't want to trust that our society was going to be able and willing to pay professionals to do everything for us," she says. Hellmann might like it a bit better if the experts ran the show, but she doesn't think it will necessarily happen. So she hopes to at least be able to provide citizens with the scientific tools to do their work effectively and safely.

So Hellmann, McLachlan, Schwartz, and another pal of theirs, Dov Sax from Brown University, decided to form a working group on the question, to start to encourage scientific study on what they saw as the inevitable movement of species. Hellmann hopes that the group can produce some kind of guide that would bring scientific information to those who might be considering loading up a U-Haul with all their favorite species and heading for the poles.

"It at least puts something out there that people can consult for decision-making," says Hellmann. "State and federal agencies, we are hoping, might pay attention to our assessment. Certainly state and federal agencies are thinking about this. But of course we don't have any authority or desire to make or enforce rules. Private individuals can do what they wish."

Hellmann is currently in the midst of exactly the kind of painstaking study that can help guide those who want to move species. Hellmann works, among other places, on Vancouver Island, studying a kind of oak savanna ecosystem that most people associate with California. The star players of these savannas are called Garry oaks or Oregon white oaks, large trees often gnarled into unique shapes. Under their canopies grow mossy meadows of wildflowers, including buttercups and star-shaped blue camas. For Canadians, this kind of ecosystem is a beloved break from the evergreens that otherwise dominate the landscape. And according to the nonprofit Garry Oak Ecosystems Recovery Team, "approximately 100 species of plants, mammals, reptiles, birds, butterflies and other insects are officially listed as 'at risk' in these ecosystems" in Canada. The range of these Garry oak savannas hugs the Pacific coast from central California to just about halfway up Vancouver Island.

These savannas are quite rare in Canada and threatened by land development. Hellmann thinks that British Columbians might be interested in establishing such ecosystems farther north on the island or even on the province's mainland as the climate warms. So one set of questions that her study is asking bears directly on whether such a move would work. For example, what are the essential components of a Garry oak savanna? Which of these are limiting its range in the North? Will the Garry oak systems be able to move themselves? If so, will the more mobile components of the ecosystem, such as the butterflies, move first? And if one were to move the ecosystem, would it be best to use the organisms from the northern edge of the range to seed the new site, or would organisms from the center of the range fare better? This last question is important because Hellmann expects that the butterflies, oaks, and other constituents of the system will prove to genetically vary as one moves from south to north. The butterflies on Vancouver Island, for example, are genetically different from their cousins on the mainland. "Would you take that whole gradient and scooch everybody?" asks Hellmann.

Getting the answers to these questions all starts with renting a house. Ecological research is a lot of work, and results that can be summarized in a sentence or two represent the hard-won outcome of years of logistical management, grueling days of fieldwork, and caffeine-fueled writing binges. To learn about the dynamics of Garry oak savannas on Vancouver Island, Hellmann had to first get grant money to do the work by putting together a proposal compelling enough to beat out its rivals. Once she got the money, she had to set up a local headquarters, in this case a house in Ladysmith, British Columbia. She then recruited a team, including Caroline Williams, a Ph.D. student from the University of Ontario, and André Burnier, an undergraduate from Brown, to do much of the daily work. With the help of satellite photos and a tour of the island in a rental car, she identified Garry oak sites and sites where Garry oak might conceivably migrate, designed several experiments, bought equipment to collect data and raise butterflies, jerry-rigged the data-collection devices so they would survive out in the field, and procured vehicles for the team. And this is only one of two headquarters. She had to go through the same rigmarole for a team at the center of the Garry oak savanna range in Oregon. The Oregon sites act as controls to which she compares findings at the edges of the range. The week I visited the northern site, Hellmann was visiting the team to see that all was well, downloading data from the field, and checking on transplanted oaks.

Together the four of us drove up and down the landward side of Vancouver Island, crossing and recrossing the range limit of the ecosystem and visiting sites on military bases, in public parks, on "Crown land" managed for forestry, and on privately owned nature reserves. From the car, the island seemed to be a blanket of conifers, with land carved out for roads and towns. The Garry oak sites were hidden treasures, tucked down winding roads, little patches of flowers, grasses and great gnarled oaks in a sea of Douglas-fir and hemlock. I could see why Canadians found them enchanting. I could also see why they might not be able to move north by themselves.

Hellmann is gathering two species of butterflies, duskywinged skippers and swallowtails, at all these sites, and breeding them, so she can look at the differences between the butterflies in different parts of the range. Essentially, she is trying to determine whether the northernmost butterflies are specially adapted to their edge-of-the-range existence, or whether they are in fact more or less miserable and dreaming of California. "I am trying to ask it, 'Where would you like to live?'" she says. If the butterflies would answer, "Ah, northern California, that is the homeland," then one might expect that as the climate warms, the Vancouver Island butterflies will become happier and more fit, reproduce more often, and push north on their own. If they would answer, "Vancouver Island! We are locally adapted," then a warming climate should make them *less* fit—and they might decline just when they would need a robust population to expand northward. If that is the case, they might need help to move north. Hellmann expects to see more local adaptation in the duskywing than in the swallowtails, as they are more isolated from their southern cousins. The duskywing doesn't fly as well, and it eats only oak leaves as a caterpillar, so many populations may live in particular Garry oak sites like little islands, never breeding with butterflies from the next savanna over.

As we drive from site to site, we stop in a couple of cemeteries. One is north of the currently northernmost Garry oak savanna, but it features a couple of really large Garry oaks, which seem to be doing just fine. Were they planted by the people who first cleared this area to serve as a cemetery? Another cemetery, at the southern tip of the island, in the town of Metchosin, is carpeted with white camas flowers and shaded by Garry oaks. Oaks may have grown continuously on this spot since before the St. Mary the Virgin Church was built here in 1862. Graveyards, like military bases, are often excellent places to look for rare species and ecosystems. Recently, a twenty-five-acre remnant of tall-grass prairie was discovered in a cemetery in urban St. Louis.[13]

As I drove up and down the island with Hellmann and her team, I learned that there's another wrinkle to the Garry oak study. Some of the sites they are looking at are probably at least partially anthropogenic. The pre-European residents of Vancouver Island also liked these systems and maintained them with fire. Apart from their aesthetic qualities, the oak meadows were easier to hunt in and provided additional calories in the form of camas bulbs. While the Garry oak meadows on rocky slopes may have looked after themselves, conservation managers have found it difficult to keep conifers from taking over Garry oak savannas on good soils. They've resorted to mowing and chopping down encroaching Douglas-fir.

To learn more, I met up with Mark Vellend, a young conservation biologist from the University of British Columbia, part of Hellman's assisted migration working group, and one of the authors of the paper that showed that gardeners are moving plants north. Vellend walked me through a few Garry oak sites and told me a story as we strolled single file between slender but ancient and gnarled oak trunks, through buttercups, shooting stars, lomatium, and camas. "Eight thousand years ago the climate was warmer and dryer on Vancouver Island," said Vellend. "Oaks and flowers might have been more widespread back then, and then later were maintained only by people burning." So, I asked him, if people didn't burn these areas after the climate cooled, would some of the flower species be extinct in Canada? He answered like a true scientist: "That's not an unreasonable hypothesis." So Garry oak savannas in Canada are a human production, threatened by human activities. And people are worried that it is "unnatural" to save them by having humans move them north? Surely assisted migration of these ecosystems would just be a continuation of the care our species has put into them for thousands of years.

One of Hellmann's sites is a little bare rocky clearing in the woods up near Campbell River, north of the last Garry oak. This site was chosen as an example of the kind of place to which people might move the oak, the butterflies, the flowers, and all the other species that make up the little fairyland savannas. Right now, though, it is already occupied. Exposed rocks were covered with thick pads of acid-green moss interspiked with blades of grass and dotted with balls of elk dung. Small bushes grew from between the rocks; on this late April day their leaves were still tiny red buds, and they were more display stands for various species of lichens. Bears visit this clearing, too, to the mild worry of researchers downloading data. It was a very attractive forest room, with walls of Douglas-fir, but it doesn't have a catchy name like *Garry oak savanna* or a fan club. I felt a bit sorry for it, almost as if the moving trucks were already on the way and the place was scheduled to be turned into a Garry oak savanna that very day. "What makes climate change different from re-establishing from a glaciation is that these northern areas are already full," said Hellmann.

The mood among the team was happy, despite the fact that several of the climate sensors, which looked like oversize watch batteries, had gotten wet and were not recording properly, even though they were carefully duct-taped inside plastic pillboxes. Oaks that they had lugged up to the site were sitting in pots, so Hellmann could see how butterflies that feed on them would do if moved to the clearing. Of course, it would be more like a real migration if the oaks were planted in the ground rather than in pots; every gardener knows that potted plants are more affected by the cold. But Hellmann, despite having permission from the government to stick those oaks right into the ground, could not quite bring herself to personally move the Garry oak past its recorded range.

She's still ambivalent. "Philosophically we are entering an era of interventionism that I am not comfortable with," she says. But on the other hand, "I have not gotten comfortable with this idea of how many species are going to go extinct. There is less stuff than there used to be. That is one thing that we should care about. I am less concerned with how it is configured than that it exists."

Hellmann worries that either way, people make too much of assisted migration. "I don't think it is a panacea for saving biodiversity under threat from climate change," she says. "There are some species that are very important, and for the species that are really important, people will do it . . . but I have a hard time imagining how we would apply it to all the beetles and the microbes, the vast majority of biodiversity. No one is going to pick them up and move them." Indeed not. It would cost a fortune, and the only monies available to finance it would likely have to come from the paltry coffers of conservation organizations. But other species, like timber trees, are worth a lot of money. So there's a third group that might be interested in assisted migration, beyond scientists and citizen naturalists: foresters.

Forester Greg O'Neill has roots in the Okanagan valley of British Columbia—both kinds. His father rode his bike out to Rattlesnake Point as a boy, a bit of provincial park sticking out into Kalamalka Lake. Greg learned to swim as a kid in Kalamalka. As an adult, he still goes skinny dipping there "on the far side"—and works for the B.C. Ministry of Forests in the nearby burg of Vernon, as a tree breeder.

At the Kalamalka Research Station and Seed Orchard, rows and rows of trees of various species at various ages sit silent and green in the summer sun. Those that are not in breeding programs designed to produce high-quality seed for the province are participating in very slow scientific experiments. If anything characterizes forestry as a science, it is its great demands on the patience of researchers. Many experiments do not produce really good data for twenty years.

O'Neill, 45, is therefore timing his masterpiece—the Assisted Migration Adaptation Trial (AMAT)—just right. The first seedlings, only inches high, were planted in 2009. O'Neill will be about retirement age when the solid results start coming in.

The AMAT takes seedlings from forty populations of sixteen species from B.C., Washington, Oregon, and Idaho and plants them in forty-eight "common gardens" all over those same areas. "So for example," explains O'Neill, "Douglas-fir from coastal Oregon will be planted as far north as the Yukon border, and Sitka spruce from the rain forest of Haida Gwaii on the Queen Charlotte Islands will be planted as far inland as the semi-desert of central Idaho."

O'Neill expects 50 percent of his seedlings to die. Trees, especially the conifers B.C. specializes in, are very genetically diverse and are often adapted to very specific local climates. Take a Douglas-fir from the coast and bring it inland, and it may very well give up the ghost before more than a few years are out. If it doesn't, it might be tiny, pest-ridden, or crooked. "Douglas-fir grows from Mexico City to central B.C., but move it seven hundred meters elevation downhill at any location, and you will be growing toothpicks," says O'Neill.

While O'Neill tortures a few experimental trees by taking them to new climates, the future will bring new climates to all the world's trees. In response, O'Neill is behind a push to "move" trees by planting seeds from the south and from lower elevations, in the hopes that the next generation of trees will be better adapted to a warmer, drier future. O'Neill doesn't think there's any time to lose. The climate is already changing, and many trees may already be maladapted for where they are rooted today. "We see some really ugly trees out there," he says. "Maybe the pest and pathogen outbreaks we are seeing are compounded by that maladaptation."

O'Neill and the foresters could leave the trees to their own devices to handle all this change. If foresters stopped replanting after they harvested and forests reseeded themselves, the wind would blow some pollen north and some south, and everywhere trees better adapted to new climates would live, while those who couldn't hack it would die. But don't imagine a slow and stately march of the forest so much as a scrappy scramble, with no trees doing very well, and not all trees moving at the same speed or even in the same direction. And for a long time to come, as local adaptation lags behind fast temperature rises, forests will likely look a bit more raggedy, stunted, and jumbled. Not ideal for making two-by-fours.

The possible changes were brought home to foresters in British Columbia by a 2006 paper in the journal *Ecology* by Andreas Hamann and Tongli Wang of the University of British Columbia. Hamann and Wang drew maps of what the climate in B.C. might look like in 2025, 2055, and 2085.[14] Crucially, they did it in a language that foresters speak: the jargon of "BEC zones." BEC stands for Biogeoclimatic Ecological Classification, the system devised in the 1960s and 1970s so foresters could talk about different types of forest using standardized language. The zones, subzones, and more than two hundred variants of the BEC system are based on vegetation, climate, and specific site features such as topography and soil type. Foresters are very adept at telling them apart. "Foresters like to be able to go into the bush, look at a few plants on the ground, the slope and the soil, and say 'Falsebox at this elevation is a giveaway. We're definitely in the IDFmw2,'" says O'Neill. So when the maps suggested that a Ponderosa-pine-dominated BEC, featuring an arid grassland tree now found only in valley bottoms in the southern part of the province, would explode into the boreal forest in the northeast of the province, foresters were extremely startled.

Hamann and Wang's maps do give the slight impression of a stately forest march, but their text makes clear the chaos they really foresee. Trees whose ranges now end in British Columbia see their current "climate envelope" move at least sixty miles north per decade. But dozens of factors, including the trees' genetic variability, the direct effect of increased carbon dioxide on growth, and "different capabilities of migrating through complex landscape" will affect whether the trees make it all sixty miles per decade.

But most new trees in B.C. are planted, not self-seeding. So the "flying BEC zones," as O'Neill calls them, can be seen either as a "what if we left them to themselves" scenario or as an instruction manual of where to plant.

According to O'Neill, the flying BEC zones were just one of the things that scared the bejesus out of foresters and policymakers in British Columbia. Pine beetles have recently hit the province hard, munching on mature lodgepole pine and turning healthy dark green trees a desiccated dead red color as it kills them. Thirteen point five million hectares are affected, an area the size of Greece.[15] Climate change is widely believed to be behind the outbreak. Usually low temperatures in the winter kill off a good chunk of the beetle population. Not so in these milder times. "People see red trees as far as the eye can see, and it becomes easier to implement some rather aggressive policies," says O'Neill. The final thing that crystallized opinion in the province was a couple of nasty forest fires in 1998 and 2003, linked to drought. Everyone agreed: something had to be done.

And so in April 2009 British Columbia became the first political unit to start systematically moving its trees. The province, like most other timber-producing areas, has rules known as *seed transfer policies*, designed to ensure that planted forests are genetically adapted to local environments. Seeds that forestry companies plant after they log an area must come from nearby. Rules vary by species, but generally, seeds must be planted within about 200 kilometers north, south, east or west and 200 meters downhill or up to 300 meters uphill from their origin.

The new rule stretches the elevation guidelines so that seeds can be planted up to 500 meters higher than where they were collected, on the theory that the trees from the warmer downhill location are adapted to a climate somewhat like what might be expected at the newly planted site some years into the future. "These changes encourage planting seed that is adapted to climates about two degrees centigrade warmer than the planting site," says O'Neill, "to account for climate change in the last century and changes anticipated in the first portion of the planted tree's lifetime."

Timing is tricky, because trees are so long-lived. If you plant a seed that is perfectly adapted the year you plant it, it may have a vigorous first few years and then slow down, as the climate changes, to something it is not prepared for. But if you plant seeds adapted to where you expect the climate to be at harvest time, they might never make it through those first few cold years. "In the end, I expect the optimum migration distance is toward the middle," says O'Neill. "Maybe one-fourth or one-third of the way through a tree's lifetime."

O'Neill is now working on a wholesale revamp of seed transfer guidelines. He plans to link them to the BEC zones, of which foresters are so fond, so that as BEC zones take wing, so do the seeds that are planted in them. He's even talking about "taking it to a new level" by putting in the odd hectare of southern seeds in places not likely to be logged and replanted for a long time. Think of it as a kind of adaptation inoculation. When the new temperatures arrive, O'Neill hopes that the genes to adapt trees to the heat will already be circulating. "Why not give them a boost?" he asks. "You could prime an area by planting a hectare, half a hectare with trees that are from one degree warmer."

Currently, *populations* of trees are being moved, but no tree *species* are being planted outside of that species' historical range. But O'Neill expects that such moves will come as a natural extension of what he's working on.

Not everyone is a big fan of O'Neill's activities. Daniel Simberloff, an ecologist at the University of Tennessee in Knoxville and a pioneer in the field of invasion biology, calls British Columbia's program "a waste of time." He sees the whole notion of assisted migration as a "bandwagon" that has recently become chic. "With respect to moving seeds around, it doesn't worry me as much as moving species," he says. But O'Neill's AMAT trial won't be able to inform policy for a long time—"He'll be dead before there is any real data from this"—and meanwhile, Simberloff says, there are just too many unknowns. "I would want to know a lot more about pathogens and insects before I moved things . . . there is very little evidence that it is going to help."

And he doesn't limit his scorn to assisted migration in forestry. A recent paper he co-authored with Anthony Ricciardi of McGill University in Montreal is straightforwardly titled "Assisted Colonization Is Not a Viable Conservation Strategy."[16]

Even assisted-migration-friendly ecologists are worried about going too fast. O'Neill's experiment "is wonderful, I am glad he is doing it," says Dov Sax, from Hellman's working group. But, he says, "the thought of planting a couple hectares of trees far to the north of where people currently harvest—that sounds a little scary to me." What if the added trees change the ecology of the forest in unexpected ways? Besides, the tradition of non-intervention is very strong. Sax calls for more study, and no precipitous moves. But he admits that his call for caution is as predictable as O'Neill's eagerness to move ahead. "You can see why people with a commercial interest are going to want to find a solution as quickly as possible. Conservationists, who have seen experiments go awry, are going to be more cautious."

So far, critics (other than those I contacted myself) have either not noticed policy changes in B.C. or feel that they have yet to cross a line. O'Neill's boss told me they have received exactly zero complaints about the new policy.

Sally Aitken, a professor of forestry genetics at the University of British Columbia in Vancouver, is all for it. She points out that the moves being considered are not completely new. Remember that during the Pleistocene repeated rounds of glaciers slid up and down the North American continent, chasing tree populations south and then allowing them to move north in a slow-motion agitation of ranges. British Columbia's plans, she says "would not put species into contact with each other that didn't interact at some point during those glacial and interglacial periods."

For Aitken, assisted migration is going to be necessary to save some species, but she despairs at rounding up the kind of resources necessary to do a thorough job of saving trees, like the threatened whitebark pine, that have no commercial importance. "In B.C. there are two hundred million seedlings planted every year," she says. "You are never going to be planting those kinds of numbers for conservation purposes. Reforestation is one of the only ways that you could accomplish assisted migration on a large scale. You have a whole system. It's all legislated, it's all tracked."

O'Neill agrees. The whitebark pine, an elegant conifer with bleached-looking wood found at high elevations, is a very appealing species, he says. "You climb up, you get to the top of your hike, and there is the whitebark pine. But the tree is hooped. It's got climate change, mountain pine beetle, and blister rust, and it's got nowhere to go." For O'Neill, pragmatism requires putting resources elsewhere. And what O'Neill thinks about what to move and what not to move has a surprising importance. His reports heavily influence B.C. policy for Crown land, and that's 95 percent of all land in the province, 27 percent or 25 million hectares of which is available for commercial forestry compared to just 13.3 million hectares in parks and preserves.

If O'Neill decides to move populations and species, it won't matter much what conservationists decide. Even if his "inoculations" are banned from protected areas, the protected areas will be swamped by the lime-green, windborne haze of pollen coming from commercial forestry land. Gene flow in conifers is particularly vigorous, and the new baby conifers in protected areas are unlikely to remain free from genes from the commercial side. "In the past, we would view any gene flow from plantations into protected areas as contamination," says Aitken. "But if we are moving genetically diverse populations north in reforestation, they may provide a source of preadapted genes into those populations. We don't know." The "contamination" may save the trees in the parks.

While many ecologists object to moving species for the very sensible reason that it is difficult to predict the consequences, it cannot be denied that sentiment plays a role. People generally like the ecosystems that surround them, and they associate the most visible plants and animals with home. When a bunch of refugees from the south show up, and when the trees and butterflies one remembers from childhood disappear to the north, it will change the look and feel of home.

Despite being a hometown boy with an obvious affection for native trees—the local ponderosa pines are his favorite—O'Neill isn't too worried about the look of the Okanagan Valley changing. I ask him how he would feel if Rattlesnake Point were to lose its pines and host, let's say, sagebrush and aloe instead. "I think it would be cool," he replies.

Assisted migration has a lot of intuitive appeal. For commercially important species like timber trees, it is inevitable. For ornamental species in a gardening context, it is a done deal. For well-loved species with rich and leisured supporters, it is likely, especially if things get really tough for the species at home. But for the vast majority of species, for Hellmann's beetles and microbes, it remains a long shot. Most species will have to find their own way to a place where they can survive and adapt to new temperatures, or else perish.

But for those species for which there is the will and the cash, the biggest obstacle they face in moving between their historical homeland and new digs may not be the valleys or suburbs in between. Their biggest obstacle may be the terror that many ecologists feel when they imagine introducing a species that might become—*dum, dum dum!*—invasive. But are introduced and "invasive" species really as terrible as we've been told? In the next chapter, we'll find out that many sojourning species aren't quite the villains they have been made out to be.

6 | Learning to Love Exotic Species

Stephens Island, off the coast of New Zealand, is a good example of the changes that so-called "invasive species" can wreak. Here, according to legend, in 1894 a single cat belonging to a lighthouse keeper—the invader—dispatched the very last members of a species called the Stephen's Island flightless wren. More recent historical research suggests that the deed was done over a couple of years not by a single cat but by a feral population descended from a "she cat heavy with kitten" accidentally let loose on the island.[1] Whether cat singular or cats plural, the world's last flightless songbird was just too helpless and too delicious to survive introduced feline hunters.[2] This is the kind of story ecologists love to tell about the ecological consequences of moving species around. A species invades, and the ecosystem collapses, species go extinct, and complexity and diversity are replaced with a monotonous and weedy landscape dominated by invaders.

But there's another side to exotic species. Consider Rodrigues Island, a tiny Indian Ocean islet about 350 miles from Mauritius. Three species that lived on Rodrigues and nowhere else—two songbirds and a fruit bat—almost went extinct when the island's forest was cut down in the 1950s and 1960s.[3] The birds and the bat missed the fruit and nectar provided by the missing trees, as well as the insects that lived in the forest shade. In the 1970s, with the three species at tiny numbers—the Rodrigues fody was down to ten birds—the island was reforested with fast-growing exotic species for timber and erosion control. The trees were chosen without regard to conservation and included some notorious pests, but almost by accident the reforestation saved the ailing species. Its lightning speed probably could not have been matched by slow-growing natives, and lightning speed was required to pull those species back from the edge. Now there are thousands of fodys and fruit bats, and the other bird, a warbler, is holding steady at 250 individuals. Meanwhile, people are gradually, laboriously transitioning the forest back to native species. Because, as useful as the exotic trees were, they're still considered invasive. The exotics turned out to help rather than hinder, but prejudice against them was so strong that instead of thanks, they are getting the ax.

That prejudice may finally be changing. While some exotic species are a huge problem, the vast majority are not. Science is finding that some are quite well behaved and innocuous, or even helpful. And spending time and money battling exotics simply because they are not "supposed" to be where they are drains time and money away from more constructive conservation projects. Ultimately, the enemy is not exotics; the enemy is us. But the culture of fighting "invasive species" is very well entrenched in conservation. It may be one of those hardy, weedy types that are so darn hard to get rid of.

The label *invasive species* is recent, stretching back just a couple of decades, but human introduction stretches back into prehistory. We have moved species around for at least as long as we have been farming. While crop plants and livestock are undoubtedly the most often moved, we are also sloppy, and prone to move species accidentally, in the root balls of nursery trees, in packing material, in ballast water, in the wheel wells of aircraft, and in the mud on our boots. Humans are also sentimental creatures. When moving from one part of the world to another, we have a history of toting with us garden plants and pets, game birds and game fish, even songbirds just to cheer us up.

Every so often one of these moved species "naturalizes," reproducing on its own in its new home. Sometimes a species naturalizes so well that it becomes a rowdy nuisance, taking over land or water previously held by natives, or eating them up or outcompeting them or fouling boat hulls or doing something else disagreeable. In general, one hears a lot more about these villains than the shier foreigners, and for many ecologists and conservationists, they have become the enemy.

Most-wanted-list members you may have heard of include kudzu, "the weed that ate the south"; zebra mussels, which clog water-intake pipes and hog all the plankton in the Great Lakes; flammable cheatgrass, which takes over plains and increases fire frequency; the Asian tiger mosquito, that stripe-legged bastard that unfairly bites at all times of day; leafy spurge, which has rendered great swaths of western prairie useless for grazing domestic livestock; and the yellow crazy ant, which forms insanely large and hungry colonies in Australia.[4] And some of our own familiar domestics can be very destructive when introduced into certain ecosystems. Goats, cats, rats, and rabbits in particular are well known for wreaking havoc on plants and animals with their appetites.

New germs and viruses can make people and animals sick; the smallpox and other diseases that killed so many American Indians and Australian Aborigines were European species, for example. Introduced mosquitoes, rats, and other species can transmit diseases, causing outbreaks. Some introduced species can cost farmers and ranchers big money, as they destroy crops or displace more palatable species on the range. Other useful ecosystem services, such as water retention in soil, can be disrupted by new arrivals.[5]

And, perhaps most dramatic of all, as on Stephens Island, aggressive introduced species can cause extinctions by eating up native species. The brown tree snake, native to Australia and nearby countries, has killed off ten of twelve native forest-dwelling birds on the island of Guam after arriving as a stowaway in cargo ships.[6] Not only have these birds disappeared, but their absence has had a cascading effect on many of the island's fruit trees, which used to be dispersed by the birds. An initial study suggests that thanks to the lack of avian dispersers, Guam's fruit trees will in future cluster together in expanding single-species rings rather than intermixing.[7]

Without doubt, some movements of species do result in consequences that nearly everybody can agree are bad, bad, bad. And people are fighting back, both in government- and in nongovernmental-organization-led efforts and on their own. In 1995 in South Africa, the lauded Working for Water program created jobs for poor people removing invasive plants that "divert enormous amounts of water from more productive uses."[8] In 1999 Bill Clinton signed an executive order declaring war against invasive species, defined as "alien species whose introduction does or is likely to cause economic or environmental harm or harm to human health."[9] All agencies were to avoid spreading them and to stamp them out, wherever possible (unless the benefits of the species outweigh the potential harm). In 2001 biologist David Pimentel and colleagues estimated the global cost of invasive species—including crop losses to exotic pests and weeds, costs of fighting invading species, and even the estimated costs of feral cats killing birds, with birds assigned a value of $30 each. The grand total was $1.4 trillion, or 5 percent of the global economy.[10]

Influential ecologists like Shahid Naeem of Columbia University "would love to get rid of every invasive species on the planet and put all the native species back in their place," as he puts it. The editor in chief of a top journal in ecology has even admitted to making nighttime raids on a neighboring garden that harbored purple loosestrife, considered a noxious invader.

One of the innumerable theaters in the war on invasive species is the Chesapeake Bay in Virginia, near the site of Jamestown, which played host to some of the first British colonists. Along the banks of the York River, crumpled beer cans and someone's soggy hunting cap bear witness to the human colonists' success. Another colonial type has also put down roots by the river: a few feet above the high-tide line sit some feathery reeds. They are the "common reed," *Phragmites australis*, said to have come from Europe and a declared enemy of the Park Service. One day in 2005 the reeds came under attack from an invasive-species strike team.

Armed with high-tech gear, these specialists travel from park to park—all-terrain vehicle in tow for the off-road areas—ready to pull, poison, or burn anything that has been declared out of place. Since their inception in 2000, the National Park Service's strike teams have treated more than one thousand square miles. But declaring a mission a success depends on the yardstick one uses: plant seeds can survive for decades, and most targeted species return sooner or later, often within a few years of treatment.

Dressed in a pale khaki uniform and thigh-high waders, strike team member Kate Jensen carefully records the exact location of the *Phragmites* using a hand-held global positioning device, which chirps merrily when it reaches enough satellites. Half an hour later her teammates—Dale Meyerhoeffer and Matthew Overstreet—arrive with a two-hundred-gallon tank of an herbicide called Habitat. The team mixed the chemical early in the morning and added a fluorescent blue dye that will make it obvious which plants have been hit.

The aim, Jensen said, is to make the area livable for native plants. She points to a handful of cattails behind the *Phragmites*: "That's what we want here. We like those." Meyerhoeffer plays out more hose so Overstreet can work his way behind a ghostly stand of dead *Phragmites* from the year before, which still shelter some persistent shoots. "I'm getting a few back here," he calls. "I'm leaving the rest for job security." There's a pause, then: "That was a joke."[11]

The Park Service's sixteen exotic-plant-management teams were conceived as a way to spread scant resources over hundreds of U.S. National Parks. The mid-Atlantic team goes after tree-of-heaven from China and autumn olive, an East Asian import once planted to fatten game birds. They also tackle privets—hedgerow plants that form dense thickets—and mile-a-minute weed, whose name betrays its alarming habit of growth.

So are the introduced reeds around Jamestown being killed for their historical inaccuracy? Rita Beard, who runs the Parks Service's strike teams, says no. "It is not just a matter of aesthetics. It is not just a matter of saving the plant communities that have been here historically. It is also about maintaining ecosystems that can withstand the ecological changes that will inevitably occur." This argument, that introduced species tend to destabilize ecosystems and reduce their diversity, goes back to the 1950s at least.

The modern scientific field of invasion biology tends to trace its origins to the 1958 publication of Charles Elton's *The Ecology of Invasions by Animals and Plants*, though it was by no means the first scientific treatment of the topic.[12] Elton's book was an expansion of a series of radio broadcasts aimed at the general public. He may have chosen his colorful and militaristic descriptions of "invasions" and bomblike "ecological explosions" of species numbers, to make the programs interesting.[13] His good-versus-evil rhetoric of species invasion may have sown the seeds for the vocabulary commonly used to talk about exotics today. But with or without the rhetoric, Elton saw these movements as having far-reaching consequences. "We must make no mistake," he wrote. "We are seeing one of the great historical convulsions in the world's fauna and flora."[14]

Elton saw species "invasions" in the context of niches. In an intact, coevolved ecosystem, every species will have a slightly different role, or niche, and often, he believed, every niche will be filled. Some animals eat grass, others leaves; some plants grow on wet soil and some grow on dry; some birds nest in dead trees, others in live ones. When new species are introduced, the theory goes, they can get a foothold and start reproducing only by finding a vacant niche or by throwing some other species out of its niche, "rather as an immigrant might try to find a job and a house and start a family in a new country or big city."

Elton noticed that some introduced species seem to do exceptionally well in new places because their new neighbors have not evolved any resistance to their wiles. The chestnut blight fungus, he noted, lived unassumingly on trees in Asia without causing any noticeable problem. American chestnuts, however, were devastated by this unfamiliar fungus.[15] (In Elton's book a 1911 map of the blight presents an irregular blotch of dead chestnuts centered on New York.[16] By 1950 nearly all American chestnuts were gone.)

In other cases, species are thought to thrive because they have found a land where their predators are absent. Later ecologists discovered that beyond these reasons, perhaps the most important variable for predicting when and where new introductions would establish was "propagule pressure"—the sheer number of seeds or organisms arriving in an area. More pressure means a higher chance of an introduced species sticking.[17]

Elton believed that the ultimate result of stirring the pot of Earth's species must be a reduction in the variety of life. "The eventual state of the biological world will become not more complex but simpler—and poorer," he wrote.[18] And this is the current conception of "invasive species"—they outcompete and eat up complex native systems, replacing them with a few dull weeds.

Concern about nonnative species stayed quiescent for several decades after Elton's book. In the 1980s it began to take off as a separate subfield of ecology, and in the 1990s academic interest in the subject exploded.[19] In 1998 a scientific paper declared alien species to be the second-gravest threat to vulnerable U.S. flora and fauna, after habitat destruction.[20] This academic trend in turn influenced the 1999 executive order and the formation of strike teams such as the one I visited in 2005. In the 1990s I remember volunteering at a Seattle-area park to pull out English ivy and holly, which were running rampant over native groundcover and shimmying up trees. It was a very satisfying experience, as is often the case when one can identify opportunities for socially sanctioned destruction. We slashed, yanked, snipped, and dug out bags and bags of vegetation and left feeling sweaty, pleasantly sore, and righteous.

In 2002 Brown University researcher Dov Sax—the same Dov Sax from Hellman's assisted migration working group—published a paper in the *American Naturalist* that overnight made him many enemies.[21] Plowing through all the literature on invasions in oceanic islands, Sax found that because invasions greatly outnumbered extinctions, the overall diversity of oceanic islands was increasing. In the case of plants, islands are now twice as diverse as they were before humans started moving things around. For example: Easter Island once had 50 native species. Since human arrival, 7 of those have gone extinct. But 68 more plants have been introduced to the island, bringing today's total number of species to 111. Sax and his coauthors were careful to point out that this bump in diversity applied only on a per-island basis. Because some species that had only lived on a single island went extinct and were replaced by common species, diversity was going down on a global scale.

Still, many ecologists were upset and confused by his results. Oceanic islands were where invasive species were supposed to be most pernicious. The popular image of endless acres of invasive grass smothering complex systems and rare species was hard to shake. But this kind of competition-driven extinction didn't show up in the record. For example, Sax found that few bird extinctions on oceanic islands were caused directly by other birds competing for resources. There were bird extinctions caused by introduced species directly killing native birds, but not by competition. And while big swaths of invasive vegetation do exist on many islands, they don't exist to the complete exclusion of the native species.

Globally, extinctions that are directly attributable to introduced species are quite rare. There are those few, mostly introduced species directly eating a native species, on remote islands or in lakes (which can be thought of as kind of aquatic "islands"). But extinctions are almost never the result of introduced species on continents.[22] Certainly introduced species have reduced native populations in numbers, sometimes quite severely, and from a genetic viewpoint these reductions can wipe out a fair bit of diversity, but as for actual extinctions? Pretty much only on islands and in lakes.[23]

Sax's paper was a particularly prominent example of recent questioning of the "invasive species" concept erected in the 1990s. Another scientist who questions the status quo is Mark Davis, an ecologist at Macalester University in St. Paul, Minnesota, whose teenage attempts at courting women with romantic strolls by the Great Lakes were stymied by an explosion of introduced alewife fish repulsively expiring in large numbers on the shore. Despite his personal beef with alewives, Davis is not a fan of the currently fashionable "good versus evil" metaphors to describe human-transported species. He feels life is in fact much messier, more dynamic, and more complex than the black-and-white battle metaphors can capture. For every pest, there are many more unobtrusive immigrants, living quietly in their new haunts, or even facilitating the growth and development of native species. This does not mean that nonnatives are never a problem, but Davis convincingly argues that they are not problematic per se.

Davis challenges much of invasion biology's conventional wisdom in *Invasion Biology*, a textbook that takes the unusual step of suggesting that scientists consider dismantling the field that is its subject. His argument is that change is the order of the day in all ecosystems, and that species move around constantly, on multiple scales. Yes, humans have done a whole lot of long-distance moving in the past few hundred years, but these moves are not essentially different from the "natural" movements of yesteryear, and they can be studied using the same scientific methods. "There is little about biological invasions that make them so unique that a specialized sub-discipline need be sustained to study them," he writes.[24]

Davis takes on other axioms of invasion biology as well, many going back to Elton. If empty niches invite invaders, then why are less diverse systems not more easily invaded?[25] If newly arrived species have an advantage because natives have not evolved resistance to them, isn't it also true that they will have no evolved resistance to the wiles of the natives?[26] Much more important, according to Davis, in predicting which species will establish in a new place is propagule pressure and disturbance. Disturbance creates a more variable landscape, with more kinds of habitats, thus increasing the chances that one niche will suit the new arrival. Disturbance also makes the availability of resources like food and nutrients variable in time. Good times will be good for everyone, native and newcomer alike, allowing a window for them to get established.[27] To use Elton's metaphor, an immigrant to a new city will have an easier time establishing him- or herself in an economic boom.

Davis also disagrees with the assumption that introduced species will automatically compete with or prey on natives. Sometimes newcomers might help natives flourish. For example, *Pyura praeputialis*, a squidgy brown sea-squirt-like creature from Australia, has increased biodiversity on Chilean rocky tidal shores by cementing itself down and creating a gelatinous landscape in which large invertebrates and algae can thrive.[28] Invasive grasses can be homes for native birds short on prairie.[29] And in at least some cases, introduced species are taking over roles once performed by extinct native species. In Hawaii, for example, a team led by Jeff Foster at the University of Illinois, Urbana-Champaign, and Scott Robinson at the University of Florida, Gainesville, found that exotic birds are dispersing the seeds of native plants since many native birds have gone extinct. In fact, exotics have almost completely taken over the seed-eating and remote-defecation business in Hawaii.[30] Without these recent immigrants, the situation in Hawaii might resemble that of Guam, with no one doing any dispersing.

Or take the story of Britain's blue tits. These charming little birds were threatened with starvation when climate change moved the date when their chicks hatched but not the date when the caterpillars they usually feed them emerge. Luckily, the tits were saved when Turkey oaks moved up from continental Europe, complete with associated gall wasps that the tit chicks find just as tasty as caterpillars. So people who wanted to see the tits survive had to embrace the Turkey oaks.[31]

Many conservationists are calling for an end to decades-long efforts to destroy tamarisks, Middle Eastern trees that look something like cedars, in the U.S. Southwest. Tamarisks have long been blamed for hogging water there, though recent research debunks the notion that they use more water than native vegetation.[32] Now endangered southwestern willow flycatchers have been found to be nesting in their branches, and so "salt cedar," as it is often called, may get a reprieve.

A philosophical conundrum comes next. The various species of tamarisk are hybridizing. Are these hybrids native or not? "To the extent that evolution can proceed by hybridization and that these things are unique, you can make a case that they are native," says ecologist and historian Matthew Chew of Arizona State University in Tempe, who has studied the history of tamarisk-eradication efforts.

When newcomers hybridize with locals, ecologists often frame the result as "genetic swamping" or even "genetic pollution."[33] Common cordgrass is the result of a spontaneous cross between an American cordgrass that traveled to the U.K. in ballast water and a U.K. cordgrass. To what country does this new species belong, if not the country of its birth—the U.K.? Yet after being initially accepted as a useful grass for stabilizing muddy coastal lands, it is now treated as an invasive because of its dubious parentage and rip-roaring success. "By taking over the mantle of the native pioneer species, *S. anglica* has altered the course of succession," says the Joint Nature Conservation Committee, which advises the U.K. government on conservation matters. "It usually produces a monoculture which has much less intrinsic value to wildlife than the naturally species-diverse marsh."[34] As the grass is considered invasive outside the U.K. as well, it is in effect a stateless species, but also a highly cosmopolitan one; it is found on mud in temperate climes all around the world.[35]

In a world with precious little money for conservation, purism about "genetic pollution" can cause conservationists to throw resources at campaigns that may have marginal value. Witness the time and energy spent on the ruddy duck. Ruddy ducks come from North and South America. They were released in the United Kingdom in the 1950s, and spread to Spain in 1982, where the last breeding population of related white-headed ducks lives. The two kinds of ducks have different reproductive strategies; white-headed ducks form hierarchies and let top ducks get all the mating opportunities, while ruddy ducks taking an aggressive every-drake-for-himself approach.[36] As a result, mating between ruddy and white-headed ducks became common, and fertile hybrids began appearing. This alarmed European conservationists, who feared that the white-headed duck would become extinct—hybridized out of separate existence.[37] The Royal Society for the Protection of Birds cheered as the U.K. government spent several million pounds on an eradication program. But what is really at risk of being lost here? Ruddy and white-headed ducks are both chestnut brown, blue-billed, and black-capped with stiff tails, but they do look different. And as their differing reproductive strategies show, they act differently. The definition of a species is notoriously problematic, but the probable reason why white-headed ducks are considered a separate species even though they can have fertile offspring with their ruddy cousins is that they have been reproductively isolated for two to five million years by being physically separate.[38] If they had been reunited "naturally," by a long-distance flight, a land bridge that they could waddle across, or some kind of duck Kon Tiki, then some scientists might have considered their mating to be within-species and therefore acceptable.

If we change our unit of focus from the messy species level to the perhaps (but not necessarily) cleaner genetic level, it is harder to get worried about the hybrids. Genes from both lines are carried forward and continue to be represented in the hybrid offspring. "What you produce is neither ruddy nor white-headed per se, but both genetic lines have continued on," says Chew. "They just have a different name. If the ducks aren't going to recognize the lines we've drawn between them, then the naming problem is ours."

What do we fear? Do we fear genuine extinction of the white-headed duck, or just extinction of the familiar category? More broadly, when we attack "invasive species," are we acting out of prudent caution to avoid likely extinctions, or do we merely fear and dislike any change? What happens to the concept of "invasive species" if you fold humanity back into nature and consider us just another way species move around, along with migration and ocean currents? Presto change-o, it disappears.

"Can't we just forget about where they came from, identify species that are causing us problems according to our values, and then deal with them?" wonders Davis. This is a hard leap to make. The "invasive species" paradigm is so easy. If a species isn't native, it is an outlaw and ought to be removed. If a species is native, it is good and should be kept. If we ditch those simple rules, then suddenly every plant and animal is a separate case, and we have to ask ourselves, "Do we want this species in this place right now?" To answer, we have to know what we want; we have to have a vision for the future of every piece of land.

But maybe the current war on invasives isn't quite as easy as we think. Just as in the war on terror, "enemy combatants" are often difficult to tell from civilians. "Native" or "invasive" status can be more difficult to agree upon than one might think. Is the dingo—which was introduced to Australia by people 5,000 years ago and may have shoved the "marsupial lion," the thylacine, toward extinction—an invasive species? If so, then why did the State of Victoria declare it an endangered species in 2008?[39] The shipworm *Teredo navalis* has been sailing the seven seas for so long that no one is sure where it originated.[40] And in fact—and brace yourself for this—*Phragmites*, the common reed that the Park Service invasive species strike team was so busy killing, isn't actually an exotic species. According to Kristin Saltonstall of the University of Maryland Center for Environmental Science, it is a global species, native to America as well as Europe. Ground sloths ate it back in the Pleistocene.[41] But a European "lineage" of the species that came over in the eighteenth or nineteenth century ended up getting aggressive and behaving like an invasive species—forming monocultures. So really, it isn't an invasive species, it's an invasive lineage. And maybe ecologists who like the 1492 baseline can use the common reed as a metaphor. Europeans weren't an invasive species, because American Indians were already here. They were just an invasive *lineage*.

While ecologists are busy examining their own prejudices against exotics, some conservationists have forged ahead and begun using exotics—on purpose. Rewilders' proxies are exotic species being used to recreate processes once carried out by extinct animals. Those promoting assisted migration are advocating moving species outside their native ranges, where many will consider them exotic. Ecologists have also introduced exotics to support rare natives: Atlantic shad now swim in rivers in the Pacific Northwest to feed endangered salmon.[42] Fast growing and hardy exotics can make excellent "nurse plants," colonizing bare areas and setting up shade and soil conditions for natives; European gorse is planted on worn-out grazing lands in New Zealand for this purpose.[43] Exotic pests and pathogens are introduced to control undesirable exotic species. Christian Giardina is hoping to bring an exotic rust to Hawaii to attack strawberry guava. Exotics sometimes make acceptable fuel for the low-grade frequent fires characteristic of some ecosystems. Exotic species like rye grass or perennial peanut can be planted to hold sites by dominating them for a few years and keeping longer-lived plants from establishing.[44] Exotic plants that are extremely good at removing metals and other toxins from the soil can be used to clean up sites: Chinese brake fern can suck arsenic out of the soil, for instance.[45] Often, exotics are used for projects like erosion control because they are simply cheaper than natives.

Exotic species may also create more diversity in the future. Naturalized species separated from their parent population will likely evolve by adapting to local challenges and by genetic drift (especially if their populations are small). Broadly successful species like the European house sparrow may turn into a dozen or more separate species over the long haul.[46] If we like biodiversity, then more species is a good thing.

Indeed, as the planet warms and adapts to human domination, it is the exotic species of the world that are busy moving, evolving, and forming new ecological relationships. The despised invaders of today may well be the keystone species of the future's ecosystems, if we give them the space to adapt and don't rush in and tear them out. These emerging, exotic-dominated ecosystems still look like trash to most ecologists. But a brave few have embraced them and given them a more positive name: *novel ecosystems*.

7 | Novel Ecosystems

Ascension Island in the South Atlantic is famous among ecologists. Usually they tell tales about single aggressive invader species bulldozing complex ecosystems. Here it was the other way around. Ascension started out as a monotonous plain of ferns; a visiting Darwin dismissed it in July 1836 as "very far inferior" to nearby St. Helena. Seven years later botanist Joseph Hooker recommended the island be improved by the importation of many new kinds of plants—what modern ecologists might see as a massive invasion. But this invasion resulted not in ecological meltdown but in the creation of a cloud forest composed of species from here and there, trapping mists, cycling nutrients, and surviving, generation after generation, all without having evolved together.[1]

According to ecology textbooks, millennia of coevolution are required to set up complex interactions between plants, animals, microorganisms, nutrients, water, and other components of ecosystems. The idea that a bunch of random plants from hither and yon could convincingly impersonate a real ecosystem rather than collapse into species-poor and poorly functioning wastelands has been markedly hard to swallow.

No one knows this better than Joe Mascaro, the graduate student who went with me to visit Ostertag and Cordell's weeded forest plots in Hawaii. Just a few years ago Mascaro was hacking down "invasive" trees in his mother's backyard, fully on board with the conventional values of ecology. Now he's learned to appreciate novel ecosystems:[2] new, human-influenced combinations of species that can function as well or better than native ecosystems and provide for humans with ecosystem services of various kinds—from water filtration and carbon sequestration to habitat for rare species. Sometimes the exotic components of these ecosystems have considerable cultural value as well.

Mascaro took me on a tour of several novel ecosystems that he studies on the Big Island. He has his sites to himself, as other ecologists consider them trashy places not worth studying. Mascaro told me about the weird things he'd found in the neglected novel forests—barrels, wire, car parts, and whole burned-out cars—trash in trashy ecosystems.

One novel forest he studies is dominated by pinelike Australian ironwood. The canopy is dense, and there is little undergrowth, apart from some sword ferns from India, trumpet tree from the American tropics, and a sprinkling of other species. Underfoot, shed ironwood "needles" gives the turf a pleasant bounce. "This soil development is a service you can get from exotics," says Mascaro, scuffing at it with his foot. On the way out he indicates a single silk oak, another Australian species.

I saw more ironwoods, tiny ones this time, at a site that dates from 1960, when a lava flow created new beachfront land. Before humans came to the islands, the first species out on new flows was always the Hawaiian tree with silky red stamens, 'ōhi'a. Today the autograph tree from tropical America (so called because one can write on the leaves by scraping off the green cuticle) and small Australian ironwoods were colonizing this flow. The interesting result is that no one can properly say that the autograph trees and ironwoods "invaded" the site. Here they were the first colonizers on brand-new land.

Mascaro counts as his mentor Ariel Lugo, an affable Forest Service scientist in his sixties with a broad grin and a white beard who helped "discover" novel ecosystems. Lugo lives and works in Puerto Rico. In 1979 he was managing a crew of researchers who were measuring the amount of ground covered by trees in pine plantations. These plantations weren't being actively managed—the original planters had more or less put in the pines and walked away. One day his researchers came back to headquarters sweaty and discouraged. "They said that they couldn't measure the trees without clearing all the new undergrowth," says Lugo.

At first Lugo thought they were shirking work or, at the very least, exaggerating. These were ecosystems dominated by pine, a nonnative species. He had been trained to expect that what was growing beneath the pines—the understory—would be less productive, less vigorous, than an understory beneath native trees. Millennia of coevolution, he had been taught, would have created an ecosystem in which almost every niche is filled, converting the available energy into trees and other species in the most efficient way. But here, the exotic-dominated ecosystem was functioning *better* than nearby native forest, if function is measured as brute production of biomass.[3]

Lugo went to see for himself. The former pine plantations were packed with living things. Nearby native-only forests of about the same age were not flourishing to the same degree. Lugo did a systematic study of the pine plantations and some equally feral mahogany plantations. The understory in the plantations was richer in species, had greater aboveground biomass, and used nutrients more efficiently than the native understories. Lugo wrote up his results and submitted the paper to a journal called *Ecological Monographs*. The scientists chosen by the journal to review the paper were horrified at the heresy that exotic ecosystems could function better than natives. Some reviewers tried to reclassify pine as a native plant to escape the troubling conclusion Lugo was reaching. In the end, it took almost a decade to get the paper past review. It was finally published in 1992.

Many of Puerto Rico's nonnative trees, like the flame tree, the African tulip tree, and the mango tree, are beloved and considered by the people to be a proper part of the landscape. *Puertorriqueños* even tried to make the vermilion-blossomed flame tree their official tree—until aghast scientists scuttled the plan by saying it was an invasive species. (Interestingly, the flame tree is threatened with extinction in its native Madagascar. If it weren't for its populations in places like Puerto Rico, it might well be doomed.) Maybe this tradition of embracing new species, a tradition not just in Puerto Rico but also in most of the world outside of ecology departments, is part of the reason why Lugo says that he finds it difficult to despise invasive trees. "My parents and their parents saw one Puerto Rico, and I am going to see another Puerto Rico, and my children will see another," he says.

Novel ecosystems are defined by anthropogenic change but are not under active human management. Some were intentionally altered by people—made into tree plantations, pastures, or agricultural fields, for example—then left to go feral. Others were never systematically altered but have been changed by humans from a distance, by the encroachment of introduced species, by climate change, by extinctions, and by a grab bag of other forces. As you might expect, novel ecosystems are now more common than intact ecosystems.

Indeed, as we've learned, all ecosystems on the planet have seen anthropogenic change. Ecologists have so far been using the term *novel ecosystems* to mean the more dramatically altered systems. A forest that hasn't changed its composition of species much in a thousand years wouldn't qualify, even though a few quiet exotic species may be tucked in among the natives, and even though the forest is sitting in an atmosphere already altered by human activity. But a forest dominated by nonnative species would count, even if humans never cut down, burned, or even visited it.

Lugo and Mascaro have seen many examples of areas where introduced and native species live together in diverse mixes rather than in the monocultures of exotics that haunt ecologists' nightmares. They've even found many novel ecosystems that are quite a bit more diverse than native forests but are shunned by ecologists. "That diversity doesn't count because they are the wrong species," says Lugo, shaking his head.

Many ecologists dislike these systems not just because they are not pristine, but also because the same successful exotics tend to show up all over the world. James Gibbs, an ecologist at the State University of New York in Syracuse, values the exquisite complexity of ecosystems that have evolved together over thousands or millions of years. "Why are we worried about the extinction of languages, the roots of music, all these weird cuisines?" he asks. "There is something about diversity and our need to steward it. It is the subtlety and the nuance and complexity that make life interesting." Novel ecosystems seem, to him, to lack this value, to be samey and artificial, "sort of like eating at McDonald's." For ecologists like Mascaro, novel ecosystems are less McDonald's than fusion cuisine.

Mascaro took me to his favorite example of a flourishing novel ecosystem, a "mango forest" tucked down a country lane that looked, smelled, and felt to me like a proper exotic jungle. The air is humid. Mangoes that were planted long ago have grown here into huge, venerable specimens, with their fruit impossibly high off the ground. Pushing into the mosquito-haunted jungle beyond the road, trees come in all sizes, from those massive mangoes to crowds of seedlings jostling for light. Hanging vines and elaborate prop roots fill in the visual space between the canopy and the floor. In everything there is something else living, in the crotch of every branch a fat basket fern, along the length of every mossy branch a line of little seedlings.

The forest features a few species I'd already met, including trumpet tree and strawberry guava. In addition, there are rose apples from Southeast Asia; *hala*, or screwpine, native to Hawaii (and pictured on the crest of the Punahou School, where Barack Obama went to high school); and a smattering of such exotics as Queensland maple from Australia and candlenut. No one knows where candlenut comes from; humans have moved it around so much that its roots are currently obscure. There are no Hawaiian birds here, but Mascaro once saw a large white owl when doing fieldwork—"it scared the crap out of me," he says—and he sees plenty of feral pigs. The soil is black and rich. Mascaro likes it here. To many traditional ecologists, this place is only to be despised. And perhaps to be ignored, since it doesn't fit the stereotype of invasive species appearing in dense monocultures. Here all the invasives are playing house together in a pattern that looks uncannily like a "healthy" ecosystem.

Not all ecologists have shut their eyes to the idea that changed ecosystems are still ecosystems. Back in 1935, when Clements's climax communities were all the rage, British ecologist A. G. Tansley balked at the exclusion of humans from all climax biomes. He suggested that if man was part of nature, then his activities in a particular area could lead to an alternative climax community, an "anthropogenic climax."[4] In this view, the prairie with its mix of grasses and grazing bison is just one possible climax. The wheat field is another. "We cannot confine ourselves to the so-called 'natural' entities and ignore the processes and expressions of vegetation now so abundantly provided to us by the activities of man," he wrote.[5] In many ways, the modern proponents of the novel ecosystem idea don't go nearly as far.

Even Charles Elton, author of *The Ecology of Invasions*, strikes a rather conciliatory tone toward the "invaders" near the end of his book. He suggests that "a careful selection of exotic forms" could have a place beside natives in man-made landscapes designed to be "rich and interesting and stable."[6]

Despite this early interest, ecologists have rarely studied areas with substantial or obvious human influence. "You walk for hours through the trashy stuff to get to your site, and you don't study the trash. And now we need to study the trash," says Lugo.

For one thing, ecologists don't yet understand why diverse novel ecosystems exist, in spite of ecological theory that predicts that heavily invaded systems will tend to be simpler than intact systems. But they have their theories.

Mascaro believes that a lot of species introductions that initially look very much like the nightmare monocultures he learned about as an undergrad will mellow out in time. Take the rose apple. It is present in the mango forest but not dominant, and the individuals we saw were all afflicted with rust disease. This wide tree with long pointy leaves, fluffy white flowers made of massed stamens, and small rose-flavored fruit hails from Malaysia and the East Indies.[7] It was introduced to Hawaii in 1825 and did very well in the lower elevations, well enough to earn the epithet "invasive." Then in 2005 a fungus or "rust" species showed up on the islands and started killing rose apple off in great numbers. An article in the journal *Plant Disease* from April 2009 says, "On Hawaii, Maui, and Oahu, trees with many dead branches are becoming common with concerns about the fire hazard of these dead trees surrounded by dry grasses."[8]

This is but one example. Lugo, like Mascaro, has found that many introduced species that initially dominate an area calm down over time. "The ballgame changes, and succession goes in a different direction," he says. "The high dominance lasts forty or fifty years. After eighty years, the species composition becomes mixed, and sometimes the species dominance goes back to the natives, with the invasive coming third or fourth on the list."

So it is hard for Mascaro to get too worked up when his colleague Christian Giardina frets about the strawberry guava, a very pervasive introduced plant that grows clonally, "like a phalanx." Giardina would like to introduce a scale insect from Brazil, the strawberry guava's home, to control it. But for many Hawaiians, strawberry guava is a familiar and tasty plant, not the enemy. Many Hawaiian kids grew up tucking folded wax-paper squares filled with salt and spices into their pockets so they could dine al fresco on strawberry guava fruit and not have to go home for lunch. The result is a "massive debate," according to Giardina, that pits ecologists against the public. Mascaro tends to think that the conflict is unnecessary. Like rose apple, strawberry guava may well run into something that stops its expansion without human help. "My sense is that plants will not stay hyperdominant forever," he says.

Mascaro's gut instinct here is similar to the *reckless invader* hypothesis, an ecological theory that suggests that many introduced species that initially run rampant will in the end be tripped up, whacked back, and humbled. The natives will evolve resistance; one of their enemies from home will catch up to it; native species will acquire a taste for it; a new introduced species will kill it. Technically, the idea is that there is a trade-off between reproductive success and stress tolerance. The shrub that puts all its energy into making baby shrubs has less energy to put into making thorns or chemicals to deter herbivory or mechanisms to keep itself alive during drought. So the prolific reproducers are also the most defenseless and vulnerable.[9]

Zebra mussels, those well-known invader villains, at first boomed in Lake Erie when they arrived in the late 1980s, to the horror of conservationists. But then native ducks learned to eat them. Soon the ducks boomed at the expense of the mussels.[10] Similarly, Elton documented the rise and fall of the Canadian water weed in Great Britain. The vigorous weed arrived in the 1840s and by the 1860s was clogging some rivers so fiercely that extra horses were required to pull barges, rowing and net fishing became impossible, a few entangled swimmers drowned, and parts of the Thames were "rendered impassable."[11] Then, for reasons unknown, it settled down into low-key coexistence with its fellow river plants. It has apparently remained well behaved in its new home ever since, apart from the occasional local bloom.

Ecologist Michio Kondoh at Ryukoku University in Seta, Japan, has proposed a nifty numerical reason for the eventual bust in many introduced species' populations. When there are few of them, they don't create much pressure to adapt on the surrounding species. When their numbers increase, however, they become an important component of the environment for many species, which then adapt to them—often by developing resistance to their attempts to eat them or steal their sun. And so they become victims of their own success.[12]

On the other hand, some introduced species have lucked into an infinite boom scenario, in which they create conditions that favor their own perpetual dominance.[13] They can do this by changing fire frequency, altering soil properties, or just packing an area so densely that no other species can get a toehold.[14] Smart people may disagree, however, on how long a species must dominate before we assume it will do so indefinitely. We've learned, after all, that nothing lies still long in nature.

No one is exactly sure how much of the Earth is covered by novel ecosystems, but one man has at least hazarded a guess. Erle Ellis at the University of Maryland in Baltimore first produced a map of the world's "anthropogenic biomes." The map is different from familiar maps of the world that break the globe up into broad ecosystem types such as "steppe," and "rain forest." The problem with these maps is that they really show the world as it was, not as it is. Think of the U.S. Midwest. Most ecosystem maps of the world would show it as a "prairie," but there is about as much prairie in the Midwest as there is oak forest in Manhattan. Ellis's own realization came when he was working in China, where one village melts into another in a thoroughly human-dominated landscape. As he puts it, "Today, the reason that trees grow in a place, or not, is mostly up to people."

Ellis's map replaces terms like *steppe* and *rain forest* with terms like *dense settlements, rice villages*, and *populated irrigated cropland*.[15] He found that 75 percent of the world's ice-free land "showed evidence of alteration as a result of human residence and land use."[16] Twenty percent of the world's ice-free land is cropland; a third is rangeland. Just 22 percent shows no sign of human occupation or use (though we know that it is unlikely to be "pristine" in any absolute sense).[17] Ellis's research suggests that the Earth shifted from mostly wild to mostly anthropogenic sometime in the early twentieth century.[18] "Nature is now essentially a part of human systems," he says.

But novel ecosystems are a bit different from the categories that Ellis worked with for his anthropogenic biomes map. Novel ecosystems are altered by human activity but are not actively managed. At my request, Ellis made a stab at estimating the amount of such lands. To get a back-of-the-envelope estimate, he looked at lands without agricultural or urban use embedded within agricultural and urban regions, which he figured were a good proxy. After all, unused lands nearest human-dominated cities and fields are very likely to be interleaved with introduced species and to see local extinctions and other changes. Using this definition, Ellis estimated that 35 percent of the world's ice-free land is covered with novel ecosystems—a huge part of the world and virtually unstudied.

Mascaro is one of the few exceptions. Back in 2006 he set out to see if what Lugo found in Puerto Rico was also happening on the windward side of Hawaii's Big Island. He studied forty-six novel forests dominated by a variety of different species and growing on lava flows of varying ages at various altitudes. He found that the novel forests, on average, had just as many species as native forests. But by and large they weren't incubating little native seedlings, as they were in Puerto Rico, perhaps because Hawaiian natives are not as scrappy as Puerto Rico natives, having been isolated for longer.[19]

But Mascaro's results didn't sour him on novel ecosystems. For one, he found that in many measures of forest productivity, such as nutrient cycling and biomass, novel forests matched or outproduced the native forests. More important, he realized that as an ecologist seeking objectivity, he had to let go of the values he had picked up during his training about "good" and "bad" species and ecosystem "health" or "proper functioning." What he saw, suddenly, was that without this value system in place, his "novel" ecosystems and "native" ecosystems were virtually indistinguishable.

Mascaro took me to a place on a back road where two ecosystems met—on the left, 'ōhi'a forest; on the right, a grove of albizia, a fast-growing tree introduced in 1917 from Southeast Asia, with an understory of strawberry guava from Brazil and a couple of natives: kolea and mamake. An ecologist unfamiliar with tropical species might not be able to tell which ecosystem was native and which was novel, but even I could tell which is poised to inherit the larger area. The line between the expanding albizia and the native 'ōhi'a trees is sharply demarcated. The densely packed albizia are much taller, and at the border between the two types of forest, the first row of albizia actually lean in toward the 'ōhi'a in a way that is hard not to read as menacing encroachment. Of course, the trees are just growing toward the sun, like every other plant on Earth. They have no intention.

Intentional or not, Stanford Hawaiian biodiversity expert Peter Vitousek would put albizia forests in the category of dangerous invaders. He argues that while novel ecosystems can be useful and "may even support native biological diversity in some important circumstances," he thinks the idea "can be taken to an extreme at which it is no longer useful; I think most of the albizia-dominated stands of Hawaii represent that extreme."

Mascaro grants the point. "I can understand where a manager wants to bulldoze an albizia forest if they are worried that it is going to exterminate an ecosystem type that is the last on Earth," he says. "I think that if we want to debate whether to use or conserve novel ecosystems, we will always have to deal with the risk they pose to other systems. But at the moment we're scarcely debating it at all."

There are reasons to debate. There are arguments for sparing novel ecosystems. Novel ecosystems have proven to be useful for—of all things—restoration of native species. Lugo once intervened to stop The Nature Conservancy from cutting down all the Leucaena trees—native to Mexico and locally called tantan trees—that formed the canopy on a former farm in the Virgin Islands. "I pointed out to them that the native species were already growing well in the understory of the tantan, because of the tantan," says Lugo. The natives were in fact using the tantan's protective shade to get established and couldn't have done so in full sun. What was most likely to spring up in the open clearing made by eradicating tantan was more tantan. "The best strategy was to let the tantan complete the ecological job of guiding succession toward a domination of native species. Just give it some additional time!"

If purity were all The Nature Conservancy cared about, they might have ignored Lugo and chopped the tantan trees down anyway. As it was, they had other goals. Perhaps they were more interested in maximizing the number of native species than in minimizing the number of nonnatives.

Novel ecosystems can also provide habitat for native animal species—crucial habitat, if all the original stuff is gone. They also often do a dandy job of providing many ecosystem services, from filtering water in wetlands to controlling erosion on hillsides, sequestering carbon from the atmosphere, and building soil. This isn't surprising when you consider that many species were introduced to new areas precisely because of their well-known abilities to provide these same services. And many accidentally introduced plants that naturalize are particularly good at sucking up sunlight and carbon dioxide and making new soil. Like human cultures that spring up in response to mass migrations and urbanization, novel ecosystems are often vital and energetic.

In addition, if what one values is not any existing species or ecosystem per se but the process of evolution, then novel ecosystems are worth protecting. More than sickly ecosystems nursed by park rangers, novel ecosystems are really wild, self-willed land with lots of evolutionary potential.

I ask Mascaro to predict the future of his fresh lava site, and he guesses it will be an ironwood forest with the occasional 'ōhi'a growing in it. "In a hundred years, I predict it will be a closed-canopy forest, from here to the ocean," he says. But he's got little more to go on than his own intuitions. Unlike the predictable succession patterns of many familiar ecosystems, novel ecosystems are headed off in unknown directions.

If you are interested in preserving evolution without human guidance, then look no further than novel ecosystems. We may have introduced the various parties to one another, directly by moving them or indirectly by changing the climate, but the rhythm of life they take up and the interplay of selection pressures they produce on one another are all up to them. Let one of Mascaro's Big Island forests work itself out, undisturbed, and what you will preserve therein will be undirected natural selection. "Do we value the fact that nature contains a list of things that were here a thousand years ago, or do we value it because it has its own processes that are not under human control?" asks Mascaro. "The value I get from nature is seeing things happen naturally. Seeing that they include parts that humans moved around doesn't devalue it for me."

As the Earth responds to the changes we humans have made, does it make sense to destroy ecosystems that thrive under the new conditions? As Lugo says, "This is nature's response to what we have done to it." Novel ecosystems may be our best hope for the future, as their components adapt to the human-dominated world using the time-tested method of natural selection. Could we hope to do any better than nature in managing and arranging our natural world for a warmer, more populous future?

These new systems likely do spell homogenization and extinction, in some places. But they can also mean ecosystem services, increased diversity, and brand-new species. And we are going to have to start studying these places. They represent the future of our planet, like it or not.

"People come up to me and say, 'It sounds like you've given up,'" says Mascaro. "I want to say, 'I never took up arms, my man.' This isn't about conceding defeat; it is about a new approach."

8 | Designer Ecosystems

Close your eyes and imagine a stream. Did you see a line of water, moving along in a single languidly curving channel with high banks? I thought so. That's the archetypal stream for ecologists, too. For decades, restoration ecologists have been busily creating streams that look just like this and hoping that these streams will boost biodiversity and reduce the sediments and nitrogen carried into bigger bodies of water.

But two researchers in Pennsylvania have recently discovered that—in the U.S. Northeast at least—this shape is an anthropogenic artifact, a legacy of the thousands of small mill dams built on eastern streams between the seventeenth and nineteenth centuries. Robert Walter and Dorothy Merritts of Franklin and Marshall College in Lancaster, Pennsylvania, pored over old maps, looked at historical documents, visited hundreds of streams, and used a cousin of radar called LIDAR to get a sense of the lay of the land underneath modern vegetation. In some places, they used a backhoe to expose sedimentary layers and check on the geological history.

They concluded that streams in the Piedmont region of the eastern United States—just to the east of the Appalachian Mountains—were more like swamps than streams when Europeans first arrived.[1] The water didn't run in a single channel but rather flowed in branching streams, got sidetracked in pools, and created a whole lot of mud that spread out over valley floors.

By the late eighteenth century, many streams had been dammed (with dams as wide as whole valleys, because the streams were so spread out), and they turned into a necklace of millponds, one every two and a half miles or so. Meanwhile deforestation on the high ground increased the water supply and inflow of soil. Millponds collected thick layers of sediment on their bottoms.

When steam power started to displace hydropower for milling, forging, and mining, many of these dams were breached. The resulting bursts of fast-flowing water cut a channel through the sediment in the old ponds, creating the deeply incised meandering channel thought of as "natural" today.

Similar work has been done in the Pacific Northwest, and the team adds that they think the same process might have taken place in Europe. "By the 1700s, there were eighty thousand mills in France," says Walter. If this reconstruction of events is true, then millions of dollars have been spent trying to return streams to an artificial state: their condition after old dams came down, rather than before they went up.

Since this revelation, the stream restoration community has become interested in bulldozing out all these old pond sediments, in essence scraping the whole system down to a pre-European layer. Several projects along these lines are under way, according to Walter. In Pennsylvania, the state is watching one such project with an eye toward enshrining it as a state-sanctioned "Best Management Practice."

Margaret Palmer, a stream restoration expert at the University of Maryland, College Park, worries that the new picture of pre-European streams will just replace one arbitrary baseline with another—neither of which takes into account the changing nature of the landscape. "Everything changes," she says. "We have cleared trees; we have dramatically changed the amount of water in these streams. If our goal is to decrease sediment load, we should focus on that and not worry about making the stream look the way it did at presettlement time, because nothing else is the same as it was presettlement." Indeed, Palmer's research suggests that while the marshy, slow-moving branched channel model may remove more nitrogen than the familiar winding single channel, neither approach removes enough nitrogen to be worth the millions of dollars that these restorations cost.

Restoring the complex ecosystems we have destroyed may be, at the moment, just too hard. We don't know enough about what they looked like or how they worked. Our restoration projects may be too small, in many cases, to capture complex processes we have lost. We can't get the magic back. The alternative, says Palmer, is not to restore to some notional and incompletely apprehended past but to design or engineer for specific, measurable goals: nitrogen reduction, sediment capture, or the maintenance of one or a small number of named species. Some goals are more compatible with each other than others. For example, interventions that make a stream better at reducing nitrogen can also have the generally unwanted consequence of making mercury more available to the fish that live in them, she says.[2]

Palmer is sufficiently doubtful about our current restoration abilities to argue that people who want to build should be required to buy and protect an identical area of a currently valuable ecosystem rather than spending the money on projects to restore less valuable systems. "If someone wants to build a Walmart, they should be required to buy land that is presently at high risk of development and save it in perpetuity," she says.

But in cases where this isn't feasible, some professionals have been tinkering with systems designed specifically for nitrogen removal. They've created "streams" that are a series of linked ponds separated by large boulders. Water can sit in each stepped pond and let nitrogen fall out before it flows on. The result looks more like a wetland than a stream, but the stepped ponds and boulders don't look like any historical system. Large boulders didn't even exist in the coastal plains where these projects are located.

These streams are not restored; they are designed. At one level most restoration projects are designer ecosystems. No restoration reproduces *exactly* the ecosystem of hundreds of years ago. And restoration ecologists use lots of "hacks"—less-than-authentic shortcuts to get a landscape looking and working the way they want. Wire baskets filled with rocks or the root balls of dead trees are chained in place to slow stream flows and create nooks and crannies for animals (though Palmer and others question whether that technique works very well). Old ships are sunk to provide places for coral reefs to live.

And certainly rewilding with proxy species creates new, designed ecosystems, even if they are inspired by the past.

But the most radical kind of designer ecosystem is not emulating any baseline at all but building de novo to achieve a particular goal. This is heady stuff for restoration ecologists, who have until recently made their living trying to recreate ecosystems at historical baselines. And according to Palmer, the balance-of-nature idea is "firmly entrenched" in the field.[3] Perhaps more than any group of scientists, restoration ecologists have been trapped by the seductive vision of healing wounded nature and returning it to a stable "natural" state. But there is a new current of energy at their meetings. They are beginning to see the possibilities of designing, engineering, cooking up something new.

Implicit in many restoration projects is the notion that a historical baseline is not just somehow morally better but ideal for restoring any number of features that a system might have lost over time, including biodiversity, ecosystem services, and recreational value. Ecologists have assumed that before humans changed them, ecosystems were always maximally efficient at such functions as purifying water, supporting diverse life, keeping sediment from washing away, and so on. They have also sometimes assumed that if you can make an area *look* like it used to, you will automatically restart all those processes and reap all those benefits.

In stream restoration, for example, hoped-for benefits include increased biodiversity, as well as the removal of nitrogen and excess sediment from the water. Nitrogen mostly comes from fertilizer, and it boosts productivity of plankton in bodies of water like the Chesapeake Bay or the Gulf of Mexico. The fat and happy plankton use up all the oxygen in the water, and the result is often an ecosystem dominated by slimy algae and depressingly lacking in shellfish, fish, or marine mammals. High sediment loads are disliked because the muddy water can clog fish's gills, smother bottom-dwellers, and block light from aquatic plants.

But Palmer and others are demonstrating that streams that look restored to the naked eye may not boost biodiversity or remove nitrogen or sediment particularly well. Restoration jobs on land often aren't much better. And scientists studying novel ecosystems have shown that historical ecosystems aren't always without equal at performing particular services. Add those insights together, and it becomes clear that depending on what you want, and given variables including size of project, budget, and how much the place has already changed, a designer ecosystem may be *better* than a recreation of a historical ecosystem.

Most people doing this kind of work are not using the phrase *designer ecosystems*. They are much more likely to use the phrase *whatever works*. Take Dee Boersma, an ecologist at the University of Washington in Seattle whose number-one conservation goal is to save the Galápagos penguin. This five-pound flightless bird is endangered; only two thousand remain. Introduced rats eat the chicks. The automatic reaction of the restoration ecologist is to try to turn back the clock and get rid of the rats. But getting rid of rats is harder than you might think.[4] So scientists are instead drilling more nesting holes into the rocks for the birds. The number of nesting sites created a ceiling on how many chicks could be born each generation. Now the population can expand and perhaps stay ahead of the reductions due to rat predation. The manipulation doesn't return penguin habitat to any particular baseline; it makes the habitat better than "normal" for the birds.

Or consider a "failed" prairie restoration job in Colorado, which resulted in a totally new kind of ecosystem dominated by a kind of grass that is usually just a bit player in prairies. Timothy Seastedt, an ecologist at the University of Colorado in Boulder was involved in a restoration of a three-hundred-acre former gravel pit near the university. The area was seeded with a mix of all kinds of species from several types of prairie ecosystems. "The outcome by 2004 was a grassland dominated by *Sporobolus airoides*, which doesn't exist as a dominant anywhere around for hundreds of miles," he says. "The locals find this to be a highly desirable-looking ecosystem. It is performing some functions, and yet it is clearly an example of a system that did not exist pre–human intervention." Designed by accident?

One advocate of designer ecosystems is Richard Hobbs of the University of Western Australia in Crawley. Hobbs is editor in chief of the influential journal *Restoration Ecology* and one of the novel ecosystem concept's greatest proponents. Just as he is keen to see what will unfold in these cosmopolitan wildernesses, he has given up on slavishly restoring ecosystems to historical states in favor of working for valuable outcomes. In a series of papers in the last decade, he concludes that pre-European human alteration of the environment and nonanthropogenic secular climate change make moot the traditional restoration baselines. He and a coauthor took the field's soul-searching public in 2009 in *Science*, one of the world's top scientific journals. "If natural states are elusive," they wondered, "if the environment is always changing and ecosystems are always coming and going, and if multiple realizations are normal, then the premises underlying ecological restoration to a historic standard come under question. Does ecological history render ecological restoration 'quaint'"?[5]

Hobbs has found himself beginning to relish the new range of options that open up when the historical ecosystem ceases to be the ideal. Most of his colleagues are still much more in thrall to historical baselines. "I play a game taking them out to the native bush," says Hobbs, with a twinkle in his eye. "Depending on whether you say it was native or not native they like it or don't like it."

Hobbs has spent some time picking apart two categories of changes that could face the restoration ecologist. *Biotic* changes are changes in the living components of an ecosystem, including the introduction of new species and the extinction of historical species. *Abiotic* changes are changes in the nonliving environment, including climate and soil chemistry. When a site shows only one type of change, a *hybrid* ecosystem often results. For example, the climate could change in a forest without killing the organisms that live there. The place would look the same, at least for a time, but its climate would be outside the historical range of variability.[6] Or the species could turn over without any real changes in the hydrology, climate, or soil properties. This hybrid would act quite a bit like its historical antecedent, just with a different cast of characters. Such hybrid systems can be restored more or less the old-fashioned way, with one's eye firmly on the past. A little weeding, some species reintroductions, perhaps a little habitat creation, and the hybrids can be dragged backward in time.

On the other hand, some hybrids might be accepted as they are, especially when introduced species have wriggled their way into the food web so well that they have made themselves indispensible to some of the native species.[7]

But change either the biotic or abiotic conditions enough—or, what is all the more likely in this messy world of ours, change both simultaneously—and one is likely to see the system move past a threshold of no return, a tipping point into a completely new system. And from such systems, return may not be possible.

Hobbs illustrates all this with the example of eucalyptus woodlands in Southwest Australia, his home turf. Historically (and *historically* here means looking back at most a few hundred years) such woodlands are composed of tall, widely spaced eucalyptus trees with an understory composed of various shrubs. Some of these woodlands have seen mild biotic change, such that the understory is now partially composed of exotic grasses. These woodlands might be able to be returned to the historical state with a big enough grant and judicious use of herbicide. Other woodlands have been grazed to the dirt, which changes the abiotic properties of the soil. Here a carefully designed planting regime, perhaps supplemented with a little fertilization, could return to the soil its historical character and eventually make things cozy for the historical shrub community again. However, there are also former eucalyptus woodlands that have crossed thresholds—in places, *all* native species have been replaced with nonnative grass; in others, the soil has become so salty due to humans fiddling with the water table that nearly nothing grows—so the modern restoration ecologist must admit that it isn't going back to the way it used to be.[8]

Faced with former eucalyptus woodland dominated by strange, ground-hugging salt-loving plants from across the seas, with the rainfall patterns unfamiliar, the soil changed, and no eucalyptus trees in sight, a restoration ecologist might be tempted to despair. Not so Hobbs. *Something* can be made of such a landscape, he reckons. "You are not going to get the previous ecosystem back, but you can still aim for something that is valuable," he says. This new ecosystem may not look familiar, but it will do something for us or for the species we care about. "We need to look to the future," he says.

But what would that "something that is valuable" be? How bold are

Hobbs and his colleagues ready to get? Will we ever know enough about how all the myriad parts of an ecosystem interlock to make one completely from scratch? Could we create small, perfect worlds for threatened species, far from their original habitats? Could we take salty former eucalyptus woodland and design a prairie that would feed native birds and also be ideal for biofuel? Could we build a forest that combines the top ten most endangered tropical trees with the top ten best at carbon sequestration on former farmland?

Ecosystems are incredibly complex; even the dullest natural area likely supports food webs that, when diagrammed, look about as intricate as a comprehensive street map of London. Ecologists admit that no one has ever been able to comprehend all the dynamics of any real ecosystem—all the competition, predation, parasitism, energy flows, nutrient cycles, range of variability, and so on. It's like trying to understand everything that happens in a city in a day, or every biochemical reaction in a human body. We just aren't there yet. So we may not live to see designer ecosystems in the sense of ecosystems designed from scratch, with everything from the bedrock up imported and no resemblance to any historical ecosystem. And maybe these will never be very common, even hundreds of years into the future. Nature still has plenty to teach us. The organisms and the relations between them that have emerged from millions of years of natural selection are likely going to outperform anything we cobble together on our computers, whether the goal is spaces for recreation, management of energy and nutrients, protection of biodiversity, or provision of services.

One of the most famous advocates of designer ecosystems was microbiologist and environmental thinker René Dubos, who died in 1982. Dubos envisioned a flourishing world covered in managed nature designed to support humans and other species. The artificial landscapes that humans created, including agricultural lands in Europe, were often beautiful and diverse, he argued.[9] Historian Roderick Nash, in the epilogue to his seminal survey of American attitudes toward wilderness, sketches out a similar future. He calls it the "garden scenario" in which "human control of nature" is both "total" and "beneficent."[10] "The fertility of the soil is well maintained; carefully managed rivers flow clean and pure. Population is not a concern because technological breakthroughs enable people to live pole to pole: in the deserts, under the sea, in the air . . . It is a planet-wide extension of Europe!"[11] Nash rejects this vision, as it leaves no room for self-willed land. " 'Good' kinds of human habitat expansion and 'smart' or 'sustainable' kinds of growth are just as invasive of wilderness as the bad kinds," he decides.[12] Nash prefers his "Island Civilization" alternative, wherein humans retreat to very dense cities, voluntarily limit their own population, and let the rest of the planet run wild.

I predict, as a best-case future, a combination of these two visions. Dubos's 1980 book *The Wooing of Earth* argued that our goal ought to be to create "new environments that are ecologically sound, aesthetically satisfying, economically rewarding and favorable to the continued growth of civilization."[13] Sounds good. I hope that the guild of restoration ecologists grows and flourishes and makes exactly these kinds of spaces. But not everywhere. Dubos himself suggests we keep parks around for those who love wilderness in the raw. I think we should keep lots of land unmanaged just to see what it does, to keep those evolutionary fires burning, and to ensure that future generations might still be able to get lost. Dubos's spaces are like the tidy kitchen garden nearest the house. I hope that much more of the rambunctious garden will be unweeded and untidy. Un-useful even.

Restoration ecologists aren't going to be renaming themselves "ecosystem designers" or "rambunctious gardeners" any time soon. I've run into Hobbs at lots of conferences over the years, and every time I see him, I ask him when he'll be ready to leave the word *restoration* behind. He's not ready yet. But he and his colleagues in the field may well transition to a role less focused on restoration to historical states. "Restoration has evolved rapidly over the past couple of decades," he says. "Increasingly we are thinking about the uncertain future." History becomes, for this new breed, "a guide instead of a straitjacket."

9 | Conservation Everywhere

One summer afternoon I bobbed on the waters of a river with an Indian name, watching a kingfisher dive for fish. Osprey perched nearby, and a few feet from my kayak a salmon jumped with an impressive splash. Was I on the Sol Duc River in Olympic National Park, perhaps, or deep in the coastal rainforest of British Columbia? No. I was in the heart of Seattle, Washington, on a five-mile stretch of the Duwamish River lined with industrial operations and designated in 2001 as a Superfund site thanks to all the toxins in the mud. From my yellow boat I could see the Space Needle and skyline, as well as Boeing's famous Plant Two, where a dozen B-17 bombers were built every day during World War II.

The Duwamish River is a mess, but the wildlife that frequents it shows that it has promise. What's interesting is the vision its supporters have for it. None of them are talking about restoring it to the way it was when Europeans first settled in Seattle in the 1850s. None of them are pushing for it to be made into a park. Instead, they see a hybrid future for the Duwamish—part habitat, part active industrial waterway.

Plant Two's windows glowed rosy in the setting sun, and from the water I could see how the massive building extended out over the river on pilings. "All the oil and toxic chemicals involved leaked through the floor-boards," said Cari Simson, a staffer at the Duwamish River Cleanup Coalition, who balanced in her own kayak as planes taking off from SeaTac airport roared low overhead. "All this mud is filled with heavy metals."

As part of the long process of the Superfund cleanup, Boeing has agreed to tear down Plant Two, seal off the portion of the river currently underneath and alongside it, pump out all the water, and then remove 100,000 cubic yards of toxic sediment.[1] Eventually they plan to install salmon-friendly habitat, including gradually sloping banks and pocket side-channels to the river, which salmon can use as rest stops as they migrate up the river to spawn.

Simson will be pleased to see the change. But she doesn't want every lot on the river to follow suit. The low-income neighborhoods on either side of the Duwamish could use the jobs that an active industrial water-way can provide. And so Simson and her colleagues want to have it both ways. The Duwamish River Cleanup Coalition has an "eco-industrial vision" for the river. It's tall order for a river mostly hidden behind defunct ce-ment factories and huge Boeing buildings, a river currently lined with signs warning against consuming the river's fish and shellfish in English, Span-ish, Chinese, Korean, Vietnamese, Cambodian, Laotian, and Russian, just to be safe.

But the entities that will have to clean up the river under the complex Superfund process, including the City of Seattle, the Port of Seattle, King County, and Boeing, share the hybrid vision for the river, or at least they claim to. Major cleanup actions won't begin for a few years, and it remains an open question how clean the Duwamish will get.

In the meantime, as my short kayak trip up the Duwamish demon-strated, the seeds of this vision are already present between defunct oper-ations rusting in the drizzle. Sure, much of the shoreline is a wild tangle of blackberries and butterfly bush growing on heavily contaminated muck, but there are also thriving businesses and restored sites, like the mouth of Hamm Creek—for many years better described as Hamm Pipe, a culvert that unceremoniously dumped into the river. Now the pipe is gone, and a "daylighted" creek softly flows into the Duwamish through a lacy scrim of reeds and grasses patrolled by herons. The vegetation that has been planted here feeds baby salmon and provides habitat for birds.

Downstream we floated by a cozily seedy marina where hip young artists live aboard their boats and past Delta Marine, a luxury yacht maker. Farther still, people waved to us from a series of tiny street-end parks that look out over the river.

Rewilding, assisted migration, and embracing some exotic species and novel ecosystems may seem like disparate strategies, but they are all at some level about making the most out of every scrap of land and water, no matter its condition. To make the most of our protected areas, we must think beyond their boundaries and complement our wildernesses with conservation everywhere else too, from industrial rivers like the Duwamish to the roofs of buildings and farmer's fields.

Some optical illusions, like the illustration that can be a rabbit or a duck depending on how you look at it, rely on a *gestalt switch*. You see an image one way, unable to see the other possibility, and then suddenly your brain flips and sees it the other way. A protected-areas-only, pristine-wilderness-only view of conservation sees a globe with a few shrinking islands of nature on it. Nature is the foreground, human-dominated lands the background. The new view, after the gestalt switch, sees impervious surfaces—pavement, houses, malls where nothing can grow—as the foreground and *everything else* as the background nature.

This background nature comes in different flavors, to be sure, from vast fields of genetically identical corn to city parks to the last hectares of South America's Atlantic Forest, where tiny golden lion tamarins swing from the trees. Not all this land is equally valuable to most conservation goals, but all of it can be improved. Those cornfields can grow strips of native plants on their edges; those city parks can provide food for migrating butterflies. Thus the project of conservation is not just defending what we have, but adding lands to our portfolio and deepening value of the lands in play.

Adding and deepening is already the bread and butter of many professional conservationists. Adding may seem impossible at first blush. Humans are always increasing in number and are likely to do so for another

190 years, according to the population experts at the United Nations. But more of us than ever are living in cities. In 2009 the world's urban population overtook its rural population for the first time. And people who live in cities often have a smaller footprint than people who live in the country. Of the less than 2 percent of the ice-free land that is paved or covered in buildings, most is rural, where housing "tends to sprawl," according to ecological geographer Erle Ellis.

Green planners have been fighting sprawl for decades in zoning board meetings and state development offices. Some argue that suburbs and exurbs will shrink once the price of gas reaches a certain level. Pavement isn't necessarily forever. Subdivisions can be undivided—especially in a recession. Even in cities, the impervious can become pervious. When Boeing's Plant Two comes down, one gigantic building will become five acres of wetland and half a mile of natural shoreline.

And then there is deepening—working the art of the possible to get more conservation value out of the other 98 percent of land. Much public land is already managed for "sustainable use," and plenty of activists are toiling away trying to improve the rules and regulations of these arrangements to eke out more conservation value. Similarly, conservation ecologists work with private landowners to make their lands work for nature as well as for the owners, often with the help of tax incentives.

Protected areas like Yellowstone are not the wrong model, but a crucial part of an expanded model. Such strictly protected areas become anchors, with overlapping zones of various protection regimes and conservation goals radiating out from them, like petals from the center of a rose.

Ideally, parks should be surrounded with areas without much development, and these wildest landscapes should be connected to each other. We need such an interwoven tissue of wild lands to sustain animals with large ranges, like many large carnivores. Recall the recipe for rewilding: big areas, well connected with corridors.

Ecologists often refer to the *species-area relationship* when discussing corridors. In a nutshell, the smaller the fragment, the fewer species it contains. As a natural area shrinks, big species go first, because the fragment just contains too few of them for them to continue on as a genetically healthy population. But small species drop out too, simply because with smaller populations, they are more likely, in a bad year, to lose 100 percent of their members and become locally extinct. When the fragment is isolated, no new individuals of the species can recolonize it, and eventually the overall number of species in a small patch falls. So small protected areas leak species. Corridors between fragments can help fill them back up.

Corridors can be rather technically defined by scientists, but I use the term to cover all those strips of land managed for connectivity—so small areas won't leak species, so migrating herds can move from summer to winter ranges and back again, so gene pools can stay large and vital. In these days of climate change, corridor advocates are also calling for corridors leading toward the poles and uphill so that the species that are sensitive to changing conditions can move themselves to more hospitable habitat.

Thus what happens outside strictly protected areas influences whether the protected areas can truly protect. Yellowstone National Park, at about 3,500 square miles, is the largest park in the lower forty-eight. But it still isn't large enough. For large species like the grizzly bear, the park cannot contain enough individuals to keep the population from becoming dangerously inbred. And as the massive fire of 1988 showed, a single large fire can threaten species that depend on old forest. Luckily, Yellowstone does not stand alone. The park is part of what ecologists call the "Greater Yellowstone Ecosystem," which also includes Grand Teton National Park, half a dozen national forests, the National Elk Refuge, Bureau of Land Management lands, private lands, and part of the Wind River Indian Reservation. Layered on top of these lands are twelve designated wilderness areas. Depending on whose map you are looking at, the whole ecosystem totals more than 31,000 square miles—almost ten times the size of the park.

And even that huge area is not an island—at least not if the Yellowstone to Yukon Conservation Initiative has anything to say about it. The U.S.-Canadian group connects up local conservation projects along the mountains between Yellowstone and the Yukon Territory by Alaska so that instead of a smattering of undertakings, everyone is supporting the same continental-scale objectives, like uniting populations of bears into genetically healthy megapopulations. And they are careful to emphasize that their goal isn't to banish humans from the region, but to achieve happy coexistence.

This coexistence is perhaps best symbolized by the graceful wildlife overpasses and underpasses they've helped build in Banff National Park in Alberta. East-west, cars zip along the road; north-south, moose, lynx, and other animals migrate and disperse. Everybody's got somewhere to go.

Yellowstone to Yukon is just one of many projects trying to create corridors and organize conservation activities at the broad landscape level. The Great Eastern Ranges Initiative in Australia aims to connect islands of protected areas along the mountain ranges in the east of the country. The Mesoamerican Biological Corridor unites protected areas from Mexico through Central America. The Path of the Pronghorn makes way for antelopes near Yellowstone. Everywhere, in the last decade or so, conservation managers are getting the message from scientists that connectivity is key.

Conservationists must patch together different kinds of land to create connected-up nature: parks, public lands of other types, private lands with special legal arrangements in place, state lands, tribal lands, and so on. There is a lot of complex research and mathematics behind designing reserves; it is a hot field in conservation biology. Ideally, reserves should be scientifically designed to achieve conservation goals agreed upon by interested parties while being sensitive to the needs of the people who now live or once lived on the sites in question. But getting people to agree on what to do with land is likely one of the toughest jobs out there. Humans have a primal and powerful attachment to land. Pick any piece of land on the face of the Earth, and likely it is someone's home, someone else's livelihood, and a third person's property, along with being an ecosystem of interest to conservationists near and far.

In the Greater Yellowstone Ecosystem, one perhaps-surprising "deepening" strategy is to keep ranches in business. Overgrazing is a pet peeve of many environmentalists, but ranches support a lot more nature than the sprawl that can replace them. Cattle often graze on native vegetation, while streams, lakes, and forested areas remain natural. Conservation easements can provide the money a ranch needs to stay operating and prevent the land from being developed or subdivided. Owners can "donate" the forfeited value and get a juicy tax break. Rancher Kasey Shepperson told reporters in November 2010 that he was happy to promise not to develop 13,900 acres of his Hat Two Ranch in Wyoming. "The easement will allow us to pass

on the property to our children faster and easier," he said. "It will also reduce mortgage demands, lessening the need to graze the property at full
capacity."[2]

Since agricultural and ranch lands make up half of the ice-free land
surface of the Earth, improving their conservation value is a good strategy.
Conservation easements are just one tool to do so, and if you want to learn
more, it is best to head to Europe, home to the world's agricultural conservation experts.

Conservationists in Europe had much less seemingly pristine land to
work with at the beginning of the conservation movement, so they have
long focused on maximizing nature in areas that are also used for something else. A few summers ago I attended the first-ever European Congress
of Conservation Biology, held in Eger, Hungary, a beautiful town in rolling
wine country. On the first morning of the conference, I went along on an
early field trip to see birds at what I was told was a nature preserve in the
foothills of the Bukk Mountains. When the group piled out of the van, I
was startled to see that we had arrived at a farm. What about the nature
preserve? And why didn't any of these European conservationists look sur-
prised? In much of Europe, a farm run in an old-fashioned way is a conservation tool, and a whole suite of species are considered farmland species.
The Royal Society for the Protection of Birds, a U.K. charity that ranks
among the oldest conservation organizations, has a program to protect
"farmland birds," birds that are "dependent on farming." One might well
wonder what the birds did before farming was invented.

According to Vera and others, they lived in open areas maintained by
herbivores. Both these grazed clearings and many of the herbivores are
long gone. So now Europeans protect such birds through agri-environment
schemes that pay farmers to roll back the recent intensification of farming, with its nearly year-round monocultures and efficient herbicides.[3]
More than 20 percent of European farms participate in such schemes.

Europeans even run their dedicated nature reserves a bit like farms.
Cambridge University conservation biologist William Sutherland has written about the UK style of management: "Visitors from outside Western
Europe are frequently astonished to discover that National Parks and nature reserves are often intensively grazed by cattle and sheep; fens are

mowed; woodland trees are routinely cut down in coppicing and that a major activity of conservationists is preventing succession by removing sapling trees and bushes."[4]

Sutherland has called for more American-style "wilderness" conservation in the United Kingdom and Western Europe, on the model of Vera's Oostvaardersplassen. But there have also been calls for Americans, Canadians, Australians, and others to put more emphasis on agri-environment schemes. Certainly such programs exist. The U.S. Environmental Quality Incentives Program has been running since 1996, focusing on reducing pollution of waterways and greenhouse gas emissions as well as habitat preservation. As of September 2010, some 72,000 square miles of farms and ranches were participating.[5] Another program that is more focused on plants and animals is the Wildlife Habitat Incentive Program, which covers some ten thousand square miles. The U.S. Department of Agriculture says that the amount of land covered by these schemes has stayed steady over time, and that most new farmers learn about their conservation programs via word of mouth, so there is clearly room to expand the land base of conservation-friendly farms.

There is an ongoing debate when it comes to conservation in agricultural lands. Habitat and other natural values can be improved by increasing the diversity and reducing the intensity of farming, but this generally also reduces yield—the amount of usable crop produced per acre. In theory, if each acre has a lower yield, the country will need more acres of farms to produce the same amount of food. So while some conservationists promote organic and other low-intensity farms, other conservationists argue for a "land-sparing" strategy, where farms are run at maximum efficiency to produce maximum yield, and the acres thus freed up can be completely dedicated to conservation.

Scientists disagree about which is the better route, and the ideal mix of strategies depends on complex variables. Jenny Hodgson of the University of Leeds and her colleagues measured butterfly densities in various English landscapes. Nature reserves had higher densities of butterflies than organic farms, which in turn had higher densities than conventional farms. The team calculates that if organic yields are equal to or greater than 87 percent of conventional yields, it is worth switching to organic to maximize butterflies. But if they are lower, it would be better to farm conventionally and convert more land to reserves—the *land-sparing* strategy. If land can't be converted to reserves, but only to lower-quality *set-asides* at field margins, then organic yields only have to exceed 35 percent of conventional to make going organic a better strategy. And if you expand beyond butterflies, the math gets even more complicated.[6]

Ivette Perfecto and John Vandermeer of the University of Michigan are among the ecologists who question a basic premise of the land-sparing argument. If agriculture intensifies, will farmers or countries really take land out of production? Or will they just grow more crops? "In more market-oriented societies," they conclude, "overproduction may lead to lowered market prices and the tendency by individual producers to increase production further to increase total farm revenue, or a shift to another commodity which may require more land (for example, extensive cattle pasture)."[7] Studies don't support the notion that more advanced farming techniques always lead to a reduction in area farmed. And even the assumption that intensive agriculture is more productive than traditional practices may not be true. Small-scale farmers with local savvy and a diverse portfolio of crops often have higher yields than large industrial monocultures. So Perfecto and Vandermeer suggest we instead focus on improving the conservation value of farms with agri-environment schemes so that species can use them either as habitat or at least as hospitable corridors between habitats.

Meanwhile, some fans of the land-sparing strategy take it to a futuristic extreme by advocating moving intensive production indoors. Entrepreneur Gene Fredericks wants to grow basil and arugula in abandoned big-box stores.[8] Columbia University professor Dickson Despommier wants to build huge skyscrapers with whole self-contained agricultural ecosystems inside.[9] There are problems with these ideas—principally that growing plants indoors takes a lot of energy while sunlight is free—but such concentrated urban agriculture may be able to work in some places, for some crops. Indoors or out, specialized high-intensity urban agriculture need not be incompatible with the landscape of small, nature-friendly farms that Perfecto and Vandermeer propose. As long as conservationists don't fall into what Perfecto and Vandermeer call "the assumption that agriculture is the enemy of conservation," there are opportunities for adding and deepening wherever food is grown.

Finding a place for nature on farms may sound like an obvious strategy. Farms and ranches are already set up for growing things. Less obvious is weaving conservation into industrial lands—the loud, soot-belching landscape of factories, processing plants, energy infrastructure, and transportation that is so often cast as the antithesis of nature. But as the Duwamish illustrates, nature and industry can coexist.

From my kayak, I could see tiny hidden green places along the river, places I'd never seen when barreling down Marginal Way or other nearby roads. A few days later I explored these tiny oases by car with Heather Trim of People for Puget Sound, an environmental group that until a few decades ago focused all their attention on preserving seemingly pristine areas but now fights to restore places such as these nubbins of waste space abutting the river. With such tiny footprints, I wondered how they could provide much conservation value. I learned that what they may lack in endangered species or, say, carbon sequestration ability, they more than make up for in recreation, aesthetic, and especially "peacefulness" values.

At the end of Duwamish Diagonal Avenue, hidden in a tangle of industrial access roads, is a small park with a picnic table. A lady in polar fleece feeds some Canadian geese as a huge barge slides by on the Duwamish, loaded with at least one hundred 48-foot cargo containers. She says she used to work nearby and comes here when she has a spare moment before her appointments at the Veterans Administration. A couple sits at the table, eating lunch after a shopping trip to the warehouse store, Costco. "We come here every time we go to Costco," says the man. "It is a little place to get off the street." "We saw seals here one time," adds the woman. It is oddly quiet, and serene, here, apart from some kind of ringing noise from Selden construction and the low white noise of big boat engines.

Other street ends are even tinier and less well maintained. One features a wild prairie of weeds with a view of Mount Rainier. Another has recently been landscaped with native plants, and a woman smoking a cigarette watches a child play at the shoreline. "It is peaceful here," she says. An employee of a metal recycling operation approaches Trim from his side of the chain-link fence separating the business from the street end as she tells me about the salmon-friendly features planned for the space now occupied by blackberry vines and a broken desk drawer. "Are there going to be trees here, and green grass?" he asks Trim, expectantly.

If Simson and Trim have their way, there will be trees, green grass, salmon, and metal recycling; there will be boat building and nest building and community building, all squeezed onto the same river.

Those who talk about greening industry usually focus on reducing the polluting outputs of industrial processes, from carbon dioxide to the polychlorinated biphenyls (PCBs), dioxins, and other chemicals that now contaminate the Duwamish River sediment. But at the same time industrial sites can become more natural by adding green space. Industrial neighborhoods like those along the Duwamish can feature natural areas, which can act as stepping-stones for moving species and as places for people to take a moment and connect with nature. Unused corners of industrial sites can be planted with native species. And roofs can be turned green. Industrial operations from the Ford Dearborn truck assembly plant in Michigan to the Hostess Cupcake factory in Hoboken, New Jersey, now feature green roofs that provide habitat for plants and bugs while reducing water runoff and counteracting the urban heat island effect, where dark roofs and pavement suck up sunlight. These green roofs often replicate shallow soil ecosystems and can attract orchids, spiders, and even ground-nesting birds that, up high, have nothing to fear from cats.

As with the green roofs, industry can obtain the greatest conservation value when it skips worrying about what particular ecosystem their site may have replaced and instead looks around for ecosystems in the region with features similar to the way their site looks now.[10] For example, large industrial buildings often have lots of exposed concrete walls, which can be used by cliff dwelling species like lichens, vines, and birds of prey. When industrial processes change the chemical composition of the soil, they can create analogues to weird and wonderful systems just waiting for the plants and animals that thrive there. Salty wastewater pools can make good homes for rare salt-loving plants and animals. Metal-contaminated sites can host the elite group of metal-tolerant plants. Quarries and gravel pits, once closed and partially flooded, can become homes for rare species like migrating waterbirds, reptiles and amphibians, and in the United Kingdom, the little garlic-smelling plant called water germander.[11] One German gravel pit was studied for a dozen years and proved to be an uncommonly effective refuge for threatened species: "22 of 230 vascular plant species, 22 of 78 moss species, 38 of 106 lichen species, and 216 of 527 animal species were at risk for extinction."[12]

Many of the new ideas being tried out in the industrial landscape are focused on places that are not active work sites. It may not be practical to have birds and trees on the factory floor, or in an active mine, but where workers have moved on, or where workers never go—these waste spaces are ripe for conservation. The same is true of waste spaces everywhere else, from urban centers to sprawling exurbs and rural lanes.

Co-opting wastelands for conservation isn't a new idea. Conservation icon Aldo Leopold put it forth in his famous book *Sand County Almanac*: "There are idle spots on every farm, and every highway is bordered by an idle strip as long as it is; keep cow, plow, and mower out of these idle spots, and the full native flora, plus dozens of interesting stowaways from foreign parts, could be part of the normal environment of every citizen."[13] Charles Elton too wrote about the importance of hedgerows, railway embankments, canals, and ditches for conservation. The quintessentially English hedgerows—long roadside and field-side hedges of hawthorn, oak, elm (Elton wrote before Dutch Elm disease killed most of them), ash, bird's nests, humming insects, and wild flowers—he argued, were "a connective tissue binding together the separate organs of the landscape."[14]

Today many highway medians are being planted with native species. Lagging behind the pack is Hawaii. Nonnative Bermuda grass has been the standard here for sixty years. But never fear—Hawaii's medians may soon be "hydroseeded" with pili grass, which native Hawaiians used for roof thatching. In hydroseeding, the seed is mixed in with water and sprayed directly on roadsides. More ambitiously, Chris Dacus, landscape architect for the Hawaii State Department of Transportation, is supervising a research project, looking at hydroseeding a mix with ten to twenty species. "We'll turn a piece of lawn that was mowed and herbicided into a no-maintenance native grassland, and we'll turn a ribbon of invasive species into a ribbon of natives—make it a vector for native species."

These little scraps of land are not going to host lions or bison. But they can be very valuable for plants, invertebrates, and even birds, amphibians, and small mammals. There is likewise a great opportunity for the world's largest chain businesses and franchises to start conservation programs. Many fast-food restaurants and big-box stores have little strips of outdoor land attached as parking lot islands, or just waste areas by the loading docks or between the road and the building. Instead of sending staff out to mow lawns on these tiny islets in the paved landscape—or even more uselessly, landscaping them with expensive ornamental plants that are pulled out and replaced several times a year as the seasons change (please no more of those horrible October mums, dying before they are set in the ground)—why not pay once to have the area landscaped with a self-sustaining mix of plants that never needs watering or weeding? In some places, one may not even have to plant. In the absence of active tending, the underlying seed bank may provide an interesting native or novel combination of species.

University of Arizona ecologist Michael Rosenzweig has gathered many examples of squeezing conservation value out of human-dominated landscapes. Rosenzweig uses the term *reconciliation ecology* to denote "the science of inventing, establishing and maintaining new habitats to conserve species diversity in places where people live, work, or play."[15] He sees possibilities for habitat creation in city parks, military bases, ranches, farms, and other spaces. Some of the unconventional strategies Rosenzweig has suggested include drilling artificial nest holes for red-cockaded woodpeckers where rotten snags are scarce, creating artificial marshes from dirt excavated from building sites, and planting native species to lure pollinators and other beneficial insects to vineyards and farms. He sings the praises of such low-investment conservation tools as bird boxes carefully designed for a species of interest, like the bluebird, perches for loggerhead shrikes, and ponds just the right size for natterjack toads. On the Duwamish I saw platforms erected for osprey, which had taken the hint and built nests there.

What's wonderful about these kinds of strategies is that private citizens do not have to wait and hope that their government or some large conservation organization will carry them out. Every owner and renter can make any space work for nearly any conservation goal, whether they have a tiny balcony, a slot in a community garden, or a ranch in Texas.

The movement to conserve nature in private gardens and yards has been enthusiastically championed by scientists, especially those at botanical gardens. The U.S. National Wildlife Federation has a *Garden for Wildlife* program in which they certify appropriately managed backyards as wildlife habitat. Many state conservation agencies run similar programs. They have increasingly urged that people let nature into their garden by planting threatened species, tearing out lawns, greening roofs, making rain gardens, and most of all, changing their aesthetic to embrace the slightly messy, the brown in the summer, and inevitably, the buggy. The new look and feel is rambunctious, diverse, and more like wild spaces.

The idea of using a small city garden as a "reserve" for nature may seem a bit silly, since the size would seem to limit its usefulness to all but the humblest of creatures. But for many small or mobile plants and animals, a range composed of lots of tiny bits of land will act somewhat like one large connected range. The larger groups that are made up of many smaller populations are called *metapopulations*. Ilkka Hanski is a metapopulation researcher at the University of Helsinki in Finland. He has done a bit of calculation on the backyards of that northerly metropolis. "We have about one million properties with a smaller or bigger lot," he says. "If people would not just have a lawn, which is unfortunately still the fashion," he says, the citizens of Helsinki could support metapopulations of many species of insects, plants, and fungi.

Plants are able to exist as a metapopulation despite being physically separate, thanks to pollinators and seed dispersers, those Irises of the floral kingdom. Even the world's largest cities are alive with pollinators. In one survey ecologist Kevin Matteson of Fordham University simply walked straight lines across New York City and stopped to observe each flower he passed—he discovered 227 species of bee.[16] Yet we are not taking advantage of the services available from these airborne genetic-mixing agents. In that same survey, more than half the flowers that Matteson encountered were showy, pest-resistant infertile hybrids, or were in gardens so neat and tidy that any new seedlings would be pulled up as weeds.

If New Yorkers planted more fertile plants and loosened up their gardening standards, bees zooming across the five boroughs could tie isolated specimens together into a metapopulation. If they were willing to plant species with less pest resistance, and accept the tattered leaves and petals that come with it, there would be more food available to the insect fauna, and the Big Apple would become a more diverse place. It would also become a buggier place with a perhaps-challenging aesthetic. As Matteson put it, a milkweed plant covered with aphids, though providing great food for butterfly larvae and aphid-eaters like ladybugs, "is not the most beautiful thing to look at."

Hanski's own garden is, he admits, "very ugly" compared to his neighbors'—by conventional aesthetic standards. The former lawn now has the look of a waist-high meadow, studded with purple flowers. After several years of letting the garden go feral, Hanski invited a biologist friend to survey the 16,000-square-foot yard for plant and insect species, then offered some ecologist dinner guests the chance to guess the total species number in the yard. The prize was a bottle of wine. "My biology friend discovered two endangered species," says Hanski, "one wasp and one beetle." All told, there were 375 species in the yard. His trained ecologist guests had all underestimated.

Hanski's biodiversity came at the cost of his lawn. For habitat and for minimizing polluting fertilizers and thirsty watering regimes, almost anything is better than a well-tended lawn. Douglas Kent, an environmental horticulturalist and landscape designer in southern California, specializes in carbon-neutral and even carbon-negative designs. Some of his ideas are a bit counterintuitive. He suggests that a lawn in southern California with lots of inputs might be better for the environment if it were simply paved over. That way one could avoid all the emissions associated with its upkeep. But he's not proposing that every backyard be consigned to concrete. There are always natural, native, landscapes to be tried. And some lawns make more sense than others. "When it comes to kids playing and these recreational values, I think the carbon costs can be justified," he says. "But those areas where the kids aren't playing and there is still grass—around tract homes, at banks, along sidewalks—that is where I want to negotiate."

Kent keeps a list of low- or no-input groundcovers. Creeping red fescue ("it languishes and just plops over and has a real earthy flow," he says) and sedges are among his favorites. And Kent says that gardening for low emissions makes for a beautiful new aesthetic experience. "There is more whimsy, more nature. It's not that Apollonian concept of real heavy structure. You kind of usher nature back a little more into your garden." Butterflies and birds like these kinds of gardens better, he says. "It is exceptionally satisfying, and there is, frankly, less work."

Apart from ripping out lawns, the most straightforward way to turn a garden into a force for conservation is to encourage the planting of native species. First of all, a focus on natives is an efficient way of dividing up the plants that gardeners are going to provide habitat for. Every area can specialize in its historical flora, and together they are more likely to cover the world's plant diversity. Secondly, local animals are familiar with and often have developed relationships with native plants. Stuffing your yard with natives makes it likelier that you will be able to support some of the more exclusive mutualisms that obtain between plants and their pollinators, seed dispersers and hosts. Third, native plants are often easier to grow and require less or no water or fertilizer because they are already adapted to your yard's climate and soils.

On the other hand, climate change complicates the premise of the "native garden." As microclimate changes, so will the plants that can live there with little or no water or fertilizer. So if gardeners get turned on to native plants because it's more environmentally friendly to grow them, they may have to think again, or maybe just start looking at native gardens a bit to the south or downhill of them for inspiration and do a little assisted migration of their own.

And there are other limits to the native garden. "Clearly we can't grow entirely native plants if you want to want to grow vegetables," says Stephen Hopper, the director of Kew Gardens, outside London. "But if every gardener put in one native tree, we could get the benefits of supporting the animals that rely on them for the various stages for their life cycle." Hopper admits that natives are often less glamorous-looking than the "large showy sterile hybrids" that so many gardeners enjoy. He recommends embedding such showstoppers in a matrix of native foliage to get the best of both worlds.

The result is a compromise. Home gardeners will balance modest natives and showy steriles. They'll also have to determine how much nature they can stand. Some nature can bite—or worse. Bushy, weedy, vital gardens will have more ticks potentially harboring Lyme disease, more mosquitoes potentially harboring West Nile virus, and more mice potentially harboring hantavirus. Individuals and communities will have to gauge their own level of tolerance for such threats. Some things can be done to lower risk beyond simplifying the environment. For mosquitoes, says Hopper, "it is really a matter of managing available free-standing water. You can minimize temporary ponds, or have permanent ponds with animals that will eat the larvae. The solution can be to increase the diversity."

As gardeners play with how much nature they can tolerate, and with what works as the climate warms, they are essentially running experiments that could inform managers of much larger tracts of land. When it comes to climate change, says Peter Raven, president of the Missouri Botanical Garden in St. Louis, gardeners can afford to be ahead of the curve. "A garden is like a painting you paint over every year," he says. "It is a lot easier in gardening than it is in many other spheres. You can adapt with new plants every year. If you are into agriculture or city planning, it is not that easy to keep redoing the painting; it can be very difficult and very expensive and very traumatic." But as city designs change and suburban lawns perhaps transform into mixed-grass prairies, as the paint-box circles of irrigated monoculture perhaps give way to a more mixed farm, backyard putterers and window-box experimentalists will be there to tell everyone what to try. "Home gardeners tend to be kind of adventurous," says Raven, "so they will continuously be pointing the way to what can be grown."

What seems to still be lacking is any organized mechanism for the conservation-minded home gardener to report to city planners or farmers what works. On the other hand, there is increasingly an Internet infrastructure for gardeners to inform scientists about what transpires in the small pieces of nature they tend and know so well. Phenologists, those who study seasonal phenomenon like blooming time, are enlisting citizen scientists to record data in projects like the U.S.-based Project Budburst, the UK's Nature's Calendar, the Netherlands' De Natuurkalender, and Nature-Watch Canada. As the climate warms, recording when your redbuds leaf out may help inform ambitious assisted migration plans. Kayri Havens, a conservation biologist at the Chicago Botanic Garden, helps run Project Budburst. "We can use it over time to look at predictive models as to where plants may need to migrate to be blooming at the same time as their pollinators."

While some goals, like large carnivore conservation, can't be well supported by organic farms, industrial green space, and rambunctious home gardens, they provide one particular value better than anyplace else. These living slivers connect people to nature, and once people learn to love nature, they will be much more likely to support conservation efforts. They'll also be healthier and happier.

When conservationists focus on "pristine wilderness" only, they give people the impression that that's all that nature is. And so urban, suburban, and rural citizens believe that there is no nature where they live; that it is far away and not their concern. They can lose the ability to have spiritual and aesthetic experiences in more humble natural settings.

Nature documentaries scrupulously edit out any trace of the modern world, tricking viewers into thinking there is a place out there, somewhere, where cheetahs and polar bears and penguins romp free. Many wildlife photographers use captive animals from game parks to create their images of wild nature. Those who do go to reserves and parks make sure that fenceposts, camera trucks, or penguin-poop-stained snow don't make the final cut. The elegant 2001 documentary *Winged Migration* used birds that filmmakers raised from eggs and imprinted on themselves. Even David Attenborough of *Planet Earth* fame has filmed polar bears in the zoo without telling his viewers.[17]

Meanwhile, plants and animals are all around us, in our backyards, along roadsides, in city parks. But this nature is much less spectacular. Ilkka Hanski warns against Americans in particular getting too used to spectacular nature. "That is likely to give the impression that what is around them is of little value. In the UK, people find it exciting to see nature that is small. They enjoy the nature in their own neighborhood."

Indeed, even cities are incredibly diverse places. Take New York's 227 bee species, and Hanski's garden of 375 species. In a thirty-year study, Jennifer Owen, a gardener and academic, has found 474 plants, 1,997 insects, 54 birds, and seven mammals in her back garden on Scraptoft Lane in Leicester, United Kingdom.[18]

It is precisely because they are chock-a-block with nonnatives that cities can rack up such impressive numbers despite being partially covered in concrete. One study of garden trees showed that while southern California has somewhere in the neighborhood of 50 to 60 native trees, the city of Los Angeles hosts 145 species, including the Mexican fan palm, the archetypal street palm one associates with Hollywood; the American sweet gum, and the southern magnolia. With eight to eleven tree species per hectare, L.A. is more diverse than many ecosystem types.[19]

Street trees are not just attractive shade-providing devices. In the annual cycles of the ginkgo and the maple, an urbanite can see the seasons turn. Birds nest in street trees; cicadas climb them, leaving their molted shells behind. Wasps rearrange the tissues of urban oaks, building galls in the shapes of balloons. Street trees are nature. And practicing seeing them that way can help everyone with the gestalt switch. If conservation is to take place everywhere, we must all learn to see nature as the background to our own lives and not just as islands far away.

If we fight to preserve only things that look like pristine wilderness, such as those places currently enclosed in national parks and similar refuges, our best efforts can only retard their destruction and delay the day we lose. If we fight to preserve and enhance nature as we have newly defined it, as the living background to human lives, we may be able to win. We may be able to grow nature larger than it currently is. This will not only require a change in our values but a change in our very aesthetics, as we learn to accept both nature that looks a little more lived-in than we are used to and working spaces that look a little more wild than we are used to.

10 | A Menu of New Goals

Why do you care about nature? What kind of appeal would make you most likely to donate to a conservation organization? If you were nominated to manage a piece of land near your house, what would your goals for that land be? A consequence of throwing out the "pristine wilderness" ideal is that conservationists, and society at large, now have to formulate alternative goals for conservation. This may be in part why we are so reluctant to move on. After all, "putting things back the way they were" seems to handily cover any other goals we might have. The perfect restoration to some Edenic baseline would always conserve all the correct species, all the natural interactions between them, all the ecosystem services that the land provided, and all the beauty that time and chance or God had put there.

Once you admit that you can't put things back the way they were, you often find yourself having to choose between goals that all sound pretty good. Throw the real limitations of budgets, politics, and time in there, and the choices become ever more brutal. In this chapter, we'll hear about a place in which we can't have both elephants and biodiversity; a situation in which we must choose between ensuring a frog species's ultimate survival or leaving it in its native ecosystem; and an experiment in which whole ecosystems are pitted against one another in a battle royale.

The final lesson is that no single goal will work in all situations. Unfortunately, this means that for every piece of land, its owners, its managers, governments, and other people who care about it will have to come together and hash out a common set of goals. This can be extremely difficult.

GOAL 1: PROTECT THE RIGHTS OF OTHER SPECIES

In the late 1940s conservation icon Aldo Leopold called the recognition of the inherent value of an ecosystem the *land ethic*. The land ethic extends to "soils, waters, plants and animals" the same moral obligations we currently have to members of our own human communities.[1] The idea is that we humans, plants, and animals are all in this living business together. "When we see land as a community to which we belong, we may begin to use it with love and respect," he wrote.[2] In modern terms, the land ethic espouses a *biocentric* view of life, which gives other species and ecosystems moral status.

Norwegian philosopher Arne Naess coined the term *deep ecology* in the 1970s. According to Naess, those who practice shallow ecology look after the Earth as an extension of looking after themselves. They'll husband resources carefully and fight pollution, but only because it ultimately benefits themselves and other humans.

Deep ecologists, like Leopold, believe that all living things have intrinsic value and deserve to be protected for their own sakes. Humans are not specially privileged species but mere nodes in the grand web of life, properly defined more by their relationships to other species than by their individual characteristics. In fact, each human can and should expand his or her conception of the self to include all these linkages, so that taking care of ourselves becomes the same thing as taking care of the environment.[3]

In the 1980s, with Naess's blessing, the phrase *deep ecology* was expanded to encompass all kinds of philosophies that shared an essential belief in the intrinsic value of nature. Deep ecologists feel that humans must reduce their current intensive impact on the Earth. Rich Westerners, especially, must quit tapping into nature at such a furious pace to satisfy the frivolous desires of their consumer society. Human beings must reduce their population so that we can live more lightly on the Earth. These are all moral obligations to the natural world, not mere choices. If we do not do these things, we are trampling on the rights of other entities as surely as if we were denying people their human rights by enslaving them or even killing them.

The exact possessor of these rights can be difficult to pin down. Many people have an intuition that animals have rights, just as humans do. But there are many cases where the rights of individual animals conflict with the familiar conservation goal of protecting populations or species of animals or plants. If cats are killing all the albatross nestlings on an island, cats may have to be killed to protect the ecosystem. Sometimes protecting diversity means buying ammunition.

Basing an environmental ethic on the rights of animals is tricky. It leaves out plants, mountains, and landscapes. Aldo Leopold didn't envision his famous "land ethic" as applying to individual organisms so much as to the land collectively. In his essay on the subject, he argues for the "right to continued existence, and, at least in spots, their continued existence in a natural state" for soil, water, plants, and animals.[4] That caveat "at least in spots" implies that not every drop of water, every deer, every wildflower, and every cup of soil has a separate right to exist. Rather, somehow, the land as a unit has a right to run itself without human meddling in some places.

Different contemporary biocentric ethicists lay out different rules of what has intrinsic value—and how much intrinsic value it has. We are used to the idea that individual lives are fundamentally valuable; it is the basis of the sense that murder is wrong. It is harder to set up values for amorphous collections like "ecosystems" or "the land" or for nonliving entities like "the soil" or a stream. Some ethicists, however, certainly hold that these entities have their own intrinsic value. Some even propose that the entire Earth itself holds value as a single human does, or that the qualities of being "natural" or "wild" themselves are a source of value. Conservation projects with biocentric goals may look different depending on who holds the rights. In general, however, human uses of the land won't have a privileged place.

GOAL 2: PROTECT CHARISMATIC MEGAFAUNA

Conservationists often talk about the power of *charismatic megafauna* to get the public to care about the environment. Charismatic megafauna are large animals that humans like and really don't want to see go extinct. At the very top of the charisma heap are whales, dolphins, elephants, gorillas, tigers, and pandas: big mammals with big eyes. The World Wildlife Fund urges us to donate to their general fund by "adopting" an animal of our choice. The donation is recognized with a stuffed animal and a certificate. The most popular choice among donors, as of April 2011 was the tiger, followed by the polar bear and the WWF's old standby, the panda.[5]

At first glimpse, focusing on just large mammals may seem a bit juvenile. Aren't all those lichens, nematodes, and parasites also worth something? But ecological theory predicts that many of the most popular species will be also be *keystone species*—species that have a great effect on how an ecosystem works and what it looks like. Conserving them can also mean *umbrella conservation* for species that live alongside them. Handily, many of the charismatic megafauna have large ranges, so conservationists can argue for the protection of large areas, which can then also shelter the little creeping things, the plants, the molds, and the microbes, that don't make it onto World Wildlife Fund tote bags.

But when keystones push ecosystems in undesirable directions, as in the case of elephants in some South African parks, it becomes clear which of the species in a given ecosystem have first place in the hearts of humans. In 2007 I visited Addo Elephant Park, South Africa, where elephants walk silently, communicating in companionable purrs. The loudest noise is the crackle of the tough foliage they are eating. Addo is a huge exception to the general state of elephants. In most places elephants are being poached in record numbers, thanks to a boom in the illegal ivory trade. University of

Washington biologist Samuel Wasser estimates that 8 percent of African elephants are killed each year to make ivory baubles for Far East markets.[6] Elephants are being killed faster than they can reproduce, and as a consequence, populations are declining almost everywhere across Africa—except in tiny Addo, where the elephants are bursting at the seams.

"You're crowding Agatha and she's going to have to press into the bush to get by," said Katie Gough from the backseat of the car. Gough, based at Nelson Mandela Metropolitan University in Port Elizabeth, South Africa, had been studying these animals for four years and could tell most of them apart by the wear and tear on their ears or by their idiosyncratic wrinkles. She was right about Agatha, who, slowly moving her enormous body into the thorny shrubs, turned her head and gave us occupants of the car a look that everyone read—scientific prohibitions on anthropomorphization be damned—as reproachful.

Agatha's home has—along with herds of elegant kudu, zebras with tawny rumps, and immense ostriches sprinting along the road—too many elephants. In 1954 22 animals lived in a park of about 9 square miles. They were the remnants of a herd that one hired hunter had hunted nearly to extinction in 1919. He was carrying out the orders of local orange growers who were sick of elephants gorging themselves on their crops. In 2007 there were around 460 animals packed into about 100 square miles—or roughly double the 1954 density.

The effects that too many elephants have on their environment were easy to see. When I climbed the stairs over a fence from an elephant area into a pachyderm-free zone, the landscape switched from patchy shrub lands to a Lilliputian forest containing a wide variety of plants, including spectacular aloes. This miniature forest can exist only where elephants are at low densities.

Thus if your goal is to preserve an entire ecosystem and not just the elephants within it, pachyderm numbers have to be controlled. Africans can become justifiably irritated when interested parties abroad tell them how to manage their elephant populations. Well-meaning and sometimes technically expert outsiders are constantly offering opinions on whether to cull animals, whether to try contraception, whether some kinds of ivory should be legally sold, and so on. Often onlookers will treat the whole continent as a single case, when each country and each area has its own problems to solve.

In 1994 culling of elephants in South Africa was stopped because of the objections of local and foreign animal rights groups. Elephant densities have since increased, and in Kruger Park, in the north of the country, large bulls flex their muscles by pushing over baobab and marula trees. And after a decade and a half of debate, in 2008, South Africa announced that culling would resume. This news was not received well. Some claimed that culling was inhumane, even unethical.

Hector Mogame, executive director of Conservation Services at South Africa National Parks, in Pretoria, doesn't see it this way. "The issue of ethics is about power," he told the Society for Conservation Biology in Port Elizabeth in 2007. "The viewpoint of opposition to lethal control is usually favored by affluent people—people with money." Citing the furor over the plan to resume culling, he says the debate is about the people on the ground being trumped by the rich and powerful.

Advocacy for individual species can become extremely political and highly emotional. And "umbrella species" notwithstanding, focusing on the charismatic doesn't always bring other species along. A world in which our only goal was preserving elephants might be a world without many species of succulent plants.

GOAL 3: SLOW THE RATE OF EXTINCTIONS

Perhaps a more sophisticated approach is to treat all species as equally valuable. This is the assumption behind such legislation as the Endangered Species Act. Under the law, a fly or a newt is as worthy of protection as a jaguar. For many conservationists, the goal of conservation is to halt extinctions (or more subtly, to return the rate of extinctions to its "background rate" before human activity vastly increased their number). This is the idea behind maps of conservation hotspots: zones where lots of endangered species live together that would make especially efficient protected areas.

Hugh Possingham, a slight, slightly manic Australian mathematical ecologist, believes every species is equally valuable. In his mathematically oriented work, each species is equal to "1," in the sense that every extinction is weighted the same. Possingham is a pragmatist, and he believes in triage. In his papers he compares different conservation land-buys in different places, which is more complex than one might think. Land prices vary around the world, as does species richness. Many investments have diminishing returns over time: once a large chunk of one ecosystem is protected, turning a tiny bit more into a park won't save many additional species. On the other hand, some interventions begin to pay off seriously only after a certain investment threshold is reached. "If you were trying to get all the rats off an island, unless you invest enough to get them all off, you might as well not even bother," explains Possingham. On top of all this is the problem that data on costs are infamously scanty—so much so that many earlier analyses just used land area as a proxy for costs, an astonishing simplification.

Possingham tries to be as rigorous as possible, and sometimes that means not everything gets saved. "A lot of people get upset with that. It basically says some regions aren't working at all. They are too expensive, the threats are too huge, or there are not enough species in them."

Consider, for example, the Mount Lofty woodlands of Australia, where eucalyptus trees shelter rare orchids, spiny echidnas, and cockatoos. Surely it is worth preserving such species from the exotic predators such as foxes and cats that threaten them? But in a trade-off between spending on the Mount Lofty ranges and on the mountainous regions of the South African fynbos, a species-rich shrub land, Possingham's algorithms give the money to the fynbos—among other regional investments. The Australian woodlands get nothing, despite the fact that Possingham, an avid birder, would bitterly regret losing part of the original range of the endangered regent honeyeater. So focusing only on stopping extinctions, with every species equally weighted, might mean that if the budget is tight, your favorite species may not get saved.

The goal of slowing extinctions has another strange implication. Consider the many dedicated conservationists working on captive breeding of amphibians, which are declining in alarming numbers worldwide, especially in the tropics, where introduced chytrid fungus is killing them off with unbridled gusto. If zoos manage to keep breeding populations of amphibians going in zoos while they go extinct in the wild, what do they have exactly? Could they wait for the fungus to burn out and then return the frogs to their native ranges? How long before the ecological niches that the frogs occupied out in the forest are filled in by other species? What happens if climate change destroys their habitat wholesale while they are in zoos? What if you end up with just a bunch of frogs in plastic boxes?

"Let's assume for the moment that the spiraling decay, including global warming, continues unabated," proposes Alan Pounds, a tropical amphibian biologist and chytrid specialist. "I would say that under such circumstances captive breeding programs can save amphibian diversity in about the same sense that a museum of Incan art can save Incan culture." Narrowly focusing on stopping extinctions, in other words, saves species but not necessarily ecosystems.

GOAL 4: PROTECT GENETIC DIVERSITY

A narrow focus on slowing the rate of species extinctions puts a lot of weight on the species concept. Using species as our unit of concern means that we must often wrestle with whether two groups of organisms are or are not the same species, which means wading up to our necks into the vexed question of what defines a species. Although most biologists agree that species are real entities—that they exist without humans around to assign them—the distinctions are not clear-cut. For example, genetic studies have shown that some brown bears are more closely related to polar bears than they are to some other brown bears. According to some interpretations of the species concept, this means that if brown bears are a species, then polar bears are not.

This can be a problem for policies, such as the Endangered Species Act. The Endangered Species Act is more flexible than you might think, given its name. The act includes in its definition of species "subspecies" and "distinct population segments" but unhelpfully offers no definitions for either of these categories. The government agencies that enforce the act do provide some guidance, but the researchers called on by the government to determine objectively whether various groups of organisms are eligible for protection are mostly left to their own devices. If a group of organisms you care about is not deemed to be a species or a subspecies, it might just lose its ticket to protection.

A way around these problems is to forget about species and focus on genetic diversity. Preserving genetic diversity preserves the raw source of the diversity of life. All populations of the same species are not genetically interchangeable. From a genetic perspective, that is an argument for protecting more than one pride of lions or forest of cedars. Sometimes there can be more genetic diversity between two populations of one species than between two closely related species. If we choose to spend millions to save the Preble's meadow jumping mouse, which only some taxonomists declare a separate subspecies from the generic meadow jumping mouse, will we have less money to spend on preserving the already-low genetic diversity of the monk seal or American bison? After all, with the world's climate changing, species with more genetic variants to play with may be more likely to come up with adaptations that help them thrive in a warmer world.

Few efforts are specifically focused on protecting genetic diversity. One of them, called EDGE (Evolutionarily Distinct and Globally Endangered), seeks to save the most genetically weird animals in the world, arguing that by losing the spiny echidnas and river dolphins, we lose millions of years of evolution not represented in any other gene pool. The EDGE project gives each species a score derived from its position on the evolutionary tree. A lone species out on a long branch gets a higher score because it is the sole bearer of genes that represent a very long period of evolution. Take the three-toed sloths, which parted company from the rest of the sloths some 15 million years ago. "There are two species of three-toed sloth that only diverged one million years ago," says Nick Isaac, a research fellow at the Zoological Society who helps to run the EDGE program. "If one went extinct, we would lose one million years, but if we lose both, we lose 15 million years." Or, says Isaac, "you could make an analogy with art. You are in a spaceship leaving Earth with three paintings. Do you take three Rembrandts, or do you take one Rembrandt, one Leonardo, and one Picasso?"

Weirdness may also be valuable for its own sake. The creeping, insect-eating, and highly venomous mammal known as the solenodon is high on EDGE's list. "The solenodon are the only species able to inject venom with their teeth," notes Isaac.

But focusing only on genetic diversity tends to lead one down the road to rows of freezers set at −80 degrees Celsius containing genetic samples from organisms around the world. If the genes are more important than the containers they are in, then you don't even need to keep living populations going in zoos, in theory. All you need are the sequences. But I think few people would really be happy with a world in which bluebirds existed only as frozen tissue samples.

GOAL 5: DEFINE AND DEFEND BIODIVERSITY

If the idea of saving the world's frogs in a bunch of separate plastic boxes or as frozen tissue samples doesn't appeal to you, it may be because such a vision saves all the units but severs all the ecological links between them. In that case, a reasonable goal may be to protect biodiversity. *Biodiversity* is a term widely used by ecologists and conservationists, and most definitions include the variety of species that exist, *and* the variety of genes within each species, *and* the variety of ecosystems on Earth. One could say that *biodiversity* is shorthand for *complexity*. Biodiversity is probably the most widely shared value among conservationists and ecologists, and it embraces a whole ecosystem or even the whole Earth at once. Biodiversity fans don't just like species A, B, and C, they like how A creeps up on B on soft paws in the snowy dawn, how B nibbles on C, blissfully unaware it is being stalked, and how C grows on the high mountainside, covered in frost. It is not enough that the snow leopard, the bharal, and the grass *Stipa orientalis* exist. We want them to exist together, preferably in the Himalayas, where they are now. The idea is that evolution has produced a beautiful web of interrelations, inscrutable in its complexity and inherently valuable.

Nature protection aimed at protecting biodiversity emerged in the early twentieth century as ecologists began to notice that the most beautiful places were not always the richest in species. Muir and many early parks-boosters wanted Yosemite and Yellowstone protected for essentially Romantic, religious reasons, because they were beautiful, soul-lifting landscapes. Now ecologists call for humble swamps, lowland forests, coastal areas, and low-key streams to be protected because of the complexity of life there.

Biodiversity is a slippery concept, though, philosophically and scientifically. How many elements of the web of interactions can disappear or be replaced with new species before it becomes a new web? If we care about complexity, then are keystone species that make a big difference in an ecosystem more valuable than "redundant" species without which nothing much would change in the web? And what of the fact that recent research is upending the balance-of-nature theory that historical ecosystems are "saturated"—that every possible niche in the food web is taken and that therefore no new species can move in without displacing one already there? If Gleason is right that ecosystems are "mere accidental groupings," then why get so worked up about them?

Meanwhile most of the world's real complexity is hidden and not highly valued by our societies, despite what we might say. Take parasites (which in at least one ecosystem, a California estuary, physically outweigh the top predators) and microbes. We are our own thriving ecosystems of bacteria, fungi, and a whole menagerie of others. Yet we feel no obligation to preserve the ecosystems currently native to our own bodies. Does taking an antibiotic, or even probiotic yogurt, contradict the value of maintaining complex ecosystems?

Biodiversity may be the most problematic conservation goal precisely because it embraces so much: several levels of biological organization, from genes to whole landscapes. Nevertheless, it may come closest to capturing what people like about nature.

GOAL 6: MAXIMIZE ECOSYSTEM SERVICES

Ecosystem services arguments come from the "what have you done for me lately" school of ecology. Bits of land and the species therein are valued to the extent that they help out humanity. We're talking here about marshes filtering water and dampening floods, bees pollinating crops, trees becoming timber, mushrooms or fish or deer feeding people, and so on. In the past, humans have treated these resources as inexhaustible and therefore valueless. After all, there are two dimensions to price: supply and demand. Demand for clean water, for food, and for breatheable air will always be high, but as long as supply was considered infinite, the price on the species and ecosystems that provided them was zero.

With a global population now approaching 7 billion and the Earth's terrestrial surface and volume of fresh water stubbornly remaining constant, the supply of many valuable services may now be low enough to create a price for them. Conservationists who work on ecosystem services are trying to point out to governments and industries that the resources on which they depend are finite. They then hope to put in place policies— financial incentives, taxes, and the like—so that ecosystems will be valued in plenty of time to save them. The alternative, they say, is to overshoot, to pack the seas full of fishing boats, the mountains with loggers, and the plains with developers until we pull an Easter Island and realize that we not only have nothing left to eat, we also don't have enough wood left to build canoes to escape our imprudence.

Ecosystem services arguments for conservation are fashionable at the moment. In 2005 the United Nations, the World Bank, and a large group of nongovernmental organizations and universities put out the Millennium Ecosystem Assessment, a giant report about the state of the planet. The assessment used the ecosystem services approach to make it clear that planetary changes mattered to more than hippie nature lovers and third-graders with crushes on whales. Perhaps in part because of this focus in such a prominent report, the scientific literature on ecosystem services has exploded in recent years, and several huge conservation projects have taken it on as a way of thinking about environmental issues.

And some actual dollars have been spent. A commonly cited example comes from Costa Rica, where in 1997 the government installed a suite of policies designed to slow the high deforestation rate, then the worst in the world. Landowners began to receive payments for environmental services, if they stopped cutting down tropical rain forest or began replanting the forest. The money for these payments—now some U.S. $15 million to $18 million a year—comes from various sources, including a 3.5 percent tax on all fuel and from hydropower companies interested in preserving forests for their ability to regulate water flow through the land. Today 8 percent of the land is earning payments, and Costa Rica has among the lowest deforestation rates in the world.

Despite ecosystem services' recent acceptance by the global fraternity of policy makers, it has its critics. Legal scholar John Echeverria at the Vermont Law School in South Royalton says that paying landowners not to damage the environment sets up an expectation of reward for refraining from bad behavior and a financial obligation for future taxpayers. Instead, he suggests, landowners should be expected to do the right thing and punished when they don't—with the caveat that some landowners who have to lose considerable sums to protect the environment should be compensated, as they already are under laws like the Endangered Species Act. "The implicit message of agreeing to pay is that they should be entitled to proceed to destroy nature," says Echeverria.

Another drawback of this approach is that if a series of concrete ditches or a weedy, disliked species could perform an ecosystem service of interest better than the current landscape, there's no reason not to pave over or start seeding monocultures of elephant grass. For it is by no means always the case that the most biodiverse places provide the best services.

Aldo Leopold had this figured out. "One basic weakness in a conservation system based wholly on economic motives is that most members of the land community have no economic value. Wildflowers and songbirds are examples. Of the 22,000 higher plants and animals native to Wisconsin, it is doubtful whether more than 5 per cent can be sold, fed, eaten, or otherwise put to economic use."[7]

For decades, ecologists have been running experiments designed to test the idea that higher biodiversity always improves ecosystem function. This would make it easier to protect more species under the mantle of ecosystem services. But they have been unable to prove that biodiversity by itself, apart from any characteristics of the species making it up, is "good" for ecosystems and thus presumably for ecosystem services. First off, the results of the experiments—typically small plots with manipulated numbers of plants—weren't what they were cracked up to be. More diverse ecosystems were more productive on average because they were more likely to include the most productive plant. Monocultures of these superstars were often even more productive than the most diverse plots. Secondly, the experimenters tended to define a highly productive ecosystem as "good" or "functioning" as if turning sunlight into biomass were the purpose or job of an ecosystem. Of course an ecosystem doesn't have a purpose any more than an organism does. And high productivity isn't always what humans prefer either. High productivity in lakes often means more algae and less fish.[8]

The difficulty of linking biodiversity to ecosystem services wouldn't be a problem if the promoters of ecosystem services really valued nature only insofar as it contributes to human well-being. No problem, they would say. In this case our models supported protecting the forest, and in this other case our models supported logging it and replacing it with rows of solar panels. We followed the money.

I don't think most ecosystem services promoters actually think this way. I believe that most of them believe that biodiversity has intrinsic value, but they see ecosystem services as a way to get it protected when the people in charge don't share their feelings. "You can easily completely miss biodiversity," says Stanford biologist and ecosystem services advocate Gretchen Daily. "If you are focused on carbon sequestration, you could plant fast-growing eucalyptus all over the planet." Nevertheless, she says, ecosystem services are the best way to gently guide people toward protecting biodiversity. "I think it is going to be a long haul for biodiversity for its own sake. I see conservation as a race to buy time. For me, ecosystem services is a strategy to buy time as well as getting buy-in."

One way that ecosystem services proponents reel in nature that doesn't make anybody money is with a fascinating economic concept: *existence value*. Existence value is the value derived from just knowing that a species or ecosystem exists. In *Walden*, Thoreau talks about the necessity of knowing that there are unexplored places, "land and sea . . . infinitely wild, unsurveyed and unfathomed by us because unfathomable." "We need to witness our own limits transgressed, and some life pasturing freely where we never wander," he says.

One study from 1999 found that "a review of the literature on passive use values, such as existence and bequest values, provided by Wilderness protection suggests that the nonrecreation benefits of Wilderness are larger in percentage terms and in the aggregate than the recreation benefits of Wilderness."[9] Thousands of nature fans in the lower forty-eight enjoy the mere knowledge that Alaska exists, so much so that they feel that they have a stake in land-use decisions made there. As Leopold puts it in his *Almanac*, "Is my share in Alaska worthless to me because I shall never go there? Do I need a road to show me the arctic prairies, the goose pastures of the Yukon, the Kodiak bear, the sheep meadows behind McKinley?"[10]

Existence value seems to stray close to the idea of intrinsic value. Are the beauties of Alaska valuable *to me* because they exist? Or is existence value a way for me to admit or assert that they are intrinsically valuable?

The ecosystem services concept is thus in many cases better conceptualized as a tool to achieve other goals rather than a goal unto itself. But in particular cases, protecting the services provided by ecosystems will be a real concrete goal of conservation and restoration. Certainly a savvy coastal community will protect the wetlands that buffer storms from their houses, provide a nursery for their seafood, and filter synthetic fertilizer out of their bay. Here taking an ecosystem services approach can reveal the common interests shared by nature lovers and business people. Everybody wins. But other ecosystems don't provide enough bottom-line value to justify protection by their services alone.

GOAL 7: PROTECT THE SPIRITUAL AND AESTHETIC EXPERIENCE OF NATURE

Even if you can't swallow the biocentric idea that nature has rights, you can still call upon sentiment and religious reasons to argue for its preservation. We like the way nature looks, smells, and sounds. We like the way a pine-needle carpet springs underfoot. We like knowing the names of birds and trees. We feel that nature is a place to refresh our spirits or to contemplate something that is grander than ourselves.

Many of us have a spiritual connection to certain landscapes, either within the framework of an organized faith that includes spiritual places, or in our own personal spiritual lives. These connections can range from a certain hillside where someone scattered the ashes of their parents to Shinto shrines that include natural sites to precincts like the Black Hills in South Dakota that are sacred to the Lakota Indians.

Hawaiian ecologist Christian Giardina told me that preference for native ecosystems boils down to faith. For him, the native biodiversity of Hawaii is important partially because it underpins Hawaii's traditional culture, which continues to thrive. In the "Kumulipo," a traditional genealogical chant, plants and animals are named as ancestors of the Hawaiian people. Thus native species are not just used to make culturally significant objects such as canoes or leis; they are family. (Interestingly, this makes it more difficult to garner the support of the native Hawaiian community for conserving species not mentioned in the "Kumulipo," such as the monk seal. The monk seal may already have been nearly hunted out and limited to outlying islets when the chant was composed.) Even though Giardina does not have native Hawaiian ancestry himself, he finds preserving the biological basis of Hawaiian culture important enough to work full time for it. For Giardina, seeing the native plants and animals of Hawaii replaced by those from other places is an irreparable loss, akin to losing a culture. "Do you just, as a planet, put your hands up and say we are going to lose the language, we are going to lose the culture, and it is all going to be McDonald's and Swatch?"

All of this is something worth taking seriously and figuring into conservation plans. Like many of the other values we've looked at, it is ultimately something that humans like and want, and thus is no different from our desire to save tigers or our desire to have marsh-purified water. Many discussions of ecosystem services include aesthetic and cultural values, even apart from recreation values.

However, aesthetic and spiritual values are not limited to native or pristine-seeming places. There is an unfortunate tendency among many of us to allow ourselves to be moved or to find beautiful only that which we believe to be pristine. The hydroelectric plant at Niagara Falls pours over the falls carefully agreed-upon water minimums to keep people coming back. They could turn the falls off completely with the flick of a switch. Would people still ooh and ah if they knew this? And why not? If one rusty beer can spoils a whole day's search for the beauty in nature, then there isn't much beauty left. But I think there is, if we just adjust our perception.

Half a million Sandhill cranes gather at the Platte River in Nebraska every March before their final push north for the winter. At night, this gray bird with a red mask and a seven-foot wingspan roosts on sandbars in the middle of the river, where it can be sure to hear the plashing approach of any predators. But the Platte is heavily used by agriculture and industry, and that reduction in water has changed the river. Without fast-moving icy spring flows to scythe vegetation off islands, heavy machinery must clear room for the cranes, which are now squeezed onto a much smaller stretch of the river. The abundant food in postharvest cornfields all around makes it possible for so many to gather together.

The result is a man-made and nature-made spectacle. Tucked into a plywood blind—a kind of rudimentary cabin with viewing windows meant to keep the birds from spotting their audience and spooking—I peered one March into the plum dusk. On the far bank, cottonwoods were silhouetted on a powder-blue and rose sky. Deer played in the last of the light. A train whistle sounded.

After a long wait, at some unpredictable moment during the slow sunset, a few of the enormous, evolutionarily ancient birds appeared above the river, wheeling in circles as they weighed the risks of landing for the night. And then suddenly crane upon crane upon crane, some missing a few feathers, like tattered pterodactyls, joined them. They are a flocking species, and they poured riverward in airborne lines; the sky was strewn with them in whorls and unfolding arabesques, and then there were so many that they drifted in a mist, circling: a philharmonic of rusty cranks. Eventually, after half an hour of ear-splitting aerodynamics, they landed for the night.

Was this fantastic display somehow counterfeit because the cranes numbers are "artificially" concentrated? Nope. Not in my opinion. Humans and birds have collaborated to create this beauty. This conscious and responsible and joyful cohabitation is the future of our planet, our vibrant, thriving, rambunctious garden.

JUGGLING GOALS

There is no one best goal. Even after we agree to pursue all sorts of goals, we still have complex compromises to make between ideologies in contested places and between local and global interests. Society must decide what its goals are on multiple scales, then allocate the best-suited land to these various goals and get going, not shying away from the occasional bold experiment. Here, land for soulful contemplation, plus water filtration. There, land for the tiger and for ten endangered plant species. Over there, a mixed-bag refuge for island species that have winked out on their home atolls. And there, farms with wide boundaries left to go wild and highway medians covered in flowers.

Being up front about what we want from nature isn't even enough. We also must be open about the costs. Right now it is considered impolite in conservation circles to mention what something might cost or even keep track of how much a project is costing. This sounds crazy, but it is based on a sense that it is distasteful to say we can't save everything because we don't want to spend the money. But ignoring costs blinds us to the cheap and cheerful projects that provide big conservation bang for the buck.

Perhaps there is one solution that applies to all these different goals: preserve open land. Don't ignore green, growing land just because it isn't your ideal native landscape. Protect it from development, even if it is just a "trash ecosystem." Build your cities in tight and up high, and let the scenery take over the suburbs.

In a nutshell: give up romantic notions of a stable Eden, be honest about goals and costs, keep land from mindless development, and try just about everything.

In Polynesian Hawaii, territory was usually divided into ahupua'a, wedge-shaped slices of land running from the highest point on the island to the shore and even some ways offshore.[11] Thus every parcel contained several different ecosystem types and all the natural resources therein.

Ecologist Peter Vitousek has recently been inspired by the idea of these ahupua'a. Vitousek, you might remember, felt that embracing novel albizia forests in Hawaii was going too far. He's famous for cataloging the native biodiversity of Hawaii and the negative effects of introduced species on the nutrient cycles of the island. I expected him to be completely focused on Hawaii as it was before humans. But he too has been thinking along new and exciting lines. "My thinking has changed, certainly," he says. "I never thought of anything human as 'bad,' but [now] I'm more inclined to categorize nonnative species into those that pose existential threats to native species or ecosystems, those that probably aren't seriously threatening, and those that might be useful."

In his recent work, he has begun to appreciate the unique history of the landscape as maintained by the Polynesians who first came to the islands. Polynesian Hawaii was a heavily managed land with a denser population than today, but still the kind of place where one could "pick fruit from the trees, go surfing, and make love in the afternoon." Such a landscape has, for Vitousek, joined the vision of the untouched islands as a scene worth preserving. "What I would love to see, if I had the power the chiefs used to have, would be an ahupua'a restored to prior to human arrival, an ahupua'a restored to the peak of human use of the island, and an ahupua'a restored to the era of early European contact. We could show multiple eras in the history of the land."

The rambunctious garden is this ahupua'a vision writ across the whole Earth. In different places, in different chunks, we can manage nature for different ends—for historical restoration, for species preservation, for self-willed wildness, for ecosystem services, for food and fiber and fish and flame trees and frogs. We've forever altered the Earth, and so now we cannot abandon it to a random fate. It is our duty to manage it. Luckily, it can be a pleasant, even joyful task if we embrace it in the right spirit. Let the rambunctious gardening begin.

ACKNOWLEDGMENTS

Ann Finkbeiner, who taught me how to write about science at Johns Hopkins, told me not to write a book unless I was *obsessed* with the subject. I thank her for the excellent advice, and I thank my darling husband, Yasha, for sharpening my ideas with his philosophical expertise and reading countless drafts.

My editor at Bloomsbury USA, Kathy Belden, was wonderful to work with, and always right about how the thing should be organized. My agent, Russell Galen, sold the book in the first place, and so has my undying thanks.

Scientists who let me tag along on fieldwork and took time out to show me places include Jessica Hellmann, Caroline Williams, and André Burnier from Notre Dame; Mark Vellend at the University of British Columbia; Susan Cordell and Christian Giardina, both of the U.S. Forest Service Institute of Pacific Islands Forestry in Hilo; Rebecca Ostertag of the University of Hawaii at Hilo; Joe Mascaro at the Carnegie Institution for Science in Stanford; Matt Hayward at the Australian Wildlife Conservancy and the whole Hayward family; Rafal Kowalczyk at the Mammal Research Institute in Poland; Bogdan Jaroszewicz of the University of Warsaw's

Geobotanical Station; Graham Kereley, Adrian Shrader, and Katie Gough at Nelson Mandela Metropolitan University in Port Elizabeth, South Africa; Greg O'Neill at British Columbia's Ministry of Forests, Mines and Lands; the National Park Service mid-Atlantic invasive species strike team crew of summer 2005: Kate Jensen, Dale Meyerhoeffer, and Matthew Overstreet; Frans Vera of Staatsbosbeheer in the Netherlands; Ken Aho of the University of Idaho; Heather Trim of People for Puget Sound; and Cari Simson of the Duwamish River Cleanup Coalition. University of Missouri journalism professor Bill Allen took me to see the cranes. Thanks, Bill!

People who read portions of the manuscript include (but are not limited to) Matthew Chew, who through tough love helped me improve my history section; Kevin Maier, my brother-in-law and a professor of English at the University of Alaska, Juneau; Daniel Botkin, professor emeritus at the University of California, Santa Barbara; Tomasz Samojlik of the Mammal Research Institute in Poland; Mark Davis at Macalester College in Minnesota; Matthew Hayward, Jessica Hellmann, Greg O'Neill, Richard Hobbs of the University of Western Australia and Ariel Lugo of the USDA Forest Service, International Institute of Tropical Forestry, in Río Piedras, Puerto Rico; Dov Sax of Brown University; Connie Barlow of the Universe; Sally Aitken of the University of British Columbia; Rebecca Ostertag, Susan Cordell, Joe Mascaro, Frans Vera, and Josh Donlan of Advanced Conservation Strategies in Midway, Utah; and Elise Fogel.

Also thanks to the editorial staff at *Nature*, where I am a retained correspondent, for letting me report the stories that became the foundation for this book: in particular, Helen Pearson and Oliver Morton (now at the *Economist*), Alexandra Witze (now at *Science News*) and Geoff Brumfiel, for continued encouragement and patience with my obsessive interest in this topic.

I delivered this book two weeks after I delivered my daughter Adele. The world she will see as an old woman in 2100 will be much changed. I believe it can be diverse and thriving and beautiful nonetheless. But it won't be easy. Thanks to all those scientists and activists whose passion and hard work will make the difference.

Notes

Chapter 1: Weeding the Jungle

1. Forster, "Changes in Atmospheric Constituents."
2. Kelly, "With Homeowner in Doghouse."
3. Kaplan, "Moose Use Roads as a Defence Against Bears."
4. Ziegler, *Hawaiian Natural History*, 359.
5. Allen, "Pacific Currents."
6. Ziegler, *Hawaiian Natural History*, 157.
7. Ibid., 195, 198.
8. Ostertag, "Invasive Woody Species Removal," 504.
9. Ibid., 513.
10. Ibid., 511.
11. Ibid., 504.
12. According to Alan Ziegler's authoritative book on Hawaiian ecology, harvesting the best canoe-making koa put selective pressure on the tree over time. "Most *Koa* seen today are multi- rather than single-boled, and these several trunks are usually relatively so thin or crooked that they could hardly have served to form the old medium or large Hawaiian canoes. Roughly 1,500 years of selection of only single-trunked straight individuals has resulted in an essential loss of this morphological variant, and the species has evolved

unto the present multiple-trunked and somewhat spindly tree. It has even been suggested that the cessation about A.D. 1300 of the apparent extensive two-way journeying between the Hawaiian and Society Islands could have been due to the exhaustion of *Koa* massive enough to furnish the large hulls needed for voyaging canoes." Ziegler, *Hawaiian Natural History*, 327.

13. http://www.australianwildlife.org/AWC-Sanctuaries/Scotia-Sanctuary.aspx.
14. Flannery, *Future Eaters*, 86–87.

Chapter 2: The Yellowstone Model

1. Liccardi, personal communication.
2. Schullery, *Searching for Yellowstone*, 8.
3. Ibid., 31–41.
4. Hitt, "Toward an Ecological Sublime," 604–08.
5. Nash, *Wilderness and American Mind*, p. 24.
6. Emerson, *Nature*, 29.
7. Schullery, *Searching for Yellowstone*, 38.
8. Thoreau, *Walden*, 1, 20.
9. Ibid., 162.
10. Ibid., 112.
11. Ibid., 7.
12. Nash, *Wilderness and American Mind*, 91.
13. Ibid., 125.
14. Ibid., 129.
15. Johnson, "John Muir As I Knew Him."
16. Nash, *Wilderness and American Mind*, 127.
17. Muir, *Our National Parks*, 50.
18. Ibid., 61.
19. Ibid., 55.
20. Yosemite was given to the State of California to be run as a park in 1864, before Muir even got there. See Perrottet, "John Muir's Yosemite." But Muir and Robert Underwood Johnson made sure even more of the area was protected as a National Park in 1890.
21. Schullery, *Searching for Yellowstone*, 77.
22. Nash, *Wilderness and American Mind*, 143.
23. Cronon, "Trouble with Wilderness," 479.
24. Turner, *Frontier in American History*, 13–42.
25. Muir, *Our National Parks*, 48.
26. Will, "Nervous Origins," 294.

27. Schullery, *Searching for Yellowstone*, 97.

28. Roosevelt, "American Wilderness," 71.

29. Roosevelt, *Outdoor Pastimes*, 327.

30. Schullery, *Searching for Yellowstone*, 111.

31. Leopold, "Wildlife Management."

32. Schullery, *Searching for Yellowstone*, 168.

33. www.nps.gov/policy/MP2006.pdf.

34. Public Law 88-577 (16 U.S.C. 1131–36), 88th Cong., 2nd Sess., September 3, 1964.

35. Dyke, *Conservation Biology*, 10–21.

36. Ibid., 10; Dowie, *Conservation Refugees*, 11.

37. Quoted in Foreman, *Rewilding North America*, 3.

38. Everglades National Park in Florida was designated a park in 1934, but according to the Parks Service "it took park supporters another 13 years to acquire land and secure funding." See Dyke, *Conservation Biology*, 10; Cronon, *Trouble with Wilderness*, 475–76; http://www.nps.gov/ever/historyculture/con sefforts.htm.

39. Dowie, *Conservation Refugees*, 2, 9–10.

40. Ibid., 6–7.

41. Ibid., 10.

42. Ibid., 11.

43. Ibid., xx–xxii.

44. Ibid., xxvii.

45. Wu, "From Balance of Nature," 441.

46. Marsh, *Man and Nature*, 38.

47. Worster, *Nature's Economy*, 210.

48. Ibid., 214–15.

49. Kingsland, *American Ecology*, 194–96.

50. Ibid., 218.

51. E.g. Herbert Bormann and Gene Likens.

52. Kingsland, *American Ecology*, 224–27.

53. Ibid., 226.

54. Botkin, *Discordant Harmonies*, 33.

55. Ibid., 37–41.

56. Beninca, "Chaos in a Long-term Experiment," 822.

57. Botkin, *Discordant Harmonies*, 9.

58. Lisiecki, "Pliocene-Pleistocene stack."

59. Martin, *Twilight*, 72.

60. Botkin, *Discordant Harmonies*, 62.

61. Davis, *Invasion Ecology*, 71.

62. Botkin, *Discordant Harmonies*, 61.
63. http://toxics.usgs.gov/highlights/drying_deserts.html.
64. Flannery, *Future Eaters*, 76.
65. Ibid., 76–77, 183.
66. Jackson, "Vegetation, Environment and Time," 553.
67. Turner, "Disturbance and Landscape Dynamics," 2838.
68. Leopold, "Wildlife Management."
69. Scullery, *Searching for Yellowstone*, 18.

Chapter 3: The Forest Primeval

1. Okołów, *Białowieża National Park*, 6.
2. Jaroszewicz, "Białowieża Primeval Forest," 3.
3. Ibid., 4.
4. Ibid., 4.
5. Jędrzejewska, "Comrades of Lithuanian Kings," 9–11.
6. Jaroszewicz, "Białowieża Primeval Forest," 6.
7. Pucek, "European Bison," 25.
8. Samojlik, "Hunting Gardens," 56.
9. Schama, *Landscape and Memory*, 65.
10. Pucek, "European Bison," 27–28.
11. Schama, *Landscape and Memory*, 67; Pucek, "European Bison," 29.
12. Schama, *Landscape and Memory*, 67–71.
13. Ibid., 72–73.
14. Pucek, "European Bison," 29.
15. Nash, *Wilderness and American Mind*, 99.
16. Martin, *Twilight*, 1–2, 30–33, 38.
17. Ibid., 1–9.
18. Gilbert, "Pre-Clovis Human Coprolites," 786–89; Dalton, "Oldest American Artefact"; Gill, "Pleistocene Megafaunal Collapse," 1103.
19. Steadman, "Asynchronous Extinction," 11763.
20. Guthrie, "Radiocarbon Evidence," 746–49, Veltre, "Patterns of Faunal Extinction," 47.
21. Guthrie, "Radiocarbon Evidence," 748.
22. Turvey, "Steller's Sea Cow," 94.
23. Martin, *Twilight*, 149.
24. Gill, "Pleistocene Megafaunal Collapse," 1101.
25. Ibid.
26. Johnson, "Megafaunal Decline and Fall," 1073.

27. Martin, *Twilight*, 11–26.
28. Ibid., 52.
29. Ibid., 141.
30. Flannery, *Future Eaters*, 118.
31. Martin, *Twilight*, 30; Flannery, *Future Eaters*, 117–18.
32. Flannery, *Future Eaters*, 115; Miller, "Ecosystem Collapse in Pleistocene Australia."
33. Wade, *Before the Dawn*, 208.
34. Flannery, *Future Eaters*, 55.
35. Ibid., 55–56.
36. Ibid., 56.
37. Ibid., 243.
38. Ibid., 196–97.
39. Ibid., 197.
40. Ibid.
41. Ibid., 245.
42. Ibid., 248–50.
43. Martin, *Twilight*, 42.
44. Ibid., 50, 124.
45. Duncan, "Invasion Ecology."
46. Johnson, "Megafaunal Decline and Fall," 1073.
47. Gill, "Pleistocene Megafaunal Collapse," 1102.
48. Ibid.
49. Smith, "Methane Emissions from Extinct Megafauna."
50. Mann, *1491*, 94.
51. Ibid., 93.
52. Ibid., 44.
53. Ibid., 25, 259.
54. Ibid., 249–51.
55. Ibid., 264–65.
56. Ibid., 304.
57. Woods, "First Century of Reports," 1.
58. Mann, *1491*, 289, 298–99.
59. Ibid., 321.
60. Ibid., 315–318.
61. Turney, "Early Human Occupation at Devil's Lair."
62. Flannery, *Future Eaters*, 217–36.
63. Ibid., 238.
64. Ibid., 14.
65. Worster, *Nature's Economy*, 208–09.

66. Ibid., 218.

67. Ibid., 241.

68. Abbey, *Desert Solitaire*, 305.

69. Farnsworth, *What Does the Desert Say.*

70. Abbey, *Desert Solitaire*, 333–34.

71. Zakin, *Coyotes and Town Dogs*, 144–45.

72. Rosenthal, "New Jungles Prompt a Debate on Rain Forest."

73. Corbyn , "Ecologists Shun Urban Jungle."

74. McKibben, *End of Nature*, 55.

75. Ibid., 40.

76. Ibid., xxii.

Chapter 4: Radical Rewilding

1. Vera, "Large-Scale Nature Development."

2. But they argue that North American ecosystems might not have always functioned this way: "Prior to the megafauna overkill in the Pleistocene, the role of large carnivores as top-down regulators may not have been as important as it is today. At that time in North America, huge herbivores (including mammoths, mastodons, giant camels, and giant ground sloths) dominated many ecosystems, and probably controlled the distribution and abundance of many plant species and habitat types, as megaherbivores such as elephants still do in Africa. Moreover, highly social, migratory ungulates, such as bison, grazed and browsed in huge numbers. Carnivores were probably not effective regulators of the megaherbivores and the migratory ungulates. Today, however, top predators appear to regulate many ecosystems." Soulé, "Rewilding and Biodiversity," 6.

3. Ibid., 9.

4. Wills, "Brighty, Donkeys and Conservation in the Grand Canyon," 113.

5. Martin, *Twilight*, 188–92.

6. Ibid., 193–94.

7. Steadman, "Late Quaternary Extinction."

8. Donlan, "Re-wilding North America."

9. Ibid.

10. Barlow, *Ghosts of Evolution.*

11. Ibid., 41–45.

12. Rubenstein, "Pleistocene Park."

13. Other proxies are already out there as well. Some were introduced with surprisingly little controversy. In Australia, the disappearance of large herbivores

some 50,000 years ago led to the disappearance of many species of dung beetles. This created a problem when European colonists introduced livestock into the country. The remaining native dung beetle species just couldn't cope with the influx of poop, and the built-up manure bred an intolerable number of flies. So in the 1960s the Australian government began introducing exotic dung beetle species from Africa and Europe. In 2001 the scientist behind the project got a Medal of the Order of Australia.

14. Seddon, "Guidelines for Subspecific Substitutions."
15. http://www.arabian-oryx.gov.sa/en/mahazat.html.
16. Vera, "Large-Scale Nature Development."
17. Hodder, *Can the Pre-Neolithic Provide*, 6.
18. Ibid., 7.
19. Ibid., 7–8.

Chapter 5: Assisted Migration

1. Pongratz, "Effects of Anthropogenic Land Cover Change."
2. Fang, "Climatic Limits."
3. Wilson, "Changes to Elevational Limits."
4. Gehrig-Fasel, "Tree Line Shifts in the Swiss Alps."
5. Harsch, "Are Treelines Advancing?"
6. Parmesan, "Poleward Shifts in Geographical Ranges."
7. Parmesan, "Globally Coherent Fingerprint."
8. Nelson, *Shrubs and Woody Vines*, 391.
9. Schwartz, "Conservationists Should Not Move," 78.
10. McLachlan, "Framework for Debate."
11. Hoegh-Guldberg, "Assisted Colonization."
12. Van der Veken, "Garden Plants Get a Head Start."
13. "Prairie in the City."
14. Hamann, "Potential Effects of Climate Change."
15. http://www.for.gov.bc.ca/hfp/mountain_pine_beetle/facts.htm.
16. Riccardi, "Assisted Colonization."

Chapter 6: Learning to Love Exotic Species

1. Galbreath, "Tale of Lighthouse-keeper's Cat," 199.
2. Flannery, *Future Eaters*, 61–62.
3. Fox, "Using Exotics as Temporary Habitat."

4. Pilcher, "Crazy Ants to Meet Their Doom."

5. Davis, *Invasion Biology*, 104–05.

6. Kareiva and Marvier, *Conservation Science*.

7. Rodgers, in press.

8. http://www.dwaf.gov.za/wfw/default.asp.

9. http://www.invasivespeciesinfo.gov/laws/execorder.shtml.

10. Pimentel, "Economic and Environmental Threats," 14.

11. No doubt it was. But sometimes invasive species eradicators do think more about job security than the ideological mission they are charged with. One Australian ecologist told me, "The guys charged with eradicating pigs from Western Australia's jarrah forest regularly captured pigs from elsewhere to restock the forest when capture rates were too low."

12. Davis, *Invasion Biology*, 8–9.

13. Ibid., 7.

14. Elton, *Ecology of Invasions*, 31.

15. Ibid., 21–22, 116–17, quote on 117.

16. Ibid., 21.

17. Davis, *Invasion Biology*, 17–21.

18. Elton, *Ecology of Invasions*, 51.

19. Davis, *Invasion Biology*, 10.

20. Wilcove, "Quantifying Threats," 609.

21. Sax, "Species Invasions Exceed Extinctions," 766–83.

22. Unless you want to count humans as an introduced species to many parts of the world.

23. Davis, *Invasion Biology*, 115.

24. Ibid., 191.

25. Ibid., 185.

26. Ibid., 48.

27. Ibid., 40–41.

28. Castilla, "Invasion of a Rocky Intertidal Shore," 8517–524.

29. Davis, *Invasion Biology*, 120.

30. Kaplan, "Alien Birds."

31. Complicating the story is the fact that in the last interglacial before this one, Turkey oaks *were* found in Britain. So you could argue that they are native anyway. Hobbs, "Novel Ecosystems," 602.

32. Stromberg, "Changing Perceptions," 179.

33. Davis, *Invasion Biology*, 78.

34. http://www.jncc.gov.uk/page-1680.

35. http://www.nwcb.wa.gov/weed_info/Written_findings/Spartina_anglica.html.

36. Henderson, "Control and Eradication," 388.

37. http://www.rspb.org.uk/ourwork/policy/species/nonnative/ruddyducks.asp.

38. Henderson, "Control and Eradication," 388.

39. The dingo has become a sort of accidental proxy for the extinct top predators of Australia. One study found that dingoes now maintain the diversity of Australian plants and small mammals as a keystone species just as Soulé and Noss believe top predators maintain diversity in North America. The researchers found that areas where dingoes were excluded by fences had far fewer of the cute-and-furries we met at Scotia. The researchers suggest that the dingoes keep introduced foxes in check, foxes that would otherwise eat the little marsupials for lunch. Dingo-free areas also had less grass cover, presumably because they weren't there to curb the herbivory of the kangaroos. The researchers conclude that "the dingo's functional role as a top predator is ecologically more significant than the classification of this species as an undesirable alien pest." Letnic, "Keystone Effects of an Alien Top-Predator." See also "Dingo Protected in Victoria."

40. Davis, *Invasion Biology*, 21.

41. Martin, *Twilight*, 111.

42. Schlaepfer, "Potential Conservation Value."

43. Ibid.

44. Ewel, "Place for Alien Species."

45. Ibid.

46. Schlaepfer, "Potential Conservation Value."

Chapter 7: Novel Ecosystems

1. Wilkinson, "Parable of Green Mountain."

2. The term *novel ecosystem* seems to imply that all the ecosystems that humans didn't alter are nonnovel. But as we know, all the planet's ecosystems are changing all the time. Every ecosystem is in some sense novel, if looked at over a long enough time span. So, oddly, the term tends to perpetuate the very distinction that gave these systems such a bad name in the first place—it tends to treat human-influenced systems as qualitatively different somehow from systems not influenced by humans. For this reason, some researchers do not like the term, but it seems to be here to stay.

3. *Ecosystem function* is an oft-used but rather nebulous term. It seems to mean something like "what ecosystems do," from making more soil with leaf litter, to making biomass out of sunlight, to moving nitrogen from the atmosphere into plants. Unfortunately, it often seems a bit circularly defined. Proper ecosystem function seems to be defined as either whatever the ecosystem was

doing before humans messed it up or "what we want an ecosystem to be doing." Any deviation, even making *more* soil, *more* biomass, or moving *more* nutrients than before, can then be described as "degraded function."

4. Worster, *Nature's Economy*, 239–40.
5. Quoted ibid., 240.
6. Elton, *Ecology of Invasions*, 155.
7. http://www.hort.purdue.edu/newcrop/morton/rose_apple.html.
8. Uchida, "Recurrent Epiphytotic."
9. Davis, *Invasion Biology*, 69.
10. Ibid., 69.
11. Elton, *Ecology of Invasions*, 115.
12. I've observed that while introgression of genes into native plants from hybridizing with an introduced species is often despised as "pollution," genetic changes made in response to the presence of introduced species are celebrated as the plucky native species "fighting back." On some level, though, both are genetic changes that would not have taken place in the absence of the human-mediated introduction and should logically therefore be equally abhorred—that is, if all changes that flow from human action are to be regretted.
13. Davis, *Invasion Biology*, 70.
14. Ibid., 117.
15. Ellis, "Putting People in Map," 441.
16. Ibid., 439.
17. Ibid., 441–42.
18. Ellis, "Anthropogenic Transformation."
19. Mascaro, "Limited Native Plant Regeneration."

Chapter 8: Designer Ecosystems

1. Walter, "Natural Streams."
2. Palmer, "Restoration of Ecosystems Services," 575.
3. Palmer, "Reforming Watershed Restoration."
4. Mark Davis's textbook on invasion biology recounts an experiment that underscores the difficulty of total rat eradication. Scientists released a single Norway rat on a twenty-two-acre island. "It took 18 weeks of concerted trapping efforts to capture this individual, even though the animal could be located via radio telemetry for the first 10 weeks, and nine different trapping and detection methods were used, including trained dogs, live traps, snap traps, buried traps, peanut butter bait, and poison bait." Davis, *Invasion Biology*, 145.

5. Jackson, "Restoration Ecology," 568.

6. Hobbs, "Novel Ecosystems," 601.

7. Ibid., 603.

8. Ibid., 603.

9. Nash, *Wilderness and American Mind*, 241.

10. Ibid., 380.

11. Ibid., 380–81.

12. Ibid., 381.

13. Quoted ibid., 242.

Chapter 9: Conservation Everywhere

1. http://boeing.mediaroom.com/index.php?s=43&item=1196.

2. Gearino, "Deal Reached."

3. Sutherland, "Blueprint for Countryside."

4. Ibid.

5. http://www.nrcs.usda.gov/programs/eqip/index.html#intro.

6. Hodgson, "Comparing Organic Farming."

7. Perfecto, "Agroecological Matrix," 5787.

8. Powell. "New Agtivist."

9. Despommier, *Vertical Farm*.

10. Lundholm, "Habitat Analogues."

11. Ibid., 971.

12. Ibid.

13. Leopold, *Sand County Almanac*, 48.

14. Elton, *Ecology of Invasions*, 158.

15. Rosenzweig, *Win-win Ecology*, 7.

16. Matteson, "Distribution of Floral Resources."

17. Williams, "Picture Perfect."

18. Brown, "Me and My Garden."

19. Weller, "Interactions of Socioeconomic Patterns."

Chapter 10: A Menu of New Goals

1. Leopold, *Sand County Almanac*, 204.

2. Ibid., viii.

3. Brennan, "Environmental Ethics."

4. Leopold, *Sand County Almanac*, 204.

5. http://www.worldwildlife.org/ogc/species_category.cfm.

6. Wasser, "Ivory Trail," 72.

7. Leopold, *Sand County Almanac*, 210.

8. Thompson, "Do We Need Pandas," 98–121.

9. Loomis, "Demand for and Supply of Wilderness," 374.

10. Leopold, *Sand County Almanac*, 176.

11. Ziegler, *Hawaiian Natural History*, 334.

BIBLIOGRAPHY

Abbey, Edward. *Desert Solitaire*. New York: Ballantine Books, 1968.

Allen, William. "Pacific Currents: Lush Hawaii Is a Zone of Mass Extinction." *Seattle Post-Intelligencer*, October 9, 2000.

Barlow, Connie C. *The Ghosts of Evolution: Nonsensical Fruit, Missing Partners, and Other Ecological Anachronisms*. New York: Basic Books, 2000.

Barlow, Connie, and Paul Martin. "Bring *Torreya taxifolia* North—Now." *Wild Earth*, Fall/Winter 2004–5, 72–78.

Barnosky, Anthony D. *Heatstroke: Nature in an Age of Global Warming*. Washington, D.C.: Island Press/Shearwater Books, 2009.

Beninca, Elisa, Jef Huisman, Reinhard Heerkloss, Klaus D. Johnk, Pedro Branco, Egbert H. Van Nes, Marten Scheffer, and Stephen P. Ellner. "Chaos in a Long-term Experiment with a Plankton Community." *Nature* 451, no. 7180 (2008): 822–25.

Bernhardt, E. S., M. A. Palmer, J. D. Allan, G. Alexander, K. Barnas, S. Brooks, J. Carr, et al. "Synthesizing U.S. River Restoration Efforts." *Science* 308, no. 5722 (April 29, 2005): 636–37.

Beschta, Robert L., and William J. Ripple. "Large Predators and Trophic Cascades in Terrestrial Ecosystems of the Western United States." *Biological Conservation* 142, no. 11, (November 2009): 2401–14.

Botkin, Daniel B. *Discordant Harmonies: A New Ecology for the Twenty-first Century.* New York and Oxford: Oxford University Press, 1990.

Brennan, Andrew, and Yeuk-Sze Lo. "Environmental Ethics." In *The Stanford Encyclopedia of Philosophy*, Winter 2009 ed., edited by Edward N. Zalta. http://plato.stanford.edu/archives/win2009/entries/ethics-environmental/.

Brown, Jonathan. "Me and My Garden: How Jennifer Owen Became an Unlikely Champion of British Wildlife." *Independent*, November 12, 2010.

Cabin, Robert J. "Science-Driven Restoration: A Square Grid on a Round Earth?" *Restoration Ecology* 15, no. 1 (March 2007): 1–7.

Campbell, L. M., N. J. Gray, E. L. Hazen, and J. M. Shackeroff. "Beyond Baselines: Rethinking Priorities for Ocean Conservation." *Ecology and Society* 14, no. 1 (2009): 14. http://www.ecologyandsociety.org/vol14/iss1/art14/.

Castilla, Juan Carlos, Ricardo Guiñez, Andrés U. Caro, and Verónica Ortiz. "Invasion of a Rocky Intertidal Shore by the Tunicate Pyura Praeputialis in the Bay of Antofagasta, Chile." *Proceedings of the National Academy of Sciences of the United States of America* 101, no. 23 (June 8, 2004): 8517–24.

Chew, Matthew. "The Monstering of Tamarisk: How Scientists Made a Plant into a Problem." *Journal of the History of Biology*, 42 (2009): 231–66.

"Conservation: Prairie in the City." *Economist*, April 8, 2009, http://www.economist.com/world/unitedstates/displayStory.cfm?story_id=13446692&source=login_payBarrier.

Corbyn, Zoë. "Ecologists Shun the Urban Jungle." *Nature*, July 16, 2010, doi:10.1038/news.2010.359.

Cressey, Daniel. "Failure Is Certainly an Option." *Nature*, May 29, 2009. doi:10.1038/news.2009.511; http://www.nature.com/news/2009/090529/full/news.2009.511.html.

Cronon, William. "The Trouble with Wilderness, or, Getting Back to the Wrong Nature." In *The Great New Wilderness Debate*, edited by J. Baird Callicott and Michael P. Nelson. Athens: University of Georgia Press, 1998.

Dalton, Rex. "Oldest American Artefact Unearthed." *Nature News*, November 5, 2009, doi:10.1038/news.2009.1058.

Davis, Mark. *Invasion Biology*. Oxford: Oxford University Press, 2009.

Despommier, Dickson. *The Vertical Farm*. New York: Thomas Dunne Books, 2010.

"Dingo protected in Victoria." Australian Broadcasting Company, October 24, 2008, http://www.abc.net.au/news/stories/2008/10/24/2400546.htm.

Donlan, C. J., et al. "Re-wilding North America." *Nature* 436 (2005): 913–14.

Dowie, Mark. *Conservation Refugees: The Hundred-Year Conflict between Global Conservation and Native Peoples*. Cambridge and London: MIT Press, 2009.

Duncan, Richard. "Invasion Ecology." Presented at the International Congress of Ecology in Brisbane, Australia, on August 19, 2009.

Dyke, Fred Van. *Conservation Biology*. Dordrecht, Netherlands: Springer, 2008.

Easterling, W. E., P. K. Aggarwal, P. Batima, K. M. Brander, L. Erda, S. M. Howden, A. Kirilenko, J. Morton, J.-F. Soussana, J. Schmidhuber, and F. N. Tubiello. "Food, Fibre and Forest Products." *Climate Change 2007: Impacts, Adaptation and Vulnerability. Contribution of Working Group II to the Fourth Assessment Report of the Intergovernmental Panel on Climate Change*, edited by M. L. Parry, O. F. Canziani, J. P. Palutikof, P. J. van der Linden, and C. E. Hanson. Cambridge, UK: Cambridge University Press, 273–313.

Ellis, Erle C., and Navin Ramankutty. "Putting People in the Map: Anthropogenic Biomes of the World." *Frontiers in Ecology and the Environment* 6, no. 8 (2008): 439–47, doi: 10.1890/070062.

Ellis, Erle, K. K. Goldewijk, S. Siebert, D. Lightman, N. Ramankutty. "Anthropogenic Transformation of the Biomes, 1700 to 2000." *Global Ecology and Biogeography*. 19, no. 5 (2010): 589–606, doi:10.1111/j.1466-8238.2010.00540.x.

Elton, Charles. *The Ecology of Invasions by Animals and Plants*. 1958; Chicago: University of Chicago Press, 2000.

Emerson, Ralph Waldo. Selections from *Nature*. In *The Great New Wilderness Debate*, edited by J. Baird Callicott and Michael P. Nelson. Athens: University of Georgia Press, 1998.

Ewel, John J., and Francis E. Putz. "A Place for Alien Species in Ecosystem Restoration." *Frontiers in Ecology and the Environment* 2 (2004): 354–60, doi:10.1890/1540-9295(2004)002[0354:APFASI]2.0.CO;2.

Fang, Jingyun, and M. J. Lechowicz. "Climatic Limits for the Present Distribution of Beech (Fagus L.) Species in the world." *Journal of Biogeography* 33 (2006): 1804–19.

Farnsworth, John. "What Does the Desert Say? A Rhetorical Analysis of *Desert Solitaire*." *Interdisciplinary Literary Studies: A Journal of Criticism and Theory* 12, no. 1 (2010): 105–21.

Flannery, Timothy. *The Future Eaters: An Ecological History of the Australasian Lands and People*. Sydney: Reed New Holland, 1994.

Foreman, Dave. *Rewilding North America: A Vision for Conservation in the 21st Century*. Washington, D.C.: Island Press, 2004.

Forster, P., V. Ramaswamy, P. Artaxo, T. Berntsen, R. Betts, D. W. Fahey, J. Haywood, J. Lean, D. C. Lowe, G. Myhre, J. Nganga, R. Prinn, G. Raga, M. Schulz, and R. Van Dorland. "Changes in Atmospheric Constituents and in Radiative Forcing." In *Climate Change 2007: The Physical Science Basis. Contribution of Working Group I to the Fourth Assessment Report of the Intergovernmental Panel on Climate Change*, edited by S. Solomon, D. Qin, M. Manning, Z. Chen, M. Marquis, K. B. Averyt, M. Tignor, and H. L. Miller. New York: Cambridge University Press, 2007.

Fox, Douglas. "Using Exotics as Temporary Habitat: An Accidental Experiment on Rodrigues Island." *Conservation* 4, no. 1 (2003).

Fox-Dobbs, Kena, Thomas A. Stidham, Gabriel J. Bowen, Steven D. Emslie, and Paul L. Koch. "Dietary Controls on Extinction Versus Survival Among Avian Megafauna in the Late Pleistocene." *Geology* 34, no. 8 (August 1, 2006): 685–88.

Fritts, T. H., and D. Leasman-Tanner. "The Brown Treesnake on Guam: How the Arrival of One Invasive Species Damaged the Ecology, Commerce, Electrical Systems, and Human Health on Guam: A Comprehensive Information Source." 2001. http://www.fort.usgs.gov/resources/education/bts/bts_home .asp.

Galbreath, Ross, and Derek Brown. "The Tale of the Lighthouse-keeper's Cat: Discovery and Extinction of the Stephens Island Wren (*Traversia lyalli*)." *Notornis* 51 (2004): 193–200.

Gearino, Jeff. "Deal Reached On Scenic Wyo. Ranch Conservation." *Casper Star-Tribune*, November 8, 2010.

Gehrig-Fasel, Jacqueline, Antoine Guisan, and Niklaus E. Zimmermann. "Tree Line Shifts in the Swiss Alps: Climate Change or Land Abandonment?" *Journal of Vegetation Science* 18, no. 4 (2007): 571–82.

Gilbert, M. Thomas P., Dennis L. Jenkins, Anders Gotherstrom, Nuria Naveran, Juan J. Sanchez, Michael Hofreiter, Philip Francis Thomsen, et al. "DNA from Pre-Clovis Human Coprolites in Oregon, North America." *Science* 320, no. 5877 (May 9, 2008): 786–89.

Gill, Jacquelyn L., John W. Williams, Stephen T. Jackson, Katherine B. Lininger, and Guy S. Robinson. "Pleistocene Megafaunal Collapse, Novel Plant Communities, and Enhanced Fire Regimes in North America." *Science* 326, no. 5956 (November 20, 2009): 1100–03.

Grayson, Donald K., and David J. Meltzer, "A Requiem for North American Overkill." *Journal of Archaeological Science* 30 (2003): 585–93.

Guha, Ramachandra. "Radical American Environmentalism and Wilderness Preservation: A Third World Critique." In *The Great New Wilderness Debate*, edited by J. Baird Callicott and Michael P. Nelson. Athens: University of Georgia Press, 1998.

Guthrie, Dale R. "Radiocarbon Evidence of Mid-Holocene Mammoths Stranded on an Alaskan Bering Sea island." *Nature* 429, no. 6993 (June 17, 2004): 746–49.

Hamann, Andreas, and Tongli Wang. "Potential Effects of Climate Change on Ecosystem and Tree Species Distribution in British Columbia." *Ecology* 87 (2006): 2773–786.

Harsch, Melanie, Philip Hulme, Matt McGlone, and Richard Duncan. "Are Treelines Advancing? A Global Meta-analysis of Treeline Response to Climate Warming." *Ecology Letters* 12 (2009): 1–10.

Henderson, Iain, and Peter Robertson. "Control and Eradication of the North American Ruddy Duck in Europe." In *Managing Vertebrate Invasive Species: Proceedings of an International Symposium*, edited by G. W. Witmer, W. C. Pitt, and K. A. Fagerstone. Fort Collins, Colo.: National Wildlife Research Center, 2007.

Hitt, Christopher. "Toward an Ecological Sublime." *New Literary History* 30, no. 3 (1999): 603–23.

Hobbs, Richard, Salvatore Arico, James Aronson, Jill S. Baron, Peter Bridgewater, Viki A. Cramer, Paul R. Epstein, John J. Ewel, Carlos A. Klink, Ariel E. Lugo, David Norton, Dennis Ojima, David M. Richardson, Eric W. Sanderson, Fernando Valladares, Montserrat Vilà, Regino Zamora, and Martin Zobel. "Novel Ecosystems: Theoretical and Management Aspects of the New Ecological World Order." *Global Ecology and Biogeography* 15 (2006): 1–7.

Hobbs, Richard, Eric Higgs, and James Harris. "Novel Ecosystems: Implications for Conservation and Restoration." *Trends in Ecology and Evolution* 24, no.11 (November 2009): 599–605.

Hodder, Kathy H., Paul C. Buckland, Keith J. Kirby, and James M. Bullock. "Can the Pre-Neolithic Provide Suitable Models for Re-wilding the Landscape in Britain?" *British Wildlife* (June 2009): 4–15.

Hodgson, Jenny, William E. Kunin, Chris D. Thomas, Tim G. Benton, and Doreen Gabriel. "Comparing Organic Farming and Land Sparing: Optimizing Yield and Butterfly Populations at a Landscape Scale." *Ecology Letters* 13, no. 11 (2010): 1358–1367. Doi:10.1111/j.1461-0248.2010.01528.x.

Hoegh-Guldberg, O., et al. "Assisted Colonization and Rapid Climate Change." *Science* 321 (2008): 345–46.

Jackson, Stephen T. "Vegetation, Environment, and Time: The Origination and Termination of Ecosystems." *Journal of Vegetation Science* 17 (2006): 549–57.

Jackson, Stephen, and Richard Hobbs. "Ecological Restoration in the Light of Ecological History." *Science* 325 (2009).

Jaroszewicz, Bogdan. "Białowieża Primeval Forest—A Treasure and a Challenge." In *Essays on Mammals of Białowieża Forest*, edited by Bogumiła Jędrzejewska and Jan Marek Wójcik. Białowieża: Mammal Research Institute, Polish Academy of Sciences, 2004.

Jędrzejewska, Bogumiła, and Tomasz Samojlik. "Comrades of Lithuanian Kings" In *Conservation and Hunting: Białowieża Forest in the Time of Kings*, edited by Tomasz Samojlik. Białowieża: Mammal Research Institute, Polish Academy of Sciences, 2005.

Johnson, Christopher N. "Anthropology: The Remaking of Australia's Ecology." *Science* 309, no. 5732 (July 8, 2005): 255–56.

————. "Megafaunal Decline and Fall." *Science* 326, no. 5956 (November 20, 2009): 1072–73.

Johnson, Robert Underwood. "John Muir As I Knew Him." *Sierra Club Bulletin* 10, no. 1 (January 1916), http://www.sierraclub.org/john_muir_exhibit/frameindex.html?http://www.sierraclub.org/john_muir_exhibit/life/johnson_tribute_scb_1916.html) November 4, 2009.

Jones, H. P., and O. J. Schmitz "Rapid Recovery of Damaged Ecosystems." *PLoS ONE* 4, no. 5 e5653, doi:10.1371/journal.pone.0005653(2009).

Kaplan, Mark. "Alien Birds May Be Last Hope for Hawaiian Plants." *Nature News*, September 28, 2007, doi:10.1038/news070924-12, http://www.nature.com/news/2007/070924/full/news070924-12.html.

————. "Moose Use Roads as a Defence Against Bears." *Nature News*, October 10, 2007, doi:10.1038/news.2007.155, http://www.nature.com/news/2007/071010/full/news.2007.155.html.

Kareiva, Peter, and Michelle Marvier. *Conservation Science: Balancing the Needs of People and Nature.* Greenwood Village, Colo.: Roberts and Company, 2011.

Kelly, David. "With Homeowner in Doghouse, Bobcats Move In." *Los Angeles Times*, September 5, 2008, http://www.latimes.com/news/local/la-me-bobcats5-2008sep05,0,2286826.story.

Kingsland, Sharon E. *The Evolution of American Ecology, 1890–2000.* Baltimore: Johns Hopkins University Press, 2005.

Ladle, Richard, and Lindsey Gillson. "The (Im)balance of Nature: A Public Perception Time-Lag?" *Public Understanding of Science* 18, no. 2 (2008): 229–42.

Leopold, A. Starker, Stanley A. Cain, Clarence M Cottam, Ira N. Gabrielson, and Thomas L. Kimball. "Wildlife Management in the National Parks." *Transactions of the North American Wildlife and Natural Resources Conference* 28 (1963): 28–45.

Leopold, Aldo. *A Sand County Almanac, and Sketches Here and There.* New York and Oxford: Oxford University Press, 1948.

Letnic, Mike, Freya Koch, Chris Gordon, Mathew S. Crowther, and Christopher R. Dickman. "Keystone Effects of an Alien Top-Predator Stem Extinctions of Native Mammals." *Proceedings of the Royal Society B: Biological Sciences* 276 (2009): 3249–56.

Ley, Ruth, Daniel Peterson, and Jeffery Gordon. "Ecological and Evolutionary Forces Shaping Microbial Diversity in the Human Intestine." *Cell* 124 (February 24, 2006): 837–48, doi 10.1016/j.cell.2006.02.017.

Liccardi, Joe. Personal communication. October 22, 2010.

Lichfield, John. "Guess Who's Coming for Dinner? Wolf Tracks Spotted in Central France." *Independent*, January 29, 2009.

Lisiecki, Lorraine E., and Maureen E. Raymo. "A Pliocene-Pleistocene Stack of 57 Globally Distributed Benthic D18O Records." *Paleoceanography* 20 (2005), PA1003, doi:10.1029/2004PA001071.

Loomis, J., K. Bonetti, and C. Echohawk. "Demand for and Supply of Wilderness." In H. Ken Cordell et al., *Outdoor Recreation in American Life: A National Assessment of Demand and Supply Trends*. Champaign, Ill.: Sagamore, 1999.

Lundholm, Jeremy T., and Paul J. Richardson. "Habitat Analogues for Reconciliation Ecology in Urban and Industrial Environments." *Journal of Applied Ecology* 47 (2010): 966–75.

Mann, Charles. *1491*. New York: Alfred A. Knopf, 2005.

Marris, Emma "Black Is the New Green." *Nature* 442 (August 10, 2006): 624–26, doi:10.1038/442624a.

———. "The Species and the Specious." *Nature* 446 (March 15, 2007): 250–53, doi:10.1038/446250.

———. "What to Let Go." *Nature* 450 (2007): 152–55, doi:10.1038/450152a.

———. "A Garden for All Climates." *Nature* 450 (2007): 937–39, doi:10.1038/450937a.

———. "What Does a Natural Stream Look Like?" *Nature News*, January 17, 2008, doi:10.1038/news.2008.448.

———. "In the Heart of the Wood." *Nature* 455 (2008): 277–80, doi:10.1038/455277a.

———. "The End of the Invasion?" *Nature* 459 (May 21, 2009): 327–28, doi:10.1038/459327a.

———. "Ragamuffin Earth." *Nature* 460 (2009): 450–53, doi:10.1038/460450a.

———. "Putting a Price on Nature." *Nature* 462 (2009): 270–71, doi:10.1038/462270a.

Marsh, George Perkins. *Man and Nature*. Cambridge, Mass.: Belknap Press of Harvard University Press, 1965.

Martin, Paul. *Twilight of the Mammoths*. Berkeley and Los Angeles: University of California Press, 2005.

Mascaro, J., et al. "Limited Native Plant Regeneration in Novel, Exotic-dominated Forests on Hawai'," *Forest Ecology and Management* 256 (2008): 593–606.

Matteson, Kevin C., and Sarah N. Dougher. "Distribution of Floral Resources and Pollinators Across an Urbanized Landscape." Presented at the Ecological Society of America meeting in Albuquerque, N.M., August 3, 2009.

McKibben, Bill. *The End of Nature*. New York: Random House, 2006.

McLachlan, J. S., J. J. Hellmann, and M. W. Schwartz. "A Framework for Debate of Assisted Migration in an Era of Climate Change." *Conservation Biology* 21 (2007): 297–302.

Miller, Gifford H., Marilyn L. Fogel, John W. Magee, Michael K. Gagan, Simon

J. Clarke, and Beverly J. Johnson. "Ecosystem Collapse in Pleistocene Australia and a Human Role in Megafaunal Extinction." *Science* 309, no. 5732 (July 8, 2005): 287–90.

Mitigation of Impacts to Fish and Wildlife Habitat: Estimating Costs and Identifying Opportunities. Washington, D.C.: Environmental Law Institute, 2007.

Muir, John. Selections from *Our National Parks.* In *The Great New Wilderness Debate,* edited by J. Baird Callicott and Michael P. Nelson. Athens: University of Georgia Press, 1998.

Nash, Roderick Frazier. *Wilderness and the American Mind.* New Haven and London: Yale University Press, 2001.

Nelson, G. *The Shrubs and Woody Vines of Florida.* Sarasota, Fla.: Pineapple Press, 1996.

O'Donnell, Stephanie, et al. "Conditioned Taste Aversion Enhances the Survival of an Endangered Predator Imperilled by a Toxic Invader." *Journal of Applied Ecology* (2010), doi: 10.1111/j.1365-2664.2010.01802.x.

Oelschlaeger, Max. *The Idea of Wilderness: From Prehistory to the Age of Ecology.* New Haven, Conn.: Yale University Press, 1991.

Okołów, Czesław, and Grzegorz Okołów. *Białowieża National Park,* translated by Wojciech Kasprzak. Warsaw: Multico Publishing House, 2005.

Ostertag, Rebecca, Susan Cordell, Jené Michaud, Colleen Cole, Jodie R. Schulten, Keiko M. Publico, and Jaime H. Enoka. "Ecosystem and Restoration Consequences of Invasive Woody Species Removal in Hawaiian Lowland Wet Forest." *Ecosystems* 12 (2009): 503–15.

Overpeck, J., C. Whitlock, and B. Huntley. "Terrestrial Biosphere Dynamics in the Climate System: Past and Future." *American Geophysical Union, Fall Meeting Abstracts* 62 (2002).

Palmer, Margaret. "Reforming Watershed Restoration: Science in Need of Application and Applications in Need of Science" *Estuaries and Coasts* 32, no. 1 (2008): 1–17, doi 10.1007/s12237-008-9129-5.

Palmer, Margaret, and Solange Filoso. "Restoration of Ecosystems Services for Environmental Markets." *Science* 325, no. 5940 (2009): 575–76.

Palmer, Margaret, H. Menninger, and E. S. Benhardt. "River Restoration, Habitat Heterogeneity, and Biodiversity: A Failure of Theory or Practice?" *Freshwater Biology* 55, suppl. 1 (2009): 205–22, doi: 10.1111/j.1365-2427.2009.02372.x.

Parmesan, C., et al. "Poleward Shifts in Geographical Ranges of Butterfly Species Associated with Regional Warming." *Nature* 399 (1999): 579–83.

Parmesan, C., and G. Yohe. "A Globally Coherent Fingerprint of Climate Change Impacts Across Natural Systems." *Nature* 421 (2003): 37–42.

Perfecto, Ivette, and John Vandermeer. "The Agroecological Matrix as Alternative to the Land-sparing/Agriculture Intensification Model." *Proceedings of the National Academy of Sciences* 107, no. 13 (March 30, 2010): 5786–91.

Perrottet, Tony. "John Muir's Yosemite" *Smithsonian*, July 2008.

Peterken, George F. *Natural Woodland: Ecology and Conservation in Northern Temperate Regions*. Cambridge; Mass.: Cambridge University Press, 1996.

Pilcher, Helen. "Crazy Ants to Meet Their Doom," *Nature News* (July 16, 2004), doi:10.1038/news040712–18.

Pimentel, D., S. McNair, J. Janecka, J. Wightman, C. Simmonds, C. O'Connell, E. Wong, L. Russel, J. Zern, T. Aquino, and T. Tsomondo. "Economic and Environmental Threats of Alien Plant, Animal, and Microbe Invasions." *Agriculture, Ecosystems and Environment* 84 (2001): 1–20.

Pongratz, J., C. H. Reick, T. Raddatz, and M. Claussen. "Effects of Anthropogenic Land Cover Change on the Carbon Cycle of the Last Millennium." *Global Biogeochemical Cycles* 23 (2009), doi: 10.1029/2009GB003488.

Powell, Bonnie Azab. "The New Agtivist: Gene Fredericks Is Thinking Inside the City's Big Box." *Grist* (September 1, 2010).

Pucek, Zdzisław. "European Bison—History of a Flagship Species." In *Essays on Mammals of Białowieża Forest*, edited by Bogumiła Jędrzejewska, and Jan Marek Wójcik. Białowieża: Mammal Research Institute, Polish Academy of Sciences, 2004.

Rehfeldt, Gerald, Nicholas L. Crookston, Marcus V. Warwell, and Jeffrey S. Evans. "Empirical Analyses of Plant-climate Relationships for the Western United States." *International Journal of Plant Science* 167, no. 6 (2006): 1123–50.

Relethford, J. H. "Genetic Evidence and the Modern Human Origins Debate." *Heredity* 100, no. 6 (March 5, 2008): 555–63.

Ricciardi, Anthony, and Daniel Simberloff. "Assisted Colonization Is Not a Viable Conservation Strategy." *Trends in Ecology and Evolution* 24, no. 5 (March 25, 2009): 248–53.

Ripple, William J., and Robert L. Beschta. "Wolves and the Ecology of Fear: Can Predation Risk Structure Ecosystems?" *BioScience* 54, no. 8 (2004): 755–66.

Rogers, Haldre. ms in press.

Romme, William H. "Fire and Landscape Diversity in Subalpine Forests of Yellowstone National Park." *Ecological Monographs* 52, no. 2 (June 1982): 199–221.

Roosevelt, Theodore. *Outdoor Pastimes of an American Hunter*. New York: C. Scribner's Sons, 1925.

———. "The American Wilderness." In *The Great New Wilderness Debate*, edited by J. Baird Callicott and Michael P. Nelson. Athens: University of Georgia Press, 1998.

Rosenthal, Elisabeth. "New Jungles Prompt a Debate on Rain Forest." *New York Times*, January 30, 2009.

Rosenzweig, Michael. *Win-win Ecology*. Oxford: Oxford University Press, 2003.

Rubenstein, D. R., D. I. Rubenstein, P. W. Sherman, and T. A. Gavin. "Pleistocene Park: Does Re-wilding North America Represent Sound Conservation for the 21st Century?" *Biological Conservation* 132 (2006): 232–38.

Samojlik, Tomasz. "Stanisław August Poniatowski's Hunting Gardens." In *Conservation and Hunting: Białowieża Forest in the Time of Kings*, edited by Tomasz Samojlik. Białowieża: Mammal Research Institute, Polish Academy of Sciences, 2005.

Sax, Dov, Steven Gaines, and James Brown. "Species Invasions Exceed Extinctions on Islands Worldwide: A Comparative Study of Plants and Birds." *American Naturalist* 160 (2002): 766–83.

Schama, Simon. *Landscape and Memory*. New York: Alfred S. Knopf, 1995.

Schlaepfer, Martin A., Dov F. Sax, and Julian D. Olden. "The Potential Conservation Value of Non-native Species." In press. *Conservation Biology* (early view, 2011), doi: 10.1111/j.1523-1739.2010.01646.x.

Schullery, Paul. *Searching for Yellowstone*. Helena: Montana Historical Society Press, 2004.

Schwartz, Mark. "Conservationists Should Not Move *Torreya taxifolia*." *Wild Earth* (Fall/Winter 2004–05): 73–79.

Seddon, Philip J., and Pritpal S. Soorae. "Guidelines for Subspecific Substitutions in Wildlife Restoration Projects." *Conservation Biology* 13, no. 1 (1999): 177–84, doi:10.1046/j.1523-1739.1999.97414.x.

Smith, Felisa A., Scott M. Elliott, and S. Kathleen Lyons. "Methane Emissions from Extinct Megafauna." *Nature Geoscience* 3 (2010): 374–75.

Soulé, M., and R. Noss. "Rewilding and Biodiversity: Complementary Goals for Continental Conservation." *Wild Earth* 8, no. 3 (1998): 18–28.

Steadman, David W., and Paul S. Martin. "The Late Quaternary Extinction and Future Resurrection of Birds on Pacific Islands." *Earth-Science Reviews* 61 (2003): 133–47.

Steadman, David W., Paul S. Martin, Ross D. E. MacPhee, A. J. T. Jull, H. Gregory McDonald, Charles A. Woods, Manuel Iturralde-Vinent, and Gregory W. L. Hodgins. "Asynchronous Extinction of Late Quaternary Sloths on Continents and Islands." *Proceedings of the National Academy of Sciences of the United States of America* 102, no. 33 (2005): 11763–68.

Stenseth, Nils Chr., Geir Ottersen, James W. Hurrell, Atle Mysterud, Mauricio Lima, Kung-Sik Chan, Nigel G. Yoccoz, and Bjørn A° dlandsvik. "Studying Climate Effects on Ecology Through the use of Climate Indices: The North

Atlantic Oscillation, El Niño Southern Oscillation and Beyond." *Proceedings of the Royal Society B: Biological Sciences* 270, no. 1529 (2003): 2087–96.

Stolzenburg, William. *Where the Wild Things Were*. New York: Bloomsbury USA, 2008.

Stromberg, Julia, Matthew K. Chew, Pamela L. Nagler, and Edward P. Glenn. "Changing Perceptions of Change: The Role of Scientists in Tamarix and River Management." *Restoration Ecology* 17 (March 2009): 177–86.

Sukhdev, Pavan. "Costing the Earth." *Nature* 462, no. 7271 (November 19, 2009): 277.

Sutherland, William. "A Blueprint for the Countryside." *Ibis* 146, suppl. 2 (2004): 230–38.

Thoreau, Henry David. *Walden: A Fully Annotated Edition*, edited by Jeffrey S. Cramer. New Haven and London: Yale University Press, 2004.

Thompson, Ken. *Do We Need Pandas?* Totnes: Green Books, 2010.

Tischew, Sabine, Annett Baasch, Mareike K. Conrad, and Anita Kirmer. "Evaluating Restoration Success of Frequently Implemented Compensation Measures: Results and Demands for Control Procedures." *Restoration Ecology* (2008), http://dx.doi.org/10.1111/j.1526-100X.2008.00462.x.

Turner, Frederick, Jackson. *The Frontier in American History*. 1920; BiblioBazaar, 2008.

Turner, Monica. "Disturbance and Landscape Dynamics in a Changing World." *Ecology* 91, no. 10 (2010): 2833–49.

Turney, C. S. M., M. I. Bird, L. K. Fifield, R. G. Roberts, M. Smith, C. E. Dortch, R. Grun, E. Lawson, L. K. Ayliffe, G. H. Miller, J. Dortch, and R. G. Cresswell. "Early Human Occupation at Devil's Lair, Southwestern Australia 50,000 Years Ago." *Quaternary Research* 55 (2001): 3–13.

Turvey, S. T., and C. L. Risley. "Modelling the Extinction of Steller's Sea Cow." *Biology Letters* 22, no. 2 (March 22, 2006): 94–97.

Uchida, J. Y., and L. L. Loope. "A Recurrent Epiphytotic of Guava Rust on Rose Apple, *Syzygium Jambos*, in Hawaii." *Plant Disease* 93, no. 4 (April 2009): 429, http://apsjournals.apsnet.org/doi/abs/10.1094/PDIS-93-4-0429B.

Van der Veken, Sebastiaan, et al. "Garden Plants Get a Head Start on Climate Change." *Frontiers in Ecology and the Environment* 6 (2008): 212–16.

Veltre, Douglas W., David R. Yesner, Kristine J. Crossen, Russell W. Graham, and Joan B. Coltrain. "Patterns of Faunal Extinction and Paleoclimatic Change from Mid-Holocene Mammoth and Polar Bear Remains, Pribilof Islands, Alaska." *Quaternary Research* 70, no. 1 (July 2008): 40–50.

Vera, Frans. *Grazing Ecology and Forest History*. Wallingford, UK: CABI, 2000.

———. "Large-scale Nature Development—The Oostvaardersplassen." *British Wildlife* 20, no. 5, suppl. (June 2009): 28–36.

Vera, Frans, and Frans Buissink. *Wilderness in Europe: What Really Goes On Between the Trees and the Beasts*. Baarn: Tirion Uitgevers B.V. & Driebergen: Staatsbosbeheer, 2007.

Vitousek, Peter M., Harold A. Mooney, Jane Lubchenco, and Jerry M. Melillo. "Human Domination of Earth's Ecosystems." *Science* 277, no. 5325 (July 25, 1997): 494–99.

Wade, Nicholas. *Before the Dawn: Recovering the Lost History of our Ancestors*. New York: Penguin Press, 2006.

Walter, Robert C., and Dorothy J. Merritts. "Natural Streams and the Legacy of Water-Powered Mills." *Science* 319, no. 5861 (January 18, 2008): 299–304.

Wasser, Samuel, Bill Clark and Cathy Laurie. "The Ivory Trail." *Scientific American* 301, no. 1 (July 2009): 68–74.

Weller, Lorraine. "Interactions of Socioeconomic Patterns with Vegetation Cover and Biodiversity in Los Angeles, CA." Presented at the Ecological Society of America meeting, in Albuquerque, N.M., August 3, 2009.

White, Lynn, Jr. "The Historical Roots of Our Ecological Crisis." *Science* 155 (1967): 1203–07.

Wilcove, David, David Rothstein, Jason Dubow, Ali Phillips, and Elizabeth Loos. "Quantifying Threats to Imperiled Species in the United States." *BioScience* 48, no. 8 (1998): 607–15.

Wilkinson, D.M. "The Parable of Green Mountain." *Journal of Biogeography* 31 (2004): 1–4.

Will, Barbara. "The Nervous Origins of the American Western." *American Literature* 70, no. 2 (June, 1998): 293–316.

Wills, John. "Brighty, Donkeys and Conservation in the Grand Canyon." *Endeavour* 30, no. 3 (2006): 113–17.

Williams, Ted. "Picture Perfect," *Audobon Magazine*, http://www.audubonmaga zine.org/incite/incite1003.html.

Wilson, Robert J., David Gutiérrez, Javier Gutiérrez, David Martínez, Rosa Agudo, and Víctor J. Monserrat. "Changes to the Elevational Limits and Extent of Species Ranges Associated with Climate Change." *Ecology Letters* 8, no. 11 (November 2005): 1138–46.

Wood, Jamie R., Nicolas J. Rawlence, Geoffery M. Rogers, Jeremy J. Austin, Trevor H. Worthy, and Alan Cooper. "Coprolite Deposits Reveal the Diet and Ecology of the Extinct New Zealand Megaherbivore Moa (Aves, Dinornithiformes)." *Quaternary Science Reviews* 27, no. 27–28 (December 2008): 2593–602.

Woods, William, and William Denevan, "Amazonian Dark Earths: The First Century of Reports." In *Amazonian Dark Earths*, edited by William I. Woods, Wenceslau G. Teixeira, Johannes Lehmann, Christoph Steiner, Antoinette WinklerPrins, Lilian Rebellato. New York: Springer, 2008.

Worster, Donald. *Nature's Economy*. Cambridge, UK: Cambridge University Press, 1985.

Wu, Jianguo, and Orie L. Loucks. "From Balance of Nature to Hierarchical Patch Dynamics: A Paradigm Shift in Ecology." *Quarterly Review of Biology* 70 (1995): 439–66.

Zakin, Susan. *Coyotes and Town Dogs: Earth First! and the Environmental Movement*. Tucson: University of Arizona Press, 1993.

Ziegler, Alan. *Hawaiian Natural History, Ecology and Evolution*. Honolulu: University of Hawaii Press, 2002.

Zimmerman, Corinne, and Kim Cuddington. "Ambiguous, Circular and Polysemous: Students' Definitions of the 'Balance of Nature' Metaphor." *Public Understanding of Science* 16, no. 4 (October 1, 2007): 393–406.

INDEX

A Note on the Author

Emma Marris grew up in Seattle. Since 2004 she has written for the world's foremost science journal, *Nature*, on ecology, conservation biology, and other topics. Her articles have also appeared in *Wired*, *High Country News*, and *Conservation*. She currently lives in Columbia, Missouri, with her husband and daughter.